Does This Count as a Career?

By Jon L. Sattler

Vacation Boy: Does This Count as a Career?
First Edition, Black & White

ISBN: 978-0-9889911-2-5

http://www.vacationboystories.com

Author and Photographer: Jon L. Sattler

Editor: Janet Dooley

Chapter contributions from Dr. Jon I. Sattler and Lisa Steadman

Cover Title Font Designed by David Simpson, a legally blind artist

Notes: *Most of these stories were written at the time they took place, spanning a period of two decades. Much may have changed in terms of political stability, levels of technology, etc. since these passages were written. Some people's names have been changed to protect the (not always) innocent.*

The photos are admittedly not of spectacular quality. Some are a bit blurry and/or were even taken with disposable film cameras, but I have included them nonetheless, hoping they help enrich the stories despite their shortcomings.

Many thanks to the family and friends who helped me pick out photos and narrow down the content of the book.

Full size color photos from the book can be seen at www.vacationboystories.com/bookphotos (this special page is not linked from the main page). While there, if you sign up for the mailing list, you'll receive a free bonus section straight from Vacation Boy's handwritten journal about hitchhiking to participate in a crazy Japanese Naked Festival.

This book is dedicated to all the people along my journeys who have helped make it all so interesting.

Table of Contents

"A ship in harbor is safe,
but that is not what ships are for."

~ William G. T. Shedd, (1820-1894)

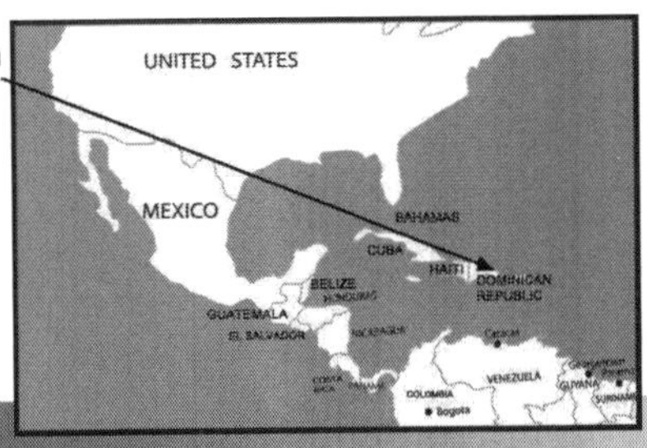

Introduction:
Vacation Boy Comes to Life

Bursting out of college with a desire to experience the world, my "career" began at Club Med in the Dominican Republic. We G.O.'s (*Gentils Orginisateurs* "nice organizers") worked seven days a week taking care of the G.M.'s (*Gentils Membres* "nice guests"). As a tour guide, I was one of the few fortunate employees who could go beyond the walls of the resort, taking the G.M.s on exotic outings like 4x4 jeep trips into the mountains to see cacao and coffee fields or whale watching in Samana.

When I wasn't occupied by my G.O. duties, I was free to take advantage of the resort facilities. I snorkeled, water skied, windsurfed, played tennis, and learned the trapeze. Between the trips I guided and the time I spent at other people's stations, my envious fellow G.O.'s started jokingly calling me "G.M. Jon," accusing me of always being on vacation. The nickname "Vacation Boy" ultimately stuck and became the email subject heading sent out to friends and family over the past 20 years to let them know I was still alive and catch them up on my goings on. At their urging, I collected these stories into this book.

Jon just prior to embarking for Club Med where Vacation Boy came to life

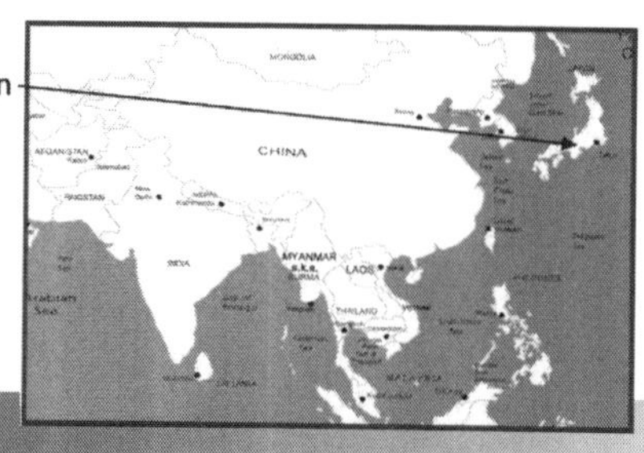

CHAPTER 1

Japanese Love Hotels

A bawdy quest for academic enlightenment

While studying abroad in Japan—in the name of research—I ended up with a bloody gash in my head, which I hid to avoid having to explain what really happened. It's time I finally reveal the details of this risqué misadventure inspired by a benign term paper assignment. If you are put off by descriptions of an explicit nature, you'd better skip to the next chapter.

Love Hotels are a curious spin-off of Japan's live-with-your-extended-family-in-(sometimes-literally)-paper-thin-walled-house society, where privacy at home is all but nonexistent. These unapologetically tacky institutions for amorous interactions mushroom up even in extremely rural areas. A few typical characteristics: they are easy to spot as they are often shaped like castles or feature other randomly exotic architecture like a Statue of Liberty, and are not shy with their use of neon lighting. They often have foreign names like "Hotel Princess" or "Hotel Belle Amour." Love Hotels rent rooms by the hour and are busiest during the day for affairs and other quick trysts. (Staying in one overnight can be a real bargain.)

Love Hotels specialize in privacy. The garage entrances usually have plastic drape flaps, which hide the people inside. Some have private garages for each room so you can go straight to the room without crossing a public garage. Payment is conducted privately through special wall panels below face level and more recently even with pneumatic tubes like a bank drive-through. They are known to have oversized bathrooms, cable radio with many stations, and any number of other sex-oriented eccentricities. Some have special theme rooms like "classroom," "jungle," "jail" or "spaceship."

I learned this doing my term paper for my Japanese language class at Nanzan University in Nagoya during my year abroad in college. Instead of writing about traditional topics like "Tea Ceremony" or "Ikebana" (flower arranging), I decided to research something that actually interested me. I was curious to know more about these mysterious, secretive institutions scattered all over Japan.

I did my research through interviews with Japanese people, in-the-know foreigners, and later via in-person visits (not what you are thinking!). Much of my firsthand research came from observations of the buildings' exteriors, going hotel to hotel photographing them for my eventual slide presentation. My buddy Rob, a *gaijin* (foreigner) friend of mine with a decent camera, accompanied me in this fun adventure. We got plenty of pictures from the outside, but—notoriously press-averse—none of the hotel personnel would let us in to photograph the interior of a room. Some told us to go away via intercom even before we got to the part about asking to be let inside. I've heard a number of these hotels allow female couples in, but not male ones, which is what they must have thought us to be.

My presentation date was drawing close, and after visiting maybe 30 hotels and not being let in to any of them, it was time to be more proactive. I talked a female *gaijin* friend of mine, Maria, into taking off from school during our lunch break to visit a place I had seen offering a "30-Minute Special" for $15. I was a poor student and that was still a lot of money for me, but I figured it would be worth it, knowing the legitimacy it would add to my report—not to mention satisfying my own curiosity.

We got there and into a room with no problem, on the way stopping to grab some bread things—as only Japanese bakeries can dream up—for lunch. Once in the room, I was delighted to be able to photographically confirm many of the features I had heard so much about: nice large bathrooms, cable radio, and many mirrors. I got a great picture of me on the bed demonstrating the ceiling mirror.

It was only when we sat down for lunch and I was completely out of film that I came across the thing I had been hoping to photograph most: the much talked about room service menu for sexual toys, whose titillating pictures made it graphically clear that dessert could come in many forms. In the interest of academic integrity I decided to take it home with me, photograph it, and then mail it back. (You may still be wondering where the head injury comes in.)

By the time we finished eating lunch, our 30 minutes were up. We called down to the reception to send up someone to collect the money through the no-see sliding pay window next to the door.

When the window slid open, an elderly woman's voice politely said, "That will be $45, please." Taken aback, we explained we were here for the 30-minute special. She responded that the special was only for Sundays and holidays. There was no way for us to pay that amount, so she went to get her manager.

When he arrived, we had to open the regular door and uncomfortably speak with him face to face. I let my much-more-blond, much-more-female, much-more-fluent-in-Japanese counterpart be the lead negotiator. After some wheeling and dealing, we settled on about $25 after confirming we had not used the bath area.

As we headed out the door and down the stairs, the manager entered the room, apparently to inspect it. Three thoughts rose up in my mind in succession:

"Uh oh, I hope he doesn't get worked up about the crumbs we dropped from lunch."

"Uh oh, what about the comb and other…um…disposable amenities Maria had pocketed?"

My pace quickened with each thought but then…

"OH SHIT, THE DILDO MENU!"

Maria and I were whispering these observations to each other as they surfaced in stream of consciousness. As we descended faster and faster, a timer was ticking in my head, playing through the imagined movements of the manager as he inspected the room. I calculated we still had some time and encouraged Maria to walk out at a normal pace to not arouse further suspicions. Probably not destined for a career as a criminal, as soon as we got to the reception/parking garage (and likely under the watchful eye of security cameras), Maria started to run. At that point I could only do the same.

As we sprinted through the garage entryway's plastic privacy flaps and up the quiet neighborhood street, the timer in my head was counting the seconds and determined we were not going to make it to the corner before the manager or someone else could potentially come out after us. We ducked into the grounds of a small temple, hoping to cut through the block. Unfortunately, there was a sizable wall between the temple and the next property over. We decided to climb over the wall and scoot out the other side.

I went first and, in the heat of the moment, did not pay sufficient attention to the clearance of a tiled roof overhanging the wall. When I jumped up, my head smashed on one of those (very hard) round tiles that abut the end of a roof. I dropped back down feeling "not so good." We decided to ditch the over-the-wall escape and, after confirming the coast was clear, went for the nonchalant walk away approach.

It was only once we were safely around the corner and almost to the subway that I touched my aching head and came down with a hand covered in blood. I had a pretty good-sized gash. Maria was concerned I had suffered a concussion.

We were on our hour's lunch break from school, so we had to hurry back to campus. Maria slid into class while I made an unavoidable stop at the school clinic. I didn't get stitches, but ended up with a sizable tension bandage crowning my head. I stupidly wore a baseball cap even indoors for several days, not knowing a decent way to explain to my Japanese host family what had happened.

Smiles of shock and awe is the best way to describe how my presentation was received at school. It was a fun presentation to give, although challenging to keep a straight face and serious demeanor, especially when some of the racier pictures flashed up, evoking gasps of laughter. Knowing the stories behind how it all came together made it that much more amusing for me. Ahh to be a student again…

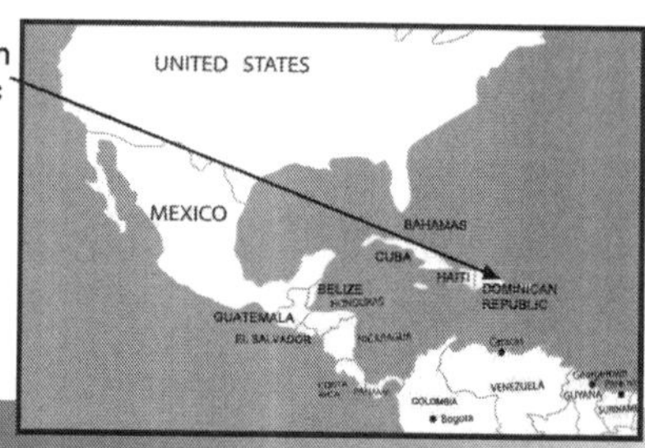

CHAPTER 2

Mosquitoes, Chickens & Tarantulas

Fun on the Dominican Republic's Chavon River

At last, I was on vacation. After taking care of guests seven days a week with no days off for six months straight at the Punta Cana resort, my Club Med career had concluded. I came to Bayaibe, a sleepy Caribbean fishing village in the southeast corner of the Dominican Republic, to begin a vacation I could call my own.

Bayaibe was the kind of town where sandy dogs lazed under the shade of breezy coconut trees, and it was difficult to break a 100 peso bill (about $8) because stores didn't have change for a bill that big. The town served as the kickoff point for boat tours heading down the coast to visit some of the most amazing beaches I've ever seen, eventually ending at the tropical outcrop of Saona. As a Club Med tour guide, I took guests out to that paradise regularly. Bayaibe was also the staging point for a different tour we did on zodiac boats, which traveled up the nearby jungle-lined Chavon River. Many of the locals who worked on both boat tours lived in or near Bayaibe.

I had come here to meet up with the French couple who ran the zodiac tours, Chantal and Christophe. They were building a thatch-roof bungalow in a bend in the dark green Chavon River. This is the river that was used in filming some of the final scenes of *Apocalypse Now.* During the course of the season, I had become friends with them and their crew and was looking forward to some down time when we were not on the clock.

"Not on the clock" was definitely a good way to describe my new status. Relying on the imprecise communication method of posting notes at a central point in town to let Chantal know I was there, I spent the day hanging out on a beach near Bayaibe relaxing and trying to grasp the idea that I was no longer working, and hopefully would not be for at least another several months.

With no sign of Chantal by nightfall, I realized I would have to stay the night. Luckily I encountered a couple people I knew as staff on the boats from my Club Med trips, and we went out to the only bar in town to cavort with other Bayaibans.

I got schooled in billiards by a young pool shark, who could barely see over the side of the table. I had impressed myself by clearing all but two balls right out of the opening break—my best pool streak ever. This kid's older friend then said in a slow deep voice, "OK, stand back, watch and learn," before the 12-year-old cleared the entire table in one go. He was incredible. His movements were effortlessly quick and smooth. Sometimes I felt he wasn't even looking at the table. The Canadian bartender Pierre summed it up saying, "If it is for work, they don't try too hard, but they will go all out to learn how to play a game well. Ever see them play baseball?"

I spent my first night of this long-awaited vacation offering myself as a gratuitous buffet to the resident mosquitoes. After futilely trying to duck the hovering mosquitoes throughout the night using the classic hide-under-the-sheet defense, my false hopes of a lazy sleep-in morning were shattered time and again starting around 4:30am when I was repeatedly awakened by the Bayaibe Chicken Tabernacle Choir. Those damn birds sounded as if they were perched directly around my bed. One chicken would cluck, another would squawk, and before I knew it every chicken in town was crowing at the top of its lungs. They would settle down, pause, and just as I was drifting off to sleep, start the whole thing over again. Ugh.

One of the boat captains I was hanging out with the night before, Carlos, woke me up for real at 7:30am so we could meet our ride to the river to rejoin Chantal and company. A group was coming from Club Med, so I would have a chance to see what the Zodiac Safari I had been leading looked like from the other side. We piled into a pickup deathtrap with food, ice, an outboard motor and other supplies needed for the tour and headed for the put-in spot on the river above the spillway.

The fact this truck could run at all was a feat of non-modern ingenuity. The driver had to use a pin to keep the cab door shut. The gas was being fed via a hose to the motor from a jug under his feet. The brakes would best be described as coaster brakes because he would press the pedal down all the way and then we'd gently glide to a stop. Supposedly, at one point this vehicle had broken in two and the guy managed to put it back together enough to drive it. On the way to the river, it died twice. His method for curing this ailment was to pound on the motor with a hammer for awhile until it miraculously came back to life.

On the way we picked up a couple more of the zodiac captains and the zodiac boats themselves before finally making it to the river—thankfully alive—where we caught up with Chantal and Christophe. When asked later why, pray tell, she trusted her operation to this guy's driving services, Chantal responded with refined Dominican practicality that he was still more reliable than any of the other guys with better trucks.

Some of my coworkers from Club Med came with the guests to try out the excursion, so I went along for the regular morning portion of the tour to spend time with them. After lunch, though, it was a wonderful sense of freedom to stay and hang out with the local staff rather than continuing on with the group. It was a pleasure making the beans for the next day's excursion with the lovely Laila, the curly-haired beauty who assisted with the tours.

Laila, Vacation Boy and the zodiac crew

In the evening, we all piled into a zodiac for a dusk cruise to the site where Chantal and Christophe were working on their future home. The river and its valley are magnificently calm at night. We passed the tree where all the cattle egrets in the area come to roost. It looked like a Christmas tree overly weighted down with bright white ornaments. Once back to the ranch, we stretched a fishing net across the river in hopes of catching something overnight.

Chantal's future house still had a long way to go. At this point, there were the beginnings of a frame, meaning a few palm columns stuck in the ground, surrounded by a field full of drying cana fronds that would later become the roof. Chantal and Christophe had been staying on site in a tent for the last several days. They managed to cobble together a cot for me with a mosquito net over the top. Good enough for me, although I didn't end up using it that night.

Before settling in, I journeyed up the mountain trail to El Gato, the village perched at the top of the hill where Laila and a couple other zodiac guys lived. On the way up, my flashlight beam crossed paths with a couple fuzzy black tarantulas, which were bigger than my hand with all the fingers spread. And one of those poisonous, horror movie clichés was right next to my foot! I became WAY more careful where I stepped.

Arriving in El Gato, I felt I had superpowers as there was no electricity and most people simply walked around in the dark or used candles or weak gas lamps. My flashlight was like a lighthouse, the brightest thing in town.

Laila was being friendlier than her ordinary shy self. We stopped by a couple candlelit stores before heading to her place for dinner. We dined on the gourmet delicacies of Chef Boyardee lasagna, then settled into a conversation between me, Laila, her inanimate brother, and later also her drunk cousin Domingo. Domingo came stumbling in, hinting I should marry Laila so she could get a U.S. passport, a suggestion which somehow didn't come as a surprise. I made the fatal mistake of declaring I didn't see myself as the marrying type. Good thinking, Vacation Boy. Laila hardly spoke to me after that. Sigh.

Oblivious, drunk Domingo was proud to be showing me the life of a *campesino (country person)*. He and I kept the incoherent conversation going well after Laila slipped away to go to sleep. He offered me his bed to sleep on while he tripped his way to the garage and passed out on a sofa.

Starting-to-sober Domingo stumbled in and out several times starting at 4:30 am on his way to the store to rekindle his buzz. He tried to get me to come with him, but I fended him off saying I was on vacation and wanted to sleep more. Laila came by at 7:00 am to wake me. She seemed annoyed I wanted to sleep in. There seems to be some kind of country ethic there that even if you don't have anything to do all day, you still have to get up early. I think I was the last person to wake up in all of El Gato.

I got up and was headed back down the mountain when Domingo spotted me from the store and came running over to give me a big, happy alcoholic hug. Apparently he never made it to his field where he first suggested he would be out working. After turning down several beer offers, I headed down to the river where the fishing net had already been hauled in. Dang, I was hoping to see how that went.

Many Club Meds have a Circus area where guests can learn the trapeze, juggling, etc., including the one where I worked in Punta Cana. The combination of a newfound love for trapeze, and the fun people running it, made the Circus Team's area one of my favorite places to hang out in my free time at the Club.

On this morning, the Circus Team was coming to me. That entire team and some other friends came on the first-ever all-GO zodiac trip as sort of an end-of-the-season party. Once GO's get out of the resort village walls—where most of them have been cooped up for months—things can get crazy and this day was no exception. Even before the first ten water fights, everyone was hammered and some of them even made it a clothing-optional trip. When we got to the swinging vine—a favorite stop on any tour—the circus team showed their true form, even pulling off double backward somersaults. I choked up a bit seeing them go at the end of the day as some of us had become like brothers working together all that time.

That night I collapsed into my rope cot by the river where yet another fitful night of sleep awaited me. Chantal's nervous dogs were new to being by the river and would go berserk at the drop of the hat, which included cows and horses moseying across the "house," or every time the machete-strapped not-terribly-bright watchman wandered up from the river to check on things.

In the middle of the night, the watchman started building a big fire right next to me.

"Why (on Earth) are you doing that?" I asked.

"Christophe told me to make some coffee for them at 7:00."

"OK, but why are you doing this at 5:30??"

"Oh, oh yeah."

He went to do something else for awhile.

At least this morning I was in time to help the watchman haul in the net we had again set the night before. We caught a few good-sized but real ugly fish. Chantal gave a couple of them away, but I cleaned the one that looked the most edible.

Breakfast was an adventure unto itself. We began by paying a visit to the farm downriver where we got fresh eggs and an even fresher chicken—still alive and clucking when we brought it back to camp. A local guy dropped a bowl of fresh honey and honeycombs he had acquired by smoking the bees out himself. It was so good!

Struggling to get the potatoes and eggs cooked over a difficult fire, it was early afternoon before we finally tore into the absolutely delicious omelet Christophe and Chantal had prepared. All along, they joked about how bad/slow the service was for their one client at their soon-to-be-world-famous restaurant.

Next we had the fish, which we had prepared "Tahitian style"–uncooked but marinated in lime juice and coconut milk. It was quite a tasty meal, but I was praying my body would take all this with good humor.

Cooking this meal with my friends forced me to confront my carnivorous eating habits head on. It is one thing to buy prepackaged Holly Farms' safely Styrofoam-encased, attractively organized meat pieces at a Piggly Wiggly grocery store (yes, I am from the South). It is another thing entirely to carry a living chicken back from the farm where it grew up and then watch as its head is lopped off with a machete on a tree root and then flips and flutters around without its head spurting blood here and there. My thought is if you can't witness something like that and be ready to eat it, you shouldn't be eating meat in the first place.

That said, I will admit freely it was the first time I had been privy to the killing of a chicken and, feeling squeamish, I was relieved when Christophe stepped up to be the machete man. Does that still make me a meat eating hypocrite?

Christophe and Chantal tried to convince me to stay longer, but I had other friends waiting for me in the capital, so they took me on one final zodiac ride and dropped me off close to the main road. Little did I know that on the hand I was waving goodbye with was a lifelong souvenir in the form of an innocent little red bump on my index finger. That dot later filled up with a soup of yellow and blue liquids, swelling my finger up to three times the size of my thumb. I suspect that painful unpleasantness originated from some sort of bite while sleeping by the river. The divot remains forever on my finger, and reminds me of otherwise pleasant memories of my time on the Chavon River.

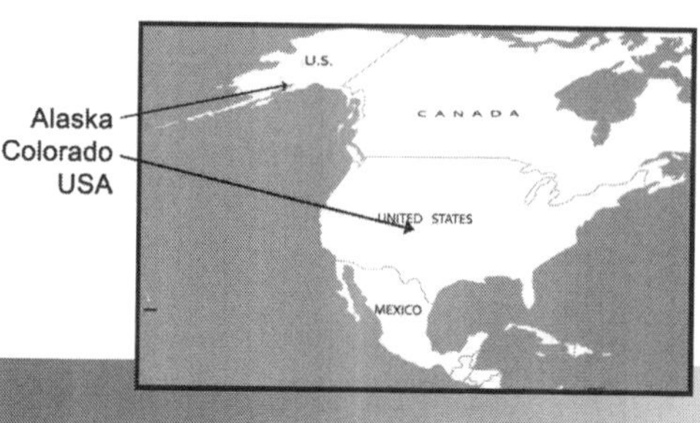

CHAPTER 3

Descending Mountains Without Shoes or Sobriety

From Colorado to Alaska

The story of why and how I ended up living a day's drive from the Arctic Circle began in Colorado.

I had spent the winter working front desk at a condo complex at the foot of Colorado's Beaver Creek ski resort, which neighbors world-famous Vail. As the Vail ski mountain season came to a close, my Colorado winter of 100+ glorious days of skiing came to a festive end.

Like resorts around the world, closing day traditions are almost religious in fervor as skiers celebrate the passing of another ski season. At Vail, locals traditionally gather at the top of the mountain where several chairlifts come together, then a giant party ensues involving beer, wine, champagne, etc. The party builds as the day advances, until the top is completely packed with skiers and snowboarders.

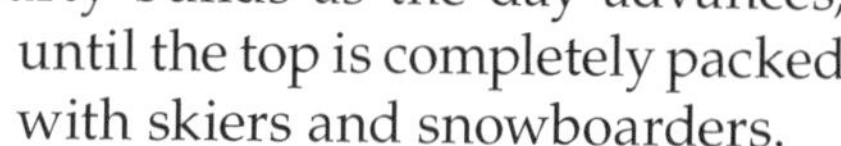

This particular spring day started with a fresh layer of snow on the ground, and more continued to dump through most of the afternoon. Locals who would have ordinarily focused all their efforts on partying were intermittently pulled away like cocaine junkies by the allure of the abundant white powder, only to regroup at the top later.

When the chairlifts at Vail finally stop running at the end of the day, there are two separate traditions. For one group, the cheers from the gathered crowd marking the stopping of the last lift is the starting gun for the wild and crazy "Chinese Downhill," where a mass of (often inebriated) locals race to the bottom of the mountain all at once. Another group stays and parties at the top until Ski Patrol eventually shoos everyone off.

My pothead housemate Jeff had his own tradition. A long time resident of the area, Jeff prided himself on being the last person off the mountain on the last day of the season. This year he invited me to join him and a couple of buddies who often shared this tradition with him. Once the Chinese Downhillers were off on their zany descent and Ski Patrol began to kick people off the mountain top, we hid in the woods. Waiting for everyone to clear out, we imbibed another bottle or so of $4 champagne, as well as a collection of other less legal items. Giving Jeff's special-occasion stash of shrooms a try pushed my normally more innocent self to an all time level of wastedness—on skis or off.

An hour or two later when we felt the coast was clear, we slipped out of our hiding place and I began the clumsiest descent of my ski career. Trying to get my legs to function normally was like herding cats. On steeper terrain, it was beyond me to link more than two turns together without falling over. Ordinarily a decent skier, I tried in vain to convince my legs to ski normally.

The slopes were completely vacant, an eerie feeling for a place that is usually mobbed. We didn't rush down. Instead we stopped on occasion to savor the moment, crack jokes and appreciate the view.

When deciding how to descend, Jeff and his friends came up with the brilliant plan of skiing down under the Vista Bahn Express lift, something ordinarily off limits. Even these hardened veteran locals had never attempted this before. Tricky on even a sober day, the lift cuts a narrow line between trees through double black diamond expert terrain.

I would have been more worried if I wasn't so busy laughing myself silly. I remember one brief moment of semi-lucidity, looking up at the chairlift suspended overhead, then down at the village as the light began to dim, pausing to pray I would get to the bottom without injuring or killing myself.

The light was transitioning from dusk to darkness when we arrived at the top of Pepi's Face, a steep final descent into Vail Village where many world class races finish. Below we could see the ski patrol's end-of-the-year party well under way on a deck outside their office. When they spotted us starting to come down the face, they all began to cheer us on. It was a glorious, albeit not entirely graceful exclamation point to the end of great season.

Alaska

From the moment the lifts stopped moving—and my vision cleared—I began to scan the horizon, looking for a destination where I could put my Japanese language skills to use before they rusted and fell off. Option #1 was to go work at a resort in the South Pacific. Option #2 was studying Aikido (a martial art) in Japan.

Pursuing Option #1 added significantly to my collection of rejection letters. I put off Option #2 for another time and instead decided on a third option: Alaska. Alaska has a high influx of Japanese tourists in the summer and seemed more convenient than Hawaii in that I could drive there.

Don't let anyone kid you, Alaska is far. To give you some perspective, if you are driving from San Antonio, Texas to Anchorage, once you get to Seattle, you are only about half way. From Colorado, I made the "convenient" drive in exactly one week and two hours. I had no idea it would take that long.

Along the way I got to see lots of frozen lakes, some bears, swarms of giant but slow-moving zombie mosquitoes, a bunch of moose (and signs warning there had already been a shocking 300+ moose kills by cars that winter alone), a fox, a wolf, a couple of huge bald eagles, and much more of the mostly flat and boring Yukon territory than I had ever hoped for. My car had a bad spark plug, which meant I could not drive over 25 MPH without the car stalling out and not restarting for at least ten minutes. It took a whole day of this monotony before I limped into White Horse, the capital of the Yukon Territory, the only city along the way with a car repair place.

While waiting for the repair shop to open in the morning, I ended up sharing a hotel room with a naïve, young Japanese guy who had been holed up there for several weeks. He had shown up there to kayak the Yukon River to its mouth, not knowing the river is usually frozen over around White Horse until at least late May. He seemed frighteningly lacking in provisions and planning for what would be a multi-month journey. I wonder if he ever made it.

Of the 3700 miles my odometer racked up, the most beautiful miles clicked off during the last stretch between Anchorage and Girdwood (easily one of the prettiest drives in America), where my journey came to an end. It would be tough to find a better place to end up. Just off Turnagain Arm and surrounded on the other three sides by mountains decorated with snow and glaciers cascading over the top, Girdwood is a gorgeous enclave about 40 miles south of Alaska's biggest city, Anchorage, which Girdwood residents pronounced "town".

Girdwood was home to famous skier Tommy Moe, about 1199 other people, some bears, even more moose, and some of the most eclectic cabin architecture you will ever see. Alaskans are proud of their independent nature (and the fact that if you divide Alaska in half, each half would STILL be bigger than Texas). In Girdwood they seemed to have gone out of their way to express their freedom through home construction. Funky colors and shapes abound in ways I never thought could appear on a singular city block.

Girdwood is a unique, incredibly scenic community which represents the best of small town Alaska. The people were very friendly. The only paved road is the one coming from the Seward Highway up to the Alyeska ski resort and on to the hotel. It is one of those places where after only a month and a half living there, I could go to either of the two bars in town and see at least someone, if not many people, I knew.

There is no home mail delivery in Girdwood and I loved the scene at the post office which consequently served as a social hub. Especially on colder days, people would leave their cars unlocked and running in the parking lot with dogs, kids or whatever inside to go check their post office box and say hi to whoever they knew inside. More people than not (myself included) were unable to get one of the coveted few PO boxes and received their mail via General Delivery.

Part of what made the summer so fun was sharing an apartment with my hilarious flightseeing pilot roommate Gary. With its 70's sensibilities exemplified in its furnishings and shag carpet, we dubbed our apartment "the Lime Green Palace". A bonus was that Gary's boss occasionally let us borrow a plane to joyride around the area. With Prince William Sound and the Chugach Range—supposedly the highest concentration of glaciers in the world—at our doorstep, it made for stunning excursions indeed.

Before I got down to the business of working, I decided to treat myself. For my birthday, I went camping in Denali National Park, home to a bunch of grizzly bears and Denali, a.k.a. Mt. McKinley, the highest mountain in North America. This would have been a great idea, except it wasn't—at least the way I went about it. In fact, my fiasco there goes on record officially as My Worst Camping Trip Ever. I am lucky I survived. What went wrong? A lot.

I started out in the Denali Park office where I was issued a bear box, a mandatory hard plastic shell for food storage, which ensures that if a grizzly decides to devour you, it will at least not get your food. I was also given some helpful information about hiking trail options, which almost proved fatal.

When asked about recommendations, the gal at the information desk told me in glowing terms about an area where she had camped two weeks earlier. It sounded perfect. The destination was a campsite that could be reached in less than a day's hike with nice views of Denali from a relatively easy-to-access mountaintop. The only thing she and I did not realize is that it had snowed a couple feet there since her visit.

Most places in the massive Denali park do not have cut trails. You have to find your own way through the brambles, fields, streams, etc. just like the original explorers. Backcountry pass in hand, I drove in, loaded my backpack and began my hike up in the area the park ranger gal had described. It was not easy going. The bottom area was swamped with water, and as the climb began, the shrubbery seemed more intent on blocking my way than indicating a trail for me to follow.

I was hiking in the new Igloo brand boots my grandparents had given me for my birthday. In retrospect, I learned that Igloo needs to keep its focus on making beer coolers and not shoes. During my arduous upward swim through the brambles—I think because of being exposed to the mud and water earlier—the soles began to separate from the shoes they were very much meant to be attached to. No, this is not something you want when hiking through the Alaskan wilderness, especially when you are about to start climbing above the snow line, which is where I suddenly found myself.

About three hours into my scramble, there was very-much-not-anticipated snow on the ground. Lots of it. My thought process was that Alaskans are tough, and when the girl had recommended this hike, there was no need for her to point out something so trivial as the fact that there was snow here because, DUH, this is ALASKA. As a newbie arriving fresh from "the Lower 48" as they call it, it was almost like Park Ranger Lisa was taunting me.

So I plodded along through the snow in my falling-apart shoes. As exhaustion began to set in, the higher I went the cold stiff wind only picked up its intensity. I already had to loop the laces of one of the boots around the sole to keep it from flapping completely open like a full-length trap door under my foot. The snow coming through the gaps did nothing to dry out my soaked-through sock.

It was hard to find a clear path to the top. At one point, I found myself scaling around a cliff where the frigid wind gusts were so strong they caught my backpack and almost spun me around sideways and off the ledge I was inching around.

In addition to cold and fear, I was getting tired. I had been at this slogfest for almost four hours and I was not near the summit nor close to anywhere I could set up my tent. I'll be honest, I was starting to give up hope and was wondering if I would ever even make it down. It was at that low point that Mother Nature decided to give me a kick in the pants, in a good way.

At a moment when I was pausing to rest and take in my situation, about 40 meters below me a bleach-white mountain goat gracefully skittered up to the top of a steep small peak below me, paused, and then scampered down the symmetric far side as easily as if it were on flat ground. It was the first sign of animal life I had seen since I began my climb. And then came another one. And then a third, and then another, all following the same precarious path. Seeing nature so gracefully in action and completely nonplussed by the harsh surroundings, was inspirational. I figured if they could do it, so could I.

The mountain goats cast a magic spell on me, bringing clarity to what I needed to do. I decided it was time to abandon hopes of making it to the top and instead focus on getting down to somewhere I could camp. I even slid down portions on my butt as it was easier than trying to walk down, especially with the state of my shoes.

The entire time during my hike, I had yet to see a single location suitable for pitching a tent. It was always too steep, too rocky, too covered with thick shrubbery or all of the above. Once below the snow line, pickings were still slim. I finally went with the best solution I could find, namely stuffing my tent into a gap in a rock cliff. It was by no means a perfect solution. The tent was still getting flapped about from the wind and the uneven rock floor wasn't exactly a king's mattress, but it was way better than anything else I had seen.

So then it was time for my birthday dinner. This was my first time camping in grizzly country and it had me on edge. I'd heard plenty of stories about the intelligence and ferociousness these magnificent beasts can bring to, ahem, bare. One thing you are drilled on before heading into bear country is how to prepare, eat and store your food. You are supposed to make a triangle, with your sleeping area in the upwind point, separating 100 feet between the downwind corners, which are used for food preparation and food storage respectively.

You prepare and eat your food in one spot, store it suspended at the proper height between two trees in the second point, and sleep in the third—after changing out of the clothes you were eating in.

This is great in theory, but another thing entirely when you are trying to do it in inhospitable terrain and weather. I made my way out on a windswept rocky ledge to set up my stove and boil water. It was nowhere near 100 feet away from my tent, but it was the only place I could find to set it up. As I sat out there shivering, waiting for my water to come to a boil, I had visions of a hungry just-out-of-hibernation bear coming around the corner, finding me in the figurative (and perhaps literal) dead end of that rock outcrop as there was only one way out other than falling 50 feet off the side.

You would think that if the only culinary prowess I needed to prepare my freeze-dried meal was to boil water and pour it in the bag, someone turning 24 that day should have been able to pull it off. However, whether because of the altitude, or the gale-force wind, or the increasingly frigid temperatures, I could not get the water even close to boiling no matter how much I tried to shelter my poor struggling stove.

I gave up and poured the warmed water into my freeze-dried meal bag, hoping for the best. After waiting for the water to work its magic, I opened the bag to find chewy beef stroganoff chunks floating in a tepid bath of almost-salty water. They were barely transformed from the congealed dry powder they resembled prior to adding the water. I began gnawing my way through the watery amalgamation, singing to myself, somewhat ironically, "Happy birthday to me, Happy birthday to me…". Even in my exhausted state, it was terrible and hard to get down. Lesson learned: truly boiling water is critical when preparing freeze-dried meals.

Tent crammed into the side of the cliff

There was no good place to hang or place my food stores, so I broke one of bear country's cardinal rules and left my bear box out there on the same ledge, hoping for the best. In the meantime it was time to finally bed down for the night. Yay. Only that didn't go well either.

Because I had no way to secure all the walls and doors of the tent, in the unrelenting wind the material FWAP, FWAP, FWAP, FWAPed like thunder all…night…long. As a silver lining, I figured the chaotic flapping about would at least discourage bears from poking their head in to dine on me during the night.

Not that it was easy to tell when it was night. Being way north this time of year it never got dark. It just got dim for awhile around 3:30 AM and then brightened back up again. I knew this because it was impossible to sleep.

Happy Birthday to meeee….Happy Birthday to meee…Happy Biiiirth…

At some point I decided it was morning enough to get up and head back to the bottom. I was glad to find my food stores intact. Along the way down, between the brambles and the water, one of my hiking shoes disintegrated completely and I found myself walking in the Alaskan wilderness wearing only a soaked sock on one of my feet. For all my trials and tribulations the day before, it thankfully only took me an hour to get back down to the blessed warm and dry sanctuary of my car.

So far I have yet to top this outing in terms of sheer misery, and I have had some doozies. What a way to treat myself on my birthday. Since then, though, when things aren't going well when I am out camping, my mind drifts back to that night in Denali and I think, "Well, at least it's not as bad as that was!"

Safely back in Girdwood, I took a waitering job at the stunning, almost brand spanking new Alyeska Prince Hotel, which was right there in the valley. It was Japanese owned and received quite a few Japanese guests considering how bleak the occupancy rate was otherwise. The employees referred to the place as "the Overlook," the empty hotel in the horror movie *The Shining*. Before long, I was able to transition from waiting tables to the much more interesting position of concierge, which also gave me more contact with Japanese guests.

During Alaskan summers, there is plenty of daylight to go around. It is invigorating. Never is that more the case than Summer Solstice, the rarely-noticed footnote on most calendars every June 21st. In Alaska—where they spend so much of the year shrouded in darkness—Summer Solstice is a big deal. It is on par with the 4th of July. It is a time when people start a round of golf, or hike up mountains, or go skiing, or rafting or anything else outdoors—all in the bright sunshine at or around midnight. Some people drive closer to the Arctic Circle where they sit atop their Winnebegos drinking beer and watching the sun spin around in the sky without ever dropping below the horizon.

In Girdwood, there is an annual tradition to have a barn burner of a party up on Crow Pass, the rugged Girdwood "suburb" where to this day some people still subsist by panning for gold. I joined what was probably all the youth in the area for the giant bonfire, live music and lots of adult beverages. Some folks broke off around 2:00 am to hike up further to go snowboarding on a nearby glacier. How cool is that?

To this day, June 21st has garnered a special spot on my calendar. I think of the good people of Alaska and celebrate in distant solidarity the longest day of the year.

At the end of the summer, I switched to a job as a camping tour guide for Japanese tourists, taking them for hikes on Matanuska Glacier and up to Denali National Park. These went WAY better than my first trip there.

I ended up recruiting Kazu and Hiro from one of my groups to go sea kayaking with me in Harriman Fjord off Prince William Sound. After agreeing to join me for the multi-day wilderness journey, these young guys asked, "What is a sea kayak?" Hmmm. Maybe not the most solid partners for this level of adventure. They even wanted to see how I pumped gas at the gas station because in Japan everything is full service and they were planning to rent a vehicle and wanted to know how to pump it themselves.

Nevertheless, they were game for this four-day kayaking trip in the remote Alaskan wilds. And so we did it, surviving just barely.

I had been scoping out a possible trip to Harriman Fjord since flying over the spectacular glacial wonderland with Gary on a joyride flight over to Valdez and Cordova. This L-shaped fjord looked to be the most protected and prettiest area around, but it wasn't an easy trip to sort out. No humans live nearby and it isn't on the way to anywhere, so there is no regular means of transportation to access it. One sightseeing tour boat visited the fjord several times a week but it created more of a danger than a possible source of help. It wasn't configured in a way for it to safely carry kayaks and it threw up a big dangerous wake on its way in and out, which could easily flip a kayaker into the icy waters. And when I say icy, I mean the kind of icy where even an Olympic swimmer would die in literally 10 minutes from the shock and exposure to the biting cold.

In Whittier we ended up hiring kayaks and crusty Captain Mike to run us out on his boat. Coming around the bend into the glassy water of Harriman Fjord took my breath away. With impressive mountains and glaciers plunging into the water, the fjord was every bit as glorious as I hoped it would be and more. Mike dropped us in what was the inside forearm of the bent arm of the fjord. When he shut down his buzzing motor to unload the kayaks and the gear, our own shuffling about and the sounds of the water gently lapping on the shoreline seemed offensively loud compared to the blissful silence beyond. Across from this magnificent campsite was an amphitheater as only Mother Nature could design, complete with its own built in thunder machine.

Glaciers, as it turns out, can be far from silent. Day or night, we would occasionally hear a distant echoing CRACK of the shifting ice, occasionally followed by the splash of newly minted icebergs collapsing into the ocean. We had to be wary of these icefalls when kayaking because when ice calves off, it can ignite a deadly mini-tsunami from the impact.

Once we got out and began exploring, we approached the glaciers from a cautious distance, weaving through the fields of ice floating in the water. The icy water had carved these mini-icebergs into interesting yet often dangerously sharp ice sculptures. Gliding amongst them, the noise of the water lapping up under ledges that had been eroded away sounded like a chorus of toothless seniors smacking their gums, but in a relaxing way. That sound was only interrupted by the gentle splash of the stroking paddle, the occasional clunk of ice hitting the kayak hull and sometimes less pleasant scraping noises when the hull glanced along frozen knife blades, making me wince.

The ice was a favorite hangout spot for seals and sea otters. With their expressive whiskery faces, fuzzy bodies, and tendency to enjoy playing when not snoozing on their backs in the water, sea otters should be legally declared the cutest animals on earth. Quite a few of them roam the waters of Harriman Fjord. They were curious what we were doing in their neck of the woods. They would pass nearby for a look when we were kayaking around and would occasionally swim by our campsite, kicking down strokes to lift themselves vertically higher out of the water to get a better peek at what we were up to. Adorable.

Rain began to sprinkle on the afternoon of the first day and only increased in intensity for the remainder of our four-day trip. Our campsite, with copious fresh blueberries and its stunning views of glaciers plummeting into the sea, started out as a scenic wonderland. As the days progressed, though, the paths and even the ground below us melted steadily into a river of mud.

We were fine when exploring the beauty of the fjord from the comfort of the kayaks, but life on land became miserable. With ropes, we jerry-rigged a kitchen under a rain poncho and oars. At one point I timed that we were able to fill a gallon jug of water from the runoff within ten minutes. My tent's water repelling tenacity eventually gave out and a small pool formed down by my feet. Few of our things remained even remotely dry.

The water falling from the sky further ramped up its intensity. Instead of moving to a new campsite on the opposite side of the fjord for the third night as we had planned, we decided to remain where we were, knowing that if we tried to pack everything up and set it up again, things like sleeping bags that were not yet soaked through would be.

The final morning, while still appreciating the beauty of our surroundings, we were excited to know we would be getting out of there. We packed everything and began paddling over to the opposite side of the fjord to the place where we were supposed to have camped on the third night and where we had also set up the rendezvous with Mike, the boat captain.

But it took us longer to get there than we first anticipated, and well before were able to reach our destination, we heard the hum of Mike's outboard motors coming into the fjord. Paddling faster now, we tried waving but we knew he didn't see us as he continued on toward the original meeting spot. But he was still far from us.

Sensing the danger that we were about to be in if we did not connect with him, I urgently sent the Japanese guys sprinting to shore, instructing them to run up and down the beach shouting and waving while I continued to press on in the direction of the boat as fast as my arms would pull me.

Captain Mike pulled away from the second campsite and motored over to look for us at our original site. As he crossed over, it was clear he still had not seen us. He hovered on that shore for a bit, and then… he left, returning home. I could feel the hope draining from my heart as the boat picked up speed and the sound of the motor began to fade away from us out the mouth of the rain swept fjord.

But then something happened. I saw the boat slow, then stop, then turn around, then start to head right for us. We were saved!

It turned out that Mike's girlfriend, Linda, had joined him for the ride out. At the last minute she was the one who spotted the Japanese guys frantically waving and running back and forth on the beach in their yellow rain ponchos. Phew.

Kiss on the cheek to Linda and the guardian angel that pointed her eyes toward us. One of the reasons they did not linger longer looking for us was because an Alaska-grade storm was fast approaching. The wet weather we had been experiencing was but polite foreplay compared to what was about to hit. In fact if Mike did not pick us up then, the severe weather would have prevented him from returning to get us for several days.

The rain and wind and resulting choppy seas made for a slow, arduous return to port. It was almost dark when we finally arrived. Mike found a dorm room of sorts for us to stay in and dry out for the night. The storm began to hit in earnest that evening. Watching the horizontal pouring rain from the dry dorm room window brought a sense of relief that is hard to describe, especially knowing how close we had been to being stuck in that maelstrom for days with dwindling food supplies and nothing dry anywhere.

Despite the near tragic ending to this trip, Harriman Fjord still evokes a longing in me. I hope one day to return to and explore its extraordinary beauty again…when it's SUNNY.

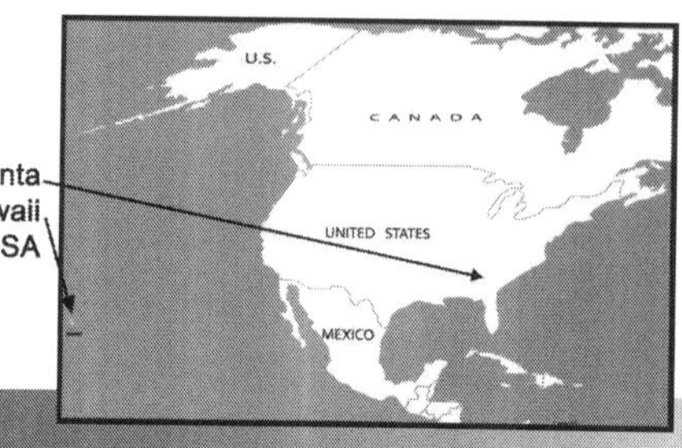

CHAPTER 4

"Get Down Here!"

An Insider's View of the Atlanta Olympics and Bombing

Aside from the RVs and busses choking the roads and the mosquitoes, which are known to have carried off small children, the only real drawback to Alaska was the inevitable event creeping up on the calendar: winter. I never had any intention of avoiding the un-esteemed, undignified, derisive title of "fair-weather Alaskan". As Jimmy Buffett so eloquently put it, "I gotta go where there ain't any snow; I gotta go where it's warm!" Knowing another winter of beaches and bathing suits would suit this warm-blooded sun worshiper just fine, I set sail for...Hawaii!

I got my bus driver's license the winter of 1996 on the island of Maui. I bet my parents beamed with pride every time they told friends that their college graduate son was a bus driver. Over the course of that winter, I carted over 1000 Japanese tourists to their hotels and later back to the airport, checking them in at either end. I got pretty good at spotting whales while driving along the ocean. It became a source of pride that I could almost always locate them before my passengers did, despite the fact I was the one driving the bus.

I also got good at spotting roaches—*in the bus*—at least in one badly infested bus the company kept assigning me. It was horrible. Every day I complained vehemently on the sheet we had to turn in about the state of the vehicle, but these complaints fell on deaf ears. Finally, to get my point across, I squashed about 17 roaches with the daily sheet and turned it in without writing anything other than "(roaches)" on the sheet. Some of them were still twitching and waving tentacles on the paper when I walked out. The next day my boss sat me down for a tete-a-tete saying how inappropriate my actions were, but I somehow never got assigned that bus again.

Bus roaches aside, I loved that winter on Maui. I finally figured out how to do a windsurfing water start. My regular surfing improved considerably as well. It got to the point that I would start feeling ill at ease if I didn't get in the water at least once every few days.

My Hawaiian life ended abruptly when I got a message on my answering machine asking me to come work in Atlanta for the Olympics. This phone call was from a woman, Eiko Mishima, who I had met years before when working as an usher at a Japanese jazz band concert at the University of Southern California, my alma mater. Mishima-san and I struck up a conversation while the concert was going on. It turned out she was from the Los Angeles office of the Japanese publishing company sponsoring the event. She was impressed by my Japanese and suggested we keep in touch. Over the years I did just that, meeting her on occasion for lunch when passing through LA. It just seemed like something I should do, although I was never sure why at the time. It turns out that jazz concert ushering job was the domino that set off a remarkable chain of events in my life.

Since I'd been looking to break out of my pattern of entry-level hospitality/tourism work, the decision to leave and go work at the Olympics was easy and immediate. As much as I enjoyed my time in Maui, I was moved out of my Hawaiian life within three weeks—rid of my job, my apartment, my car—and saddest of all—my surfboard.

In Atlanta, life started at a pleasant trot. By late May it took off running. I was working for a Japanese daily sports newspaper. It was an exciting job, especially compared to continuously pointing out the same dang pineapple field for five months in Hawaii. I started by helping set up the newspaper's office operations.

The main office was near an Atlanta commercial hub, Lennox Mall. Later we also had an office in the Main Olympic Press Center, plus an office by Stone Mountain where we printed 10,000 copies of the paper in Japanese to distribute around Atlanta and to other parts of the country. I also wore a reporter's hat, doing reporting and photography leading up to the Games, including covering the US Track and Field Trials.

One specific event during the lead up to the Games formed another life changing link in that same chain of events I mentioned earlier. That day, a lot was going on in town and the main photographers were occupied elsewhere, so I was tapped to be the photographer for a leg of the Olympic Torch Relay where Tokio, a famous (in Japan) band was running.

The next thing I knew, I found myself standing in the dark along a middle-of-nowhere country road, at 5 a.m., groggy and wondering if we were in the right place as there was no one around for miles. If anyone would have told me a mini-career would be spawned from this moment, I would have been certain they were off their rocker. But in hindsight I can see the minivan eventually pulling up across the lonely road and the Japanese businessmen getting out, smoking cigarettes and chatting. I went over to say hello and see if they were confident about this being the right location as I was only going to have one shot at this important picture.

I spoke mostly to the shorter guy in the group, who years later would end up slapping me hard across the face in a mistaken drunken rage. But that was later. Oblivious to that future, my ears perked up upon learning they were from Coca-Cola Japan and were there because they had sponsored the band/runners' trip. I mentioned I had been planning to go to Japan in the fall to try and find work relating to the upcoming winter Olympics, and that Coca-Cola was at the top of my list to call on. He maintained they only had a small office and not much promise for work, but I asked him to at least look for me when I came knocking on their door. Indeed he did. But that was also later.

For now, urgency shifted to the horizon where the arriving Torch Relay caravan lit up the night. I was given instructions from my Japanese reporter colleague to not be afraid to elbow my way through the inevitable onslaught of Japanese media that would be arriving to cover this event.

Everything happened so fast. All I remember was taking some pictures as one band member passed on the flame to his other band member and then I ran with the second one a bit, taking more pictures as we went—backup in case I had blown any of the previous precious pictures. I guess I did OK as my pictures ended up taking the better part of a page in the newspaper when it went to print later that day.

Back in Atlanta, once the Olympics began, my role shifted to being a driver/escort for a famous Japanese photographer. Not that any American (myself included) would have ever heard of him, but in Japan he is revered and as well known as George Lucas is in the U.S. I took him to practice sessions of the athletes as well as into the actual Olympic events. He didn't have an official photographer's pass, so we would often get chased off. We worked out routines where he would shoot like crazy while I delayed security guards as long as possible. VERY coincidentally, years later when travelling in New Zealand I caught a TV show about a security guard who had volunteered to work security at the Atlanta Olympics and sure enough, part of the footage showed him chasing off my photographer.

One undercurrent during the entire Olympics was watching my boss slowly become insane. Literally. He felt under extreme pressure to get everything right and his way of reacting to the pressure was to double up on his cigarette intake and halve his nightly sleep to less than four hours most nights. He never got more than four and a half hours of sleep a night over more than a three week stretch. His losing it resulted in longer and longer rants where, wreaking of cigarettes, he yelled at me, spattering spit, and going on and on about who knows what.

These one-way halitosis blasts eventually lasted 45 minutes or more where I would mostly nod and apologize and try to figure out some way to change the subject or get out of there. During one volcanic venting session he even suggested the only thing protecting me was that the VIP photographer in my charge adored me and loved the work I was doing for him. This happened to be my only responsibility. He hinted he was jealous I was getting to escort this famous guy around to nice restaurants and Olympic events, while he could only sit there and implode from fatigue.

My boss's lack of sleep and instability got a real workout the night of the bomb. That evening, sometime after 1 a.m. I had been catching up with an old friend at a restaurant in the suburbs when we noticed on TV there was some sort of panic going on in downtown Atlanta. A bomb blast had occurred in Centennial Olympic Park, right at the heart of the Games, and directly next door to the Main Press Center where our office was located. I called my boss to let him know about it. Clearly already at the helm of this for a while before I called, in a completely exasperated and horse voice he screamed into the phone as best he could at that point, "What are you doing? GET DOWN HERE!!" And hung up.

I left my friend and jumped into my dad's Acura Legend, which I had borrowed for the summer, and started streaking into town. At 105 MPH, cops were passing me left and right. Once I got into downtown Atlanta, I knew it would be impossible to get to the Main Press Center by car, so I ditched the Acura in a random parking lot and proceeded by foot. It was an eerie, confusing scene with police everywhere, police tape blocking off possible evidence, and many streets blocked off altogether. I spotted people walking away from the scene, visibly in shock, with blood on them. I gathered what information I could and snuck into the Press Center, which had been otherwise barricaded. The rest of the night was a blur of information, misinformation and press conferences. Over 100 people were injured, one woman was killed by the bomb directly, and a Turkish journalist died of a heart attack running to cover the story. It is a miracle my boss didn't end up with a similar obituary.

In the end, this summer stint was a great job. My exposure to the in-the-trenches world of the media and other facets surrounding a humongous event like the Olympics was a major eye opener and as an Olympics junkie, it was cool seeing a bunch of events in person including a number of track and field world records.

Within days after the Games were over, I was on my way to Alaska to work and play for a month. I returned to work for the same tour company I had worked for at the end of last summer, leading Japanese guests on multi-day camping trips. Between trips, I did trips of my own, including a five-day sea kayaking trip through the stunning Kenai fjords where I FINALLY caught my first real Alaskan fish and saw my first bear while camping—at the same time!

Kenai Fjords

I was convinced I would be selling my car and shipping all my goods back to South Carolina before I left, but I couldn't bring myself to do it, so I ended up storing things with a friend before taking off. Alaska is hard to give up (at least the summer part).

Mind you, this return to Alaska marked the first time I ever returned anywhere I had already lived previously. With repetition like this in my life, the next thing you know I'll have a wife, a house in the burbs, some kids, and a dog by my side.

OK, stop laughing.

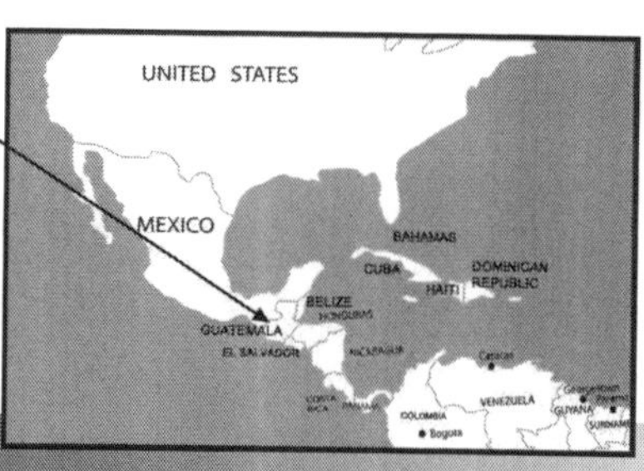

CHAPTER 5

Drunks Falling off Horses and Fun with Chicken Busses

Travels through Guatemala

Studying Spanish in Guatemala was something I'd had in the back of my head for quite some time, ever since my former math teacher Joy Ingham had told me about having done it herself. I finally had the funds and the time. I spent seven weeks living with three different families, studying Spanish at various schools. I studied entirely in Spanish with a private instructor four to seven hours a day. It was amazing how cheap this was to do.

I used my weekends to get out and explore the country with my newly made friends. Anytime I left the relative security of my Spanish lessons, I, like all Guatemalans, was subjected to the horrible "chicken busses" that roam the countryside. Almost every bus in Guatemala is an old American "Blue Bird" school bus, most of which were probably no longer considered roadworthy enough to transport America's elementary school children.

They all share some common characteristics. Most importantly, they contain some kind of stereo cranking out a Latin mix of music well beyond the volume capacity of the cheap speakers. The driver is protected in the front by a collection of stickers containing the words "God", "Jesus", "Love" and "has blessed this bus" in various combinations and orders, sometimes in numbers to the point of blocking the driver's view. Part of the mandatory maintenance program seems to require the removal of various parts of the muffler so as to be able to make the most noise as possible while belching out the maximum output of smoke. As they cram up to four adults into the space originally intended for two young children, all of these busses are filled to at least double the legal capacity, which is diligently posted right next to the sticker above the sun visor saying, "Looking out for the safety of your children". But this is the only real way to get around (other than in the back of pickup trucks) and everyone in them suffers equally, except for the people located directly next to the pukers, of which there are many.

On one of these weekend trips, three of my fellow Spanish language students and I hiked up the 3742m (12,000ft) Santa Maria volcano. While well off the beaten path, we had heard it was a hike worth doing so we grabbed a makeshift tent, some warm clothes, a few cans of food and went for it. Ironically, the highlight of the excursion for me was throwing up.

Shadow of the Santa Maria volcano on which we were camping out

At night, the four of us were packed into our two-person tent-like shelter like a can of sardines. When one person rolled over, everyone rolled over. And it was windy and cold. I woke up in the middle of the night and debated with my inner devils until I lost, succumbing to the fact that I was not going to be keeping down my dinner. I decided it would be neighborly of me to not live out this destiny on my tent mates, so I stumbled outside under a new higher ceilinged tent of stars. It had been cloudy when we got to the top, so we never had much of a view.

But now it was completely clear and the view down into the valley, under the bright almost-full moonlight, was incredible. I am not sure if I was called out there due to altitude sickness, funky food, or the pot we'd smoked earlier, but ultimately I was thankful for the unpleasant urge that pulled me out of bed. Under that moonlight I witnessed the source of a mysterious jet engine-like noise we had been hearing intermittently. It turned out that below, completely unbeknownst to us, was another smaller, erupting volcano. A shape-shifting spiraling plume climbed a tall tower into the sky, forming dragons and images of other monsters as it rose. I witnessed this in awe while pausing to vomit. I realized if the wind were blowing in a different direction, we could have been in great peril as we would have been smothered by the ash and fumes. I was particularly thankful for having been awoken in the middle of the night, because the next morning it was clouded over again and the view was lost.

The volcano below us erupting after the clouds opened up again later in the afternoon

Aside from other Guatemala highlights, such as a three-hour ride on top of a bus, and getting robbed by three kids with big knives, one particularly interesting detour was to see the Day of the Dead festivities in Todos Santos. Tucked up in a mountainous enclave away from the rest of the world, Todos Santos is a holdout of indigenous tradition. While throughout Guatemala you can find colorful indigenous groups, nowhere are they more colorful than Todos Santos, both in costume and festivities. The most intriguing celebration of all is el Dia de los Muertos, which pits sobriety (or rather the lack thereof) against horsemanship skills in what can be a battle to the death.

By 7:45 a.m. I had a good seat overlooking the course where the all-important "horse race" was to unfold. A half hour later the first contenders made their way into the arena, a straight dirt road with wooden railings along both sides. With the population being over 90 percent indigenous in Todos Santos, the people watching is fascinating and no day is that more so than the Day of the Dead, as it is a tradition for the locals to wear a newly woven "huipile" garment. Colorful clothing like this can be found throughout Guatemala, but the designs of these in Todos Santos are some of the prettiest I have seen and seemingly everyone was wearing them. Even the men wear a traditional outfit: red with white pin stripe woven pants plus a colorful striped shirt with a big vibrantly woven collar. I saw many of the men working on sewing their new outfit the night before.

The basic race concept was that the drunk men on horseback would gallop chaotically at full tilt to the opposite end of the course, stop, pause there for a bit and then race back the other way. The race started with one guy and eventually built up to about 30 of them at a time. There were no starting guns, no referees, just an ebb and flow back and forth, which carried on for about four hours in the morning and another four in the afternoon after the all-important siesta.

In terms of rules or goals, the best I could figure, these guys were completely hammered when they first got on the horses in the morning, and they would race back and forth, drinking as they went until they eventually passed out and fell off—and I mean fell hard. I probably witnessed eight to ten wipeouts and I am sure there were more I didn't see. If I gathered correctly through my observations, the best way to pass out while riding a horse is ride leaning back further and further, then at

some point just let go. One guy fell and was out cold, motionless on the side of the road, but I saw him up and at it again later. Apparently this event used to be even wilder with 100-150 participants, and they used to use live chickens for whips. Ahh the good old days.

By the time the morning's heats were up, the entire town's visiting and resident population was covered with an inch or more of dust kicked up by the horses and the falling riders. Like NASCAR racing, it seemed the real draw was seeing the guys eat it. Rumor has it someone dies most every year which is not at all surprising when you see them fall. When they do, it is supposed to bring good luck to the village for the next year, sort of like a ritual Mayan sacrifice by lottery.

I tried to get a better understanding of what was going on around me, but I could never find anyone who spoke Spanish. Mam is the first language spoken here. Even the parrot at the place I was staying spoke Mam.

As the day progressed, the burracho-meter gradually edged upwards to higher and higher levels. The drunker people got, the more fights broke out and the more people could be seen passed out in various places. In the afternoon, I made my way back down to the race. This time I caught it at ground level, which is kind of like taking a dirt shower.

"Man Down!" One of the completely *burracho* Todos Santos riders bites the dust, horse whip still in hand.

The next day, the Day of the Dead action shifted from people trying to get in the cemetery, to the actual cemetery itself. The entire town flowed in like a river past the vendors. It was a real celebration. Three different marimba groups were in full swing playing their traditional mellow Guatemalan music to the crowds. This is a day everyone gathers around the graves of their elders to reminisce, eat, drink, mourn and laugh. They clean up the gravesite and adorn it with colorful decorations. It seemed like a neat tradition that would likely never work at that level in modern, spread out American society.

It was a real joy to be joined by Japanese newspaper coworker Kahori and her friend Shoko who came down from Atlanta to share my final week in the region. I felt deeply satisfied just watching them climb out of the eight-seater plane, especially since I was never sure they were coming. I had been unable to reach them by phone for three weeks, and didn't know if they had received my detailed fax about how I suggested we meet. I love it when a plan comes together.

The two of them had no clue about where to go or what to do here, but they were game for anything, which was a good thing. We ventured down some rough and tumble back roads through what was supposed to be rainforest (can you say slash and burn?) to see the breathtaking Mayan ruins buried in the thick rainforests of Tikal.

We continued on to kick back on the relaxed islands of Belize. While it was a fun ending to my time in Guatemala, I'll admit I had never been so happy to return to Los Angeles, a city I have never been a big fan of. There is something to be said about being back on American turf where—sure you are a target for crime—but not much more than the next guy. Also it was nice not having to be careful about everything I ate.

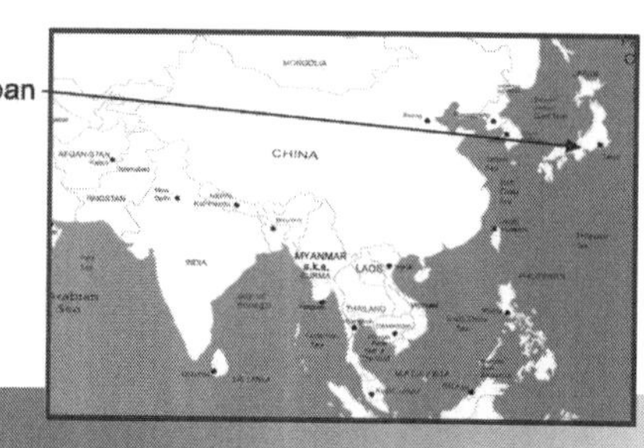

CHAPTER 6

In Pursuit of a Shower

Winter Olympics Life in Nagano, Japan

I was soon on my way to Japan, kicking off my first week in Tokyo tracking down friends and job leads. After my Guatemala experience, just walking through fancy ticket-reading turnstiles to get on a bullet train, I couldn't help but feel that while ridiculously expensive, with its automated efficiencies and predictability of every product or service you buy, in Japan you at least got what you paid for.

One only-in-Japan highlight was an afternoon of skiing at the Tokyo Ski Dome with one of my favorite people anywhere, Inoue-san, a hilarious photographer friend from the Japanese newspaper. Indoor skiing was definitely a first for me. It was set up extremely efficiently, so you could walk in wearing regular clothes and they would equip you from soup to nuts. We had a blast for the one hour we signed up for.

From Tokyo I made my way out to the prefecture of Nagano, a place with real skiing where I spent a week looking into different job and housing possibilities. I moved into a gem of a place. OK, it wasn't exactly a king's palace. There was no shower (or so I first thought), but it still suited me fine and the landlord was good to me.

The family I rented the room from used to live in the space over their shop where I had just settled. They had moved into their newly-built, adjoining house earlier that year. The husband was a smiley chain smoking elderly guy who spoke in a hard-to-follow local Nagano dialect. In the shop space beneath me, he ran some sort of medical treatment facility involving electricity and/or magnets, which I never understood.

I picked this place, assuming they were going to fill up the other rooms, thereby giving me neighbors and cooking partners. That never happened other than when my friend Nima helped rent out the extra rooms during the Olympics. All in all, the place wasn't bad, considering I was paying under $200US per month…in JAPAN. (OK, I wanted to see that in print just once). In a world of $60 melons, I have to say I am still proud of my find. My monthly rent was more like $140/ mo., but I factored in the nifty thing they have in Japan called "key money" which is a sum of money you put up as a "gift" to your dear new landlord. Sometimes this sum can be up to five times your monthly rent.

The two biggest adjustments I had to make were not having a place to bathe, which meant I had to go to a public bath house down the street and—a Westerners all time favorite—the squat toilet. Both inconveniences were resolved before too long.

My landlords did their best to make things as comfortable as possible for me. Every time I turned around a new piece of furniture, futons or other stuff would appear. The charming old guy even bought me my own (heated!) toilet adapter (I bet you didn't know there was such a thing—I can tell you I didn't) so rest easy knowing I was sitting down like the rest of you folks when it came time to take a "big" as they call it.

At one point the good doctor let it slip there was a functioning hot shower downstairs in the back side of my building, only he refused to let me use it until at least March because he insisted I would catch a cold. Baths are integral to Japanese culture and most Japanese take baths, not showers on a daily basis. The idea that a shower in winter is a way to catch a cold was an entrenched way of thinking. Once the cat was out of the bag, though, I lobbied hard for shower access. He finally relented during the New Year holidays when the public bathhouse I had been using was going to be closed for five days. Then I just had to deal with being able to see my breath (from the cold) while showering and navigating around their unpleasant dog, which they put out in their house entrance at night and whenever the weather was lousy. Also sometimes my shampoo almost froze.

I developed a system of preheating the drafty room and the shower basin by running steamy hot water before setting foot inside. Once I was done, I dried my head and the half of my body not facing the hot water before turning it off, drying the rest of me at lightning speed and scampering out and up to my kerosene-heated bedroom before the cold hit me.

It got quite chilly in the main apartment area, too, which lacked central heating. Sometimes the water in the toilet would ice over and I had to keep vegetables in the refrigerator to keep them from freezing. Even my cooking oils and toothpaste would congeal from the cold.

With housing sorted out, I started knocking on doors to find work relating to the Olympics. I picked up a few odd jobs with organizations like TIME Magazine and the Canadian Olympic Committee, which needed help with their Olympics preparations.

Not knowing how Coca-Cola works, I went to the local bottler thinking it was the same company as the people I met in Atlanta. I was shocked when only one year before the Olympics were to begin, they said they, "didn't have much in the way of Olympics-related things going on."

As an olive branch, one of the older senior managers mentioned they had a test event at the new hockey arena coming up and they could possibly hire me to work for that. Immediately I sprung into action offering my services, like taking care of international VIPs attending the hockey tournament or other high-level work. He smiled. Fast forward to me in a freezing cold parking lot yelling, "Coca-Cola for sale!" from a vending trailer. I couldn't help but laugh at myself, now Coca-Cola Boy, decked out in my bright red and white uniform hawking Cokes and can coffee. What I won't do to get my foot in the door.

It turned out to be a smart move. There were a number of people there from the (corporate) Coca-Cola Japan's main Tokyo office. On the last day of the five-day tournament, the short guy I met at the Atlanta Torch Relay showed up and remembered me. He asked if I was still looking for work and I said yes. He said, "In that case talk to this guy next to you as he needs someone to do Public Relations." And thus discussions started

getting serious. Ultimately I was hired to help with international PR for all of Coke's Nagano Olympic efforts, i.e. the Torch Relay, Coca-Cola Radio, pin trading stuff, etc. etc. based in both Tokyo and Nagano City.

Vacation Boy getting mauled by the Coke bear, a.k.a. John Henson, son of Muppet creator Jim Henson

(With his boss Jen) Vacation Boy becoming the Paralympic rabbit for an event at the Coca-Cola Pin Trading Center

But that's work. Let's instead talk about…

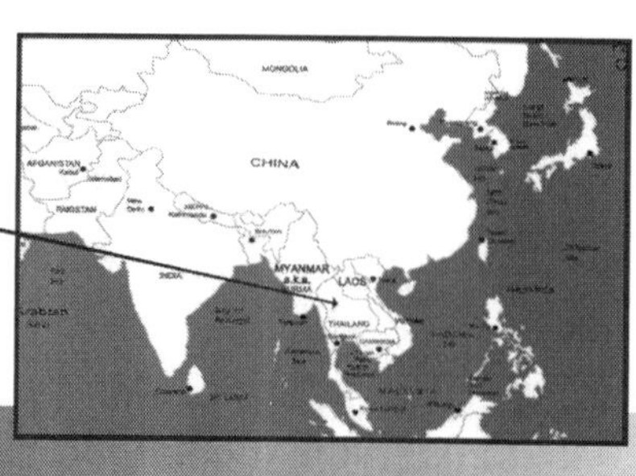

CHAPTER 7

Eluding Leeches and Losing My Pants

Travels through Thailand

To get away from the mayhem at Coca-Cola in Tokyo preparing activities relating to the 1998 Winter Olympics, I loaded my backpack and headed for a week of desperately needed respite in Thailand.

Thailand was great right from the start. Although I would normally have been concerned about arriving in Bangkok just before midnight, this time I was in good hands. Jiu, a Thai friend of mine from my days of studying abroad in Japan, not only grew up in Bangkok, but worked for the Thai Tourism Bureau. She met me at the airport, then dropped me off at a pleasant yet cheap hotel she had already reserved.

I was ready to head for the hills at sunrise, but Jiu offered to play tour guide, so we spent Sunday seeing the sites and shopping around town. Who could turn down a personal tour from a friend who works for the Thai Tourism Bureau? She generously navigated me around to all the top sites. What a treat!

All of Thailand, including Bangkok, seemed pretty well put together. The worst bus I encountered here was better than the best bus in Guatemala. The Thai people were extremely kind and not bent on trying to cheat you every chance they could. People only rarely came up to sell stuff or ask for money.

To top it off, with the strong dollar and the troubled baht, everything was insanely cheap. I felt giddy rich, like a king with a buying power I had never before experienced. Even including the flight to get there, my week in Thailand came out to be less expensive than if I had stayed in Japan for my vacation. Heck, the most expensive room on my trip was under $7 and the cheapest came in at $1.50.

I spent my first day on my own flying north up to Chiang Mai. I was apprehensive about going there since the day before two Italians had been shot in the Chiang Mai airport.

An English language paper outlined how a Thai police officer had shot them as they were waiting at the check-in counter. The cop was apparently drunk and pissed off that his girlfriend had left him to shack up with a *farang* (foreigner). He walked in and saw a group of white guys and opened fire. Fortunately, they were only injured.

Once I spent a little more time in the north, I realized why he had hit Italians. Up there, I think if you close your eyes and shot in any given direction, you would likely hit at least one Italian (although your chances of grazing a Frenchman or German would be pretty good, too.)

I bussed over to the quiet town of Pai to join up with a rafting trip leaving the next morning. Unfortunately, the next morning I overslept. I woke up ten minutes before the latest time they said I could arrive. Panicked, I threw my stuff in my bag, slapped my money down at the reception, and flew out the door and down the street. It was not until a few minutes later, already halfway down the street, that I noticed through my blurred eyes that I had no idea where I was. There were three streets in the whole town and I managed to sprint down the wrong one.

A blurry woman pointed me back in the right direction and off I went running again. I miraculously managed to arrive several minutes before my given deadline, yet all was eerily quiet. Too quiet. No one in sight. I spent the entire previous day trying to get to this location for this trip, so the prospect of blowing it by oversleeping 30 minutes was not something I was prepared to accept. I entered the neighboring restaurant and asked the people cleaning up where the rafting group was and how I could catch up with them. After a fairly involved series of events, $3 and 66 kilometers later, I managed to catch up with the group.

The group consisted of a young Dutch couple, two Thai guides and a French contingency of ten participants. There were two sturdy rafts and the inflatable canoe in which I rode. It was not far down the river I decided to apply water fight strategies I had perfected during my tour guiding days, thereby soaking the people in the other boats. The water battles from that point on were non-stop and no holds barred. Not a dry person in the group.

As we floated into the canyon-like mountains, the scenery became more and more stunning. During the two-day trip, we saw almost no signs of civilization. I had hoped to see a bit more wildlife, but I did at least spot several cool looking blue hornbills. At night, we stayed at a rustic camp mostly made of bamboo and other local foliage. The sleeping area was little more than mats on a raised platform with a thatch roof and mosquito netting, which brings up an important point. This area had a fairly high-risk rate of malaria. I was not able to acquire malaria medicine because the stupid Japanese government decided the medication is too strong, so it isn't available anywhere in Japan. Throughout my trip and another few weeks after I had to keep my fingers crossed. If I had gotten malaria I would have been pissed.

With medium-high water flow in the river, the next day's rapids were fun. Low hanging branches added extra challenges to these class II-III+ waters. By the end of the trip, the rafts were nearly empty as they passed through many of the rapids with their intended passengers floating alongside them—either by choice or by force.

Once the trip ended, my biggest challenge was deciding what I would do next, since I had no concrete plans. Although it would drive many people nuts, I enjoy travelling without a specific plan. It gives me the ultimate in flexibility. I can't be lost unless I have a location in mind where I'd like to be, right? I try to offset my lack of foresight by asking every soul along the way what they feel are the best things to see.

I was pretty sure at this point I wanted to do some kind of trekking up in the mountains to see hill tribes, but I did not know where to leave from or what there was to see. I had read in guidebooks that many trekking routes have become overused. People on my rafting trip had talked about how much they enjoyed their two-day experience, leaving from a town slightly off the more heavily beaten paths, but said when they arrived in the tribe villages, they were still swarmed by people trying to sell them handicrafts, which was exactly the type of experience I was hoping to avoid.

The river trip ended at a town called Mae Hong Son, a laid back village surrounded by mountains and situated around a quaint little lake. I liked the feel of the town and decided to stay.

While wandering about, I stopped at the Buddhist temple across the lake from my guesthouse. There, the orange-clothed, shaved-head, sandal-wearing monks had taken in a small, three-month old monkey as a pet. The spry little guy's favorite pastimes included riding on and otherwise hassling the dogs, and temporarily fleeing from his smiling, reverent caretakers. He didn't have any qualms about scurrying right up my leg to be cradled in my arms. Dressed in his Buddhist charm-bracelet-like chain, this guy was too cute. I decided I must have a monkey.

I met my affable and capable, yet unfortunately named trekking guide Sum Sok, through a series of introductions in town. The next day when it was time for the trek, he came by to inform me his other prospective client, with whom I had been hoping to be paired, had already taken off on a different trip the day before. I didn't have time to wait an undetermined amount of time to try and find someone else to share the expense with, but in my new role as currency-exchange-related windfall millionaire, I was OK with this. I dug into my deep pockets to cover the cost for a private guide, food, room, and transportation for two days: $45. Off we went.

Our day started at the market, buying the food for the trip. We then got a ride up to our starting point village where the sounds of Creedence Clearwater Revival could be heard lofting out of a house, a sure sign we still had a little ways to go to escape the grips of modern civilization. It didn't take long. We were soon surrounded by lush forests on all sides.

The difference in gear between me and my guide was comical. While I was dressed to take on the harshest of elements in my long pants, hiking boots and full backpack, my trusty guide's attire of choice for this mountainous terrain was a T-shirt, shorts, and flip flops ("they are waterproof," he said) plus a smaller bag that included all the food.

I started the hike more concerned about getting leeched than about looking around at the surrounding scenery. I asked Sum Sok, "Aren't you afraid of leeches?" He replied, "There aren't too many in the area where we're going," yet then nonchalantly pointed out a couple of ugly leech scars on his feet from his last trip, sending shivers up my spine.

It wasn't long before a creek began to intertwine with the path and then both funneled into the foot of a canyon. We paused for a moment to swim and take in the beauty. Although we were almost continually shaded by the canopy of the surrounding towering trees, it was still plenty hot so the dip in the water felt good. It was somewhere after the dip that, when extending my leg to get around a big rock, I heard a little rip around the important crotch part of my Thai cotton pants. It seemed innocent enough at the time, but the tear turned out to be a more serious parting of the pants than it first appeared. Within a couple hours, the little hole had expanded to the point that I looked like I was wearing cotton chaps with major ventilation in the middle. I was pretty embarrassed and made Sum Sok promise he'd tell me before we got to a village so I could put some actual clothes on.

The total ascent to the White Karen village took about four hours. It was stunningly beautiful much of the way. During my time in Tokyo, I starting paying attention to the percentage of greenery one sees in any given landscape (and how depressingly low the number is in Tokyo—usually less than 15%). I thought of it as the Green Count. Here, in some places, including the sky above and the path below, the Green Count was at least 90%. It was glorious. My psyche felt like chlorophyll cells being recharged by sunlight. (That simile is for my sister—I hope I didn't screw up the biology part!).

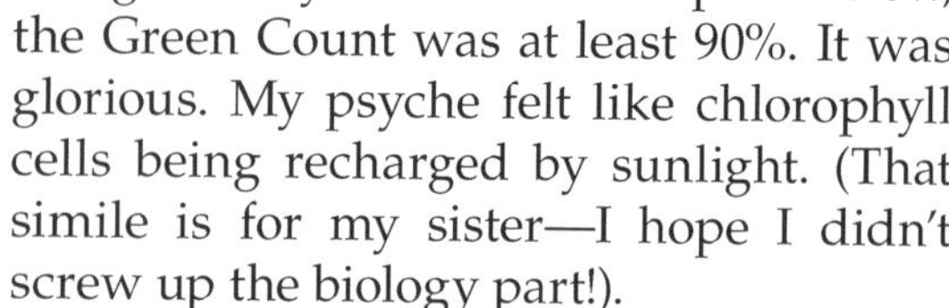

Far from a leisurely stroll, the invigorating trail crisscrossed the stream and climbed up over rocks. While getting pretty exhausted, I still thought we were making decent time until an elderly tribal lady (she had to be over 70 years old) blew by us in her flip flops as if we were standing still—and she was carrying a heavy load suspended in a bag by a strap around her forehead. I couldn't believe it. I got a picture of her scaling up a slippery rock face to assure myself later that I wasn't making it up.

Sum Sok, always out to inspire confidence, told me about how two months prior he had seen a huge snake, over 14 feet long, skirting up a slope near this part of the trail. "It was probably a king cobra," he said casually as I now found myself re-preoccupied with scanning the surrounding vegetation.

The sleepy village of the White Karen people was exactly the kind of place I was hoping to experience. No electricity, no phones, no running water, but beautiful views and wonderful people. We stayed in the home of one of the local families. There was no one running up trying to sell me things like my fellow travelers had experienced. Instead there was just one shy little girl in the house who seemed more intent on running away from me than anything else.

Mother of the Karen house where we were staying, preparing greens for the evening meal

The remainder of the evening was spent preparing food, eating food and drinking drink. These were happy people. Neighbors perpetually passed through to visit and talk about whatever.

Sum Sok was truly friends with them and it was easy to see he enjoyed their company. He had learned their language by coming up to the village for fun and spending time with them even when he wasn't leading trips. As we sat on the smooth dark wood floor together for dinner I got a chance to try a tasty local dish which I believe was made from ferns.

After dinner, everyone gathered in the kitchen around the fire for a bit of moonshine and more conversation. It was through a translated conversation that I was able to determine they had never heard of the Olympics. *This* was a vacation!

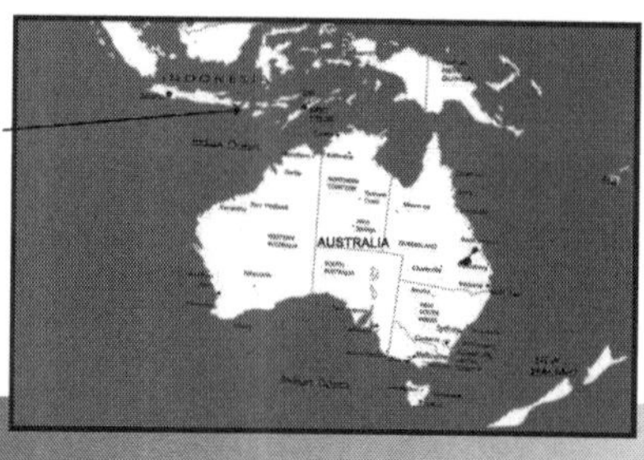

CHAPTER 8

Explosive Bali Diving

Indonesia

After a frenetic winding down of my Coca-Cola work in Japan, Vacation Boy needed a break, and luckily I had the remainder of a round-the-world ticket which needed using. The southern hemisphere beckoned me, so off to Indonesia I went. This was a big travel milestone for me since out of all my 26 years of existence and lots of traveling therein, never once had I set foot in that half of the world. Half!

The saddest looking monkey of all time. hanging out by the side of the road in Bali

Indonesia is an inexpensive place to travel on a regular day, but during this time period it was being further affected by the Asian financial crisis sweeping the region. Even without Japan's painful prices lingering in the scarred recesses of my frugal mind, it would still have felt WAY cheap. It didn't take long, however, for me to adjust to the new reality of feeling exorbitantly wealthy. When I came across a hotel in Bali that charged not rupiah but seven actual US dollars a night I remember thinking, "Who would pay such an outlandish sum?"

On another occasion on the island of Lombok, I was walking

somewhere with my full backpack when a shared taxi tried to stop and give me a ride to the town I was heading to. He tried to bilk me for what I think in hindsight was a whole 25 cents, an outrageous sum for the distance I had left to cover, so I walked the several miles myself to avoid such an affront. I can't help but laugh thinking about it now.

During my bike trip around Bali, I took a break to do some scuba diving near Lovina. Bali's diving is renowned for its vast array of colorful fish and coral. Some theories suggest that life on earth may have begun and spread from here since Bali has the highest concentration of marine species anywhere. The species count steadily dwindles as you get progressively further away.

One thing never mentioned in the glowing descriptions of Bali's diving was the possibility of being blown up. In the midst of a drift dive, where we were flying with the current like a weightless plane over the reef, BLAM!—there was a jarring explosion. I looked about frantically to see if someone's air tank had exploded or perhaps the gas tank on the boat had blown up, yet the dive leader proceeded on like nothing had happened. And later, BLAM! It happened again.

When we surfaced later I learned someone had been dynamite fishing nearby. This is a destructive practice where instead of going to the trouble of catching fish the traditional way, the "fisherman" simply tosses some TNT into the sea, waits for the explosion and then collects whatever floats to the surface. Pretty scary even if you aren't a fish and it does atrocious things to the coral. This fish hunter may have been a mile or more away, but the strength of the blast made it feel like it was next door. I could see how someone could easily pass out underwater from the concussion of the explosion if it were closer by.

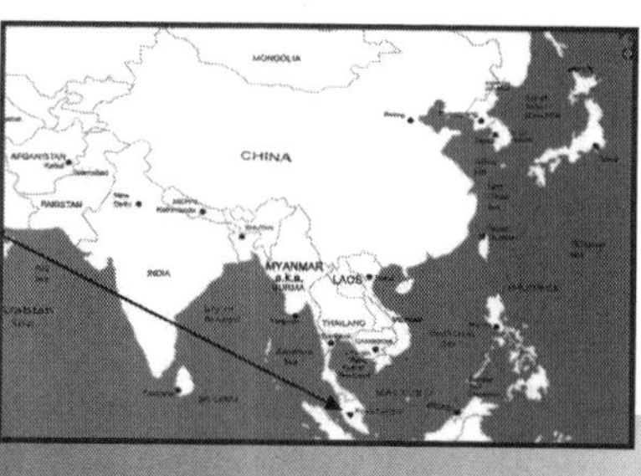

CHAPTER 9

Painful Encounters with Fish and Friends

Malaysia

Arriving at my next stop in Malaysia I immediately felt like a fish uncomfortably out of water. Things went downhill almost from the moment Lai-Hsin met me at the Penang airport accompanied by her sister and sister's friend. Lai-Hsin and I had been friends from my student days in Japan and had traveled together on a couple occasions in Japan where a romance eventually blossomed between us. Here in her native land, everything that had been right before was now out of place.

They dropped me off at a painfully over-priced, over-luxurious hotel she had reserved for me, which I did not balk at only for the sake of being polite. The hotel served as my low-security prison during my next several days of torture. Perhaps coming from the mental bliss of my Indonesia wind down in the idyllic Gili Islands (off Lombok Island) to this—a big crowded expensive city with people out to annoy me—made everything harder to bare.

For one, Lai-Hsin and her crew were addicted to their cell phones. They constantly received calls, made calls, and sent texts everywhere we went—even in a movie theater DURING the movie.

Next was the food. I have always considered myself to be a lover of pasta and noodles, but I now knew I only kind of liked them compared to these folks. Breakfast, lunch, dinner and snacks—noodles, noodles, noodles. It seemed to be the only thing they survived on.

Third was having to spend at least half my time there in the company of Lai-Hsin's new boyfriend. Yes, I was happy for her finding this new love in her homeland, but (admittedly still having feelings for her) having him incessantly petting and rubbing and holding hands with her made me uncomfortable. My one consolation in hindsight is they ultimately ended up getting happily married and are still to this day.

At the time, though, my priority was to buy a map and guidebook to plot a course out of town as fast as possible. Anywhere else would be fine.

Before I escaped, my time in Penang dragged from one awkward social situation to another. The exclamation mark came when Lai-Hsin's parents invited us to dinner at their private member's sports club. I was told several times during the meal the only reason we weren't able to eat at the nice air-conditioned restaurant upstairs was because I was not wearing a collared shirt. I kept looking for the exits.

The next day I knew I would be leaving. One thing that put me in better spirits, ironically, was my morning's horoscope. It was scary how it seemed to be talking straight to me:

"Cheer up! Your situation is not as bad as it seems to be. You are still much more fortunate than many others. And, soon your troubles will be licked."

Wow. I sat up after reading it. I knew I had been wallowing unnecessarily in my low spirits, but reading this advice was like a slap on the cheek to snap out of it and move on. So I did.

We made one last stop for, of course, noodles, before I said goodbye to my friends and sprinted (mentally) for the bus and the rainforests to which it would be taking me.

My clothes are soaked through,
Yet there is not a cloud in the sky.
Fatigue is setting in and I ask myself,
"How can I go on?"
Then I look up and see the bounteous nature around me and think,
"How could I not?"

I came up with this poem on a ten kilometer-plus hike with all my heavy gear through the rainforest of Taman Negara National Park. It was one of several such hikes I would take in this park. Despite some of the walks remaining entirely in the shade of the lush rainforest canopy, the heat and humidity were oppressive and it wasn't long before my clothes were completely saturated with perspiration.

The jungle noises were fantastic despite the occasional interference of motor boat noises from the nearby river. As long as I was moving, surprisingly few bugs were interested in biting me, although anytime I stopped, insects seemed to want to help speed up my biodegrading process. It made for short rest breaks.

Of all the amazing creatures I encountered the first day, the one that left the most indelible impression was one particular three-foot iguana/monitor lizard, namely because it scared the shit out of me. Upon seeing me, it darted off in a mad dash across the forest floor, sounding like a choo choo train as its claws skittered across the dry leaves. My heart still aflutter from the surprise even after it was long gone, I now knew that if anything in that forest wanted to attack me as badly as that lizard wanted to flee, I would be dead meat. It turned out the most dangerous creatures I would encounter in the park were not these giant lizards and not the 4-foot king cobra, nor the leaches or the persnickety rat who tried to get my food at night, but rather some tiny little fish lurking under the water. But that was later.

At night I stayed in the tree-house-like "hides" which offered the opportunity to spot wildlife below (and in the cabin itself). Pulling out the scary bunk mattresses the first night, I decided to use my metallic emergency blanket on top of it as a barrier because this was an emergency.

The second night I shared a different hide with a British guy Richard. When the rainstorm passed through that evening, we took turns playing Tarzan, showering au natural on the balcony. It did wonders for cooling off the heat of the day.

Exhausted from the day's hiking, and with no electricity to keep lights ablaze, we turned in early. Right away I shooed off a roach scurrying within my mosquito net and Richard spotted a large spider on top of his. He was happy he decided to use the netting, otherwise he might have had that eight-legged critter as his bedmate.

As night weighed heavier, the volume of the chorus of animal and insect sounds increased and it felt like the jungle was closing in on us. Contributing to that sensation was something scratching at the empty cans down on the forest floor.

Earlier we had eaten a delicious tuna with chilies sandwich. We hung the remaining food in the cabin and tossed the empty cans in a bag, down onto the rubbish pile below. Around 11 p.m. I was awakened by the sound of something ripping open and clattering about the contents of our trash bag. Then I heard something heading up the tree toward our hide, driven by the promise of more food from wherever those cans originated.

Our first four-footed visitor of the evening soon arrived—a rat. He was not at all phased by me shining a flashlight at him. After some insistent urging, he finally scurried under the door, but I had to step on his tail to get him all the way out.

Our second visitor (or perhaps the same one) showed up around 1:30 a.m. This time I was prepared. I had strategically relocated a substance in the hide which we speculated to be rat poison to some key locations. Visitor #2 eventually left, too, and I am proud to say that neither got my food.

After the previous day's rain, the leeches were out in force. Luckily they are not fast. They look like inchworms with a magnetic-like sensor that slowly points them in the direction of the blood running through your veins. If you step to one side, they change course to head towards you. Even when they did jump aboard the Vacation Boy Express, I usually could spot them and flick them off before they even reached the sock level. Not a big deal. It was those devilish fish I should have been worrying about.

The irresistible waters in which the mini-monsters lurked

I can't say I wasn't warned about the little fish. I had run into a tourist earlier in my visit who, when describing a minnow-like fish in these waters, reminded me of the soothsayer in "Monty Python and the Holy Grail" warning against the danger of the rabbit in the cave, saying, "It's got fangs!" This person's story would have been equally as hard to believe were it not for the bloody bandage on his knee. He said menacingly, "If you get in the water, you have to keep moving or, they'll get ya". Mind you, people are swimming in these waters all the time.

But that warning was several days earlier and in the persistent sweltering heat, the cool waters proved too strong a temptation to pass up, especially when my fun new Argentinean friends were stripping down to their bathing suits and leading the charge.

I had met Emma and Cecilia earlier in the day at the main swimming hole. They liked that I was the first person in their SE Asia travels who could speak Spanish, and I enjoyed being able to practice. We ended up hanging out and visiting some of the sites together, the coolest of which was the Canopy Walkway. This was an incredible 500-meter long rope bridge that wound through upper reaches of giant trees. I'd guess at some points these swaying bridges were 200 feet above the forest floor. At times you could not see the ground through the foliage below.

But back to that lake…where was I? Oh yes, Emma & Cecilia, lake, stripping, swim suits, sweltering heat…obviously I decided to join them. I was supposed to be catching the boat which would start my journey to Kuala Lumpur, but decided a quick dip would make the ride immensely more comfortable.

What started as a few minutes of refreshing bliss turned into a horror show when the girls shrieked and flinched almost simultaneously at a stabbing pain they were each feeling under the water, saying "something bit me!" In a panic we clamored out of the water and onto shore to find blood pouring from their toes. Simple pressure was not enough to make it stop. Once they used their hair bands as tourniquets and slowed the blood flow we got a look at an astonishing U-shaped divot that been removed from the tip of Cecilia's toe. These fish meant business!

Unfortunately, to make my outbound plane, I had a boat to catch. I had to leave these wounded women even before they got the blood to stop running. They did write me later to let me know that despite getting quite a scare at the time, they survived just fine.

CHAPTER 10

Screw It, I'm Going to Greece

An Unexpected Detour

In hindsight I am glad the rude and unhelpful people at the Indian embassy in Tokyo were unable to help me get an Indian visa in time, causing me to say, "screw it, I'm going to Greece." Boy I loved Greece! I showed up in Athens without a guidebook or a plan. I was completely unprepared since I had originally intended to go to India. On the 6 a.m. bus into town I was groggily searching my brain for things about Greece and Greek culture that I knew and would be interested to check out. Then it hit me, GREEK FOOD! I LOVE Greek food! Having been on Asian rations for almost a year and a half, to plunge full time into this culture of feta cheese, baklava, spanakopita and moussaka seemed like too much to ask for. Elated and fueled by this thought alone, my brain started waking up to the realization that I was arriving into the cradle of one of the world's great civilizations.

I did something in Athens I would normally consider unthinkable: a bus tour. It turned out perfect, because arriving into town early in the morning with no plan whatsoever, the half-day city tour was a great way to see some sites and get my bearings. I couldn't get enough of the Parthenon. Its stately grandeur gave me a timeless sense of peace just by gazing at it.

The comments written in the used guidebook I bought after the tour gave me all the direction I needed to put together the rest of my week. I started by venturing inland to see the byzantine monasteries of Meteora. Amazing. They are perched on and around gigantic boulders, which were remnants of rock cliffs from when the sea level reached that high.

I ended up spending a couple days wandering around the area with Tammi, a garrulous redhead from Melbourne, Australia staying in the same hostel as me. The night we met, we headed into town to see what the Kalambaka nightlife had to offer on a Saturday night. It was a fun scene trying to cavort with the locals over the pounding music of Nirvana and Offspring while trying Ouzo for the first time. Being the conservative, jet lagged and sufficiently buzzed person I was, I turned in early that night. Tammi, however, apparently stayed much later. The next day she was complaining about skin painfully missing from her back as a result of an amorous encounter. Something about a stone wall...

For me, the highlight of Meteora was visiting the Agios Triada monastery. Built in 1476 and perched atop a sheer sandstone pillar, the spectacular location was featured in the finale of the James Bond film *For Your Eyes Only.* It wasn't until the 20th century that monks, pilgrims and supplies were able to reach the monastery by means other than rope ladders and baskets.

The most outstanding feature of the monastery was Father John, a gregarious one-eyed friar who welcomed us to the apparently not-so-visited site. Dressed in a traditional black Greek Orthodox frock, he not only gave us a personal tour showing the exquisite frescos in the byzantine chapel, but invited us to join him for some local candy, coffee and conversation. He loved America and had traveled there many times when he wasn't living up on this rock.

At one point a trio from Colorado came in and Friar John invited them to join us. The mother cowered back when the friar leaned in, and pulled open his empty eye socket to show where he'd had several operations. He was a hoot.

It made for a special and intimate ambiance hanging out with him in this echoing ancient monastery, great views and all. He even sent me off with a candle he had hand made from bees wax.

Next it was time for the Greek Islands. In the Kalambaka train station, I met Ayako, a Japanese traveler from Yokohama who would become my travel partner for the next several days and eventually one of my lifelong friends. Ayako was heading the same direction, so we ended up taking on the islands together. I began by mischievously letting her struggle through our English conversation, wanting to see how long it would take her to figure out I had been living in Japan and spoke fluent Japanese. I think I made it a full hour before she figured it out and quickly switched to speaking Japanese.

Train and ferry schedules caused us to make an overnight stop on the island of Prados en route to our intended destination of Santorini. In the morning, our rough-around-the-edges-but-still-OK host at John's Rooms, Yannis, was not pleased we were leaving. He kept telling us, "Santorini…no good!" We appreciated his advice (however much we doubted it) and told him we would surely return if it was as lousy as he made it out to be.

But Santorini turned out instead to be a dreamy, poster-perfect island both from a distance and close up. The island is the remnants of an ancient volcanic crater rim, forming a crescent with the middle of the bay punctuated by its old caldera cone and surrounding lava flow. The crescent slopes up gently from the exterior of the former volcano until it plunges off as a dramatic steep cliff on the interior. From a distance, the landscape looks like it is sprinkled with snow. These are the iconic whitewashed "cave houses" often imbedded into the cliff sides that contribute to the fame of these picturesque islands. Santorini was an island done up right.

After some exploring around Oia in the quiet northern tip of the crescent, we discovered a studio apartment for rent that was to die for. With its cliff top uninterrupted view facing the sea-filled crater (even from the bed), this 'cave house' was one of the most scenic rooms I have ever seen. On a backpacker's budget $34/night is a relatively big hit, but I knew good & well it was an excellent value and an oh-so-worth-it splurge here at the end of my trip. And we split it!

Ayako and I felt like we were living in a dream, enjoying each other's company and soaking up the romantic surroundings. Our relationship would eventually continue beyond Greece as she came to visit me in the US and I visited her more than once in Japan.

I intentionally left pebbles from Santorini's beach in my shoes, so that later while living in Paris, I could evoke memories of my wonderful Greek experience. Speaking of which, the City of Lights awaited me…

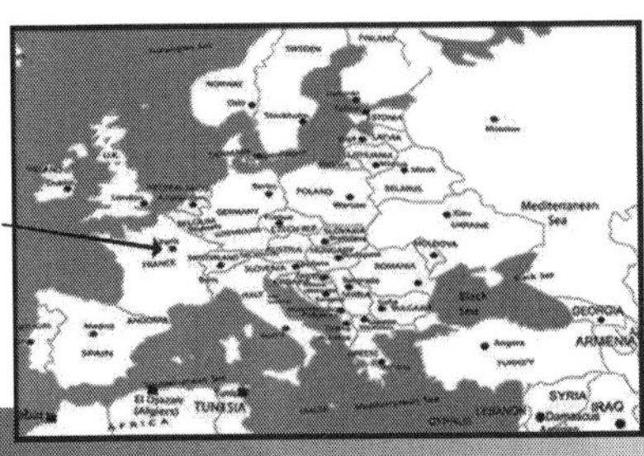

CHAPTER 11

"Is That Someone Asleep Behind the Register?"

Working the World Cup Soccer Tournament in France

As an admitted travel junkie, I was fired up when the plane touched down at Charles de Gaulle airport, knowing that upon arriving in Paris I had completed my first ever circumnavigation of the planet. That was a biggie on the bucket list.

During my Southeast Asia and Greece trip I had sporadically remained in touch with people from the American company that had run the Coca-Cola Pin Trading Center in Nagano. I knew they would be running a similar operation for World Cup in France and that they were considering having me work for them. But nothing was ever set in stone until I met with them the day after I arrived in France, whereupon they hired me and put me to work that very day. It was my fastest jumpstart ever.

What a ride that World Cup summer turned out to be! Work aside, after all the time I had been spending in Asia, it was a delightful contrast of senses to be back in Europe. Despite having lived in and visited France a number of times, I was excited to finally be making my first attempt at living in Paris.

I was in charge of Coca-Cola-can-shaped kiosks in five World Cup match cities, plus assisted at the main store in the shadow of the Eiffel Tower. We sold Coca-Cola/World Cup merchandise. The hours were grueling, but the experience was much more engaging and challenging than anything I had ever anticipated.

I came to France with low expectations because I was arriving so late in the game, and because I did not have a work visa (shh!). My goals were simply to make more money than I spent and to attend at least a couple matches. It turns out there is a BIG difference between working at Coca-Cola and working for a vendor representing Coca-Cola. In Japan I got to see a bunch of premier events, including the Opening and Closing Ceremonies and the gold medal hockey game among others. In Paris, I made it into one first-round match and that was it. Can't have everything I guess. I did make some decent money, though, and I had a great (paid for) apartment in the heart of Paris.

During the tournament, I did my own Tour de France three or four times, including one time when I drove the truck all night to get merchandise, and myself, to Bordeaux where I needed to open a kiosk first thing in the morning.

The day of The World Cup Final, I was scrambling to get back into Paris after closing up shop in Lyon. With honking horns and waving flags, the soccer revelry was already warming up even before I pulled out of town. As I approached the capital, soccer fever increased precipitously. Fans even gathered on highway overpasses waving French or Brazilian flags at the traffic passing below and the drivers would either honk and wave in support, or honk and give them the finger.

The match was scheduled to start only shortly after I would be arriving in town, which was true of everyone driving near me. I laughed when arriving at the toll gates, people started laying on their horns a few hundred yards before arriving at the booth, and didn't let up until they were through. It was the loudest continuous collective horn chorus I had ever been around.

While I was sad to have not figured out a way to attend the Final match of France vs. Brazil, at least I had a decent backup. I watched The Final on a big screen TV at an Adidas-sponsored event in the Trocadero area directly across the Seine River from the Eiffel Tower.

The arrogance of the Adidas people organizing the event was reflected in the fact that they thought they could have this big screen all to themselves in the heart of Paris with the meager security they had set up. Soon after the game started the surrounding crowds flattened the fences. The security guards were pressed back despite their use of pepper spray. The place became overcrowded to the point of being dangerous. At one point the Adidas people threatened to turn off the screen if people didn't stop trying to press in close to the front. Having been inside the stadium for the 1994 World Cup Final in Los Angeles, I began swearing to myself I would find my way back into the stadium walls for the 2002 Cup in Japan.

Eventually the crowd's tension shifted to concentrating on the game and then to extraordinary collective joy as France kicked the stuffing out of the hapless Brazilian team.

Once the game was over, all of Paris erupted in celebration. Now THAT was a party! I got warmed up by the Adidas champagne celebration directly after the game, which then spilled out into the festive streets.

I was not the only one out there feeling my champagne as I stumbled my way (a mile or so?) over to the Champs-Elysees which was a wall-to-wall people party in full swing. There was no room for the cars usually packing the boulevard. People said it was the biggest event since the liberation of France at the end of World War II. Some said it might have been bigger though, because at the end of the war there were only French, whereas this time there were many tourists visiting as well. Whatever it was, it was fun! My parting memory for the night was dancing and singing circled in a huddle with a bunch of Argentinean fans in the middle of the street.

The down side was I had to be at work at 6 a.m. the following morning. We had to completely evacuate the site we were renting by that evening, having only closed the not-small store right before the Final. Figuring it wasn't worth the hassle to try and go home, I meandered my way back to the store around 4 a.m. and just crashed there. The next thing I knew, I heard voices saying, "Is that someone asleep behind the cash register?" "Hey, it's Jon!" It was my American managers arriving. It turned out it was already 7 a.m. and I was the only one who had arrived on time. None of the French staff arrived before 8 a.m. and I'm certain some of them who did were not yet sober. Others didn't drag themselves in until almost noon looking terribly hung over but elated. It was pretty funny.

After the World Cup, I felt any rest I might consider taking was both needed and deserved. The question I had been ducking for the final several weeks (almost staying permanently crouched towards the end) was "What are you going to do now?" Good question. I hadn't worked out a good answer yet. I soon pulled out my world map, my calendar and my wallet for inspection. I felt the next nine months would be my last hurrah before settling down to go back to school and maybe even ending up with a "gasp" career...

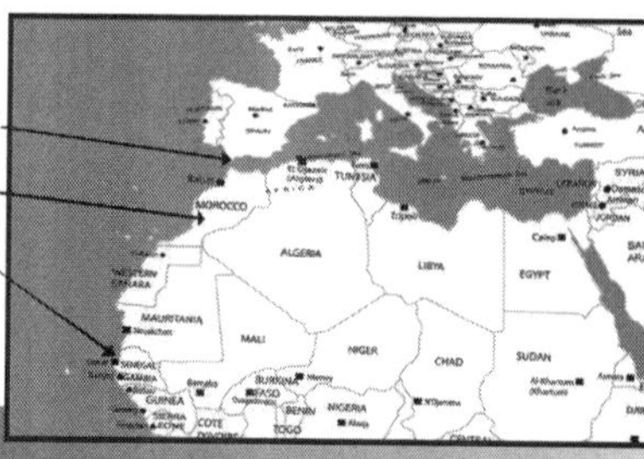

CHAPTER 12

Paris to Dakar—My Metaphorical Road Race

Welcome to Africa

The Paris-Dakar Race is a perilous off-road 4x4 and motorcycle scramble between these two capitals, passing through the heart of the desert. Racers lost for days at a time in the famous desert rally take more direct routes than I did for my Paris-Dakar run. Leaving from Paris, I began by making my first-ever visit to Spain followed by a ferry ride to the next continent down. Sailing past the famed Rock of Gibraltar was a big moment for me. I will admit to having been a bit nervous about making my first foray into Africa. I thought I would stay a week and then jump back to Europe. Two and a half weeks later…

Morocco's energy, food, colors, smells, dress and music jarred the senses and suddenly made Spain seem mundane in comparison. Most Moroccan cities of size have a vibrant core in the old section called a medina, a walled-in, narrow labyrinth of homes, shops and mosques (Morocco is mostly Muslim). Medinas are exclusively pedestrian zones (if "pedestrian" also counts hoofs!) that are so discombobulated that it is easy to lose ones bearings and have no idea where you are or how to get out.

One unforgettable excursion was seeing the mid-November meteor shower from the dunes of the Sahara Desert with some friends I had met on the way down through Spain. We had been told the best viewing would be on the sixteenth, but the fifteenth turned out to be the real show, and we saw it only because we were lucky enough to be on a freezing cold, jarring overnight bus where it was impossible to sleep, much less remain firmly planted in one's seat.

The sky gave us a display unlike any I had ever seen or even heard of. What started out as pleasant series of shooting stars turned somewhat frightening when this usually distant celestial event started coming too close for comfort. The huge firework-like meteors streaked halfway across the sky, illuminating the terrain below like lightning. Twice I saw cloud traces left from these "shooting stars" blowing in the wind uncomfortably close above.

Once the sun came up, it took a full day's effort to get to the village Merzouga at the edge of the Sahara from which a group of us headed off on camels into the sunset. I enjoyed my camel ride, imagining I could keep riding across the sands all the way to Egypt. Upon dismounting, however, the pains in my general saddle-sitting area brought some reality back to the picture.

Those of us with energy left when we arrived at our campsite soon had it dissipated by attempting to climb up a large, steep nearby dune in the dark. Back at camp, despite the cold and the wandering camels, I opted to sleep under the stars. With no moon, the stars were amazing. There were many shooting stars, but the stellar show never reached the intensity of the previous night.

In the wee hours of the morning, I hiked up a dune, planted my feet in the cool powdery-fine red Sahara sand and watched the sun rise up over the nearby mountains of Algeria. I can't remember a quieter sunrise.

My second great Moroccan memory involved a three-day hike in the upper Atlas Mountains. I found a great hiking partner in Marrakech—Ruben, an outdoorsy, longhair student from New York State. We made our way to Imlil, the main departure point for hikes in this region. We hired a guide, bought sleeping bags, picked a route, and headed up the mountain. The hike was great, although pretty cold at times. We passed a number of frozen waterfalls. Some of the scenery seemed like something I might expect to see in Nepal. The first day, passing through a little village, we came across the unusual scene of an entranced lady dancing to some funky live music while a goat was being sacrificed.

We spent the first night in a 3,200 meter refuge. In the morning, instead of hiking up Toubkal, at 4,167 meters (13,671 feet) the highest peak in North Africa, we headed the opposite way—two hours up a 3,800 meter sufficiently intimidating pass. Pretty tough day.

The native-people's village of neatly constructed mud and thatch abodes where we stayed after a six hour varied valley descent, plus all the amazing views made it all extremely worthwhile.

A half-week later, clouds arrived for the first time during my stay in Morocco. They seemed to indicate it was time for me to move on. I skipped back through Spain and dabbled in southern Portugal before moving on to the next phase of my trip: Senegal.

Senegal

Coming from a state with a large black population and a history where slavery played a significant role, I had long been interested in seeing what Black Africa looked like. I was able to establish contact with a long time Belgian friend who was doing health care-type volunteer work in poor communities in Dakar. I thought, "What the heck, how often do I get a chance to go to Senegal?" So off I went.

The antics during the plane ride alone alleviated any doubts that this detour might not be worth the effort to get there. My neighbor on the flight was a hilarious skinny guy from Guinea-Bissau with a constant big toothy grin. He didn't speak French or English, but we were somehow able to communicate a little. I laughed watching him interact with other seatmates who he also kept in stitches. He tried to suggest I abandon my plans to go to Senegal and instead come visit his country (which was in the midst of a violent uprising). "It's great, you will love it!" he said, then did an impression of someone shooting a machine gun at me and all our neighbors. It is sad to see happy people like this guy stuck in such an unfortunate situation, a reminder that the conflicts we only hear about in the news in the U.S. often catch innocent very-human bystanders like him in the crossfire.

Well into the flight, the pilot came back into the cabin and an unexpected scene unfolded. I thought myself to be surrounded by the poorest group of people I had ever seen assembled on an airplane. Now, however, everyone around me was holding up huge wads of European currency, waving it at the pilot trying to get his attention. I was witnessing what I could only assume was a tradition of the pilots exchanging money with these folks at a rate better than they could get in a bank. Large sums traded back and forth. Cash mayhem reined until the pilot ran out of bills to exchange and headed back to the cockpit, leaving many people still waving their original stash.

My Belgian friend Myrtille was living in Dakar with a typical Senegalese family of about ten people in one house. No TV, no hot water, no stove, a non-flushing toilet, lots of bugs, etc. in the home. But the lack of material possessions was counterbalanced by the warmth of the people within. I stayed with them and their relatives the entire week, eating only home cooked meals. The latter was a pleasant surprise. I figured I would spend a lot of time with an upset stomach—or worse—but the food I had in Senegal was the best of my entire trip. I shared a room and large sagging old bed with springs poking up here and there with two to four of the men in the household. Yes, to me it was "different" sharing a dilapidated mattress with a bunch of men, but for them, one more body amongst them did not seem to be a big deal.

The young woman preparing all the delicious meals was Lena, a cousin of sorts who ran the entire household. I am not sure what the actual mother contributed to the inner workings of the house as Lena was treated like a servant and in charge of everything including cooking, cleaning, sewing and raising the children. After returning home to the States, I lobbied the U.S. Embassy to permit Lena to come to America for an exchange visit. I thought I could set up some Senegal-themed dinners as bake-sale-like fundraisers to cover the cost of her trip plus some spending money to take home. A couple weeks' visit should have netted her a cash windfall enough to help her get a sewing business off the ground, a dream of hers. But since she had no children or real job of her own, and no money to speak of, the Embassy was not convinced she would return and declined her application.

While in Dakar, on top of spending a lot of time sitting around the patio of the house shooting the breeze and enjoying the warm weather, I visited one of the slums in which my friend Myrtille was doing health care work, plus a couple of popular tourist destinations. One of the extended family members, Iba, was assigned to me as my 24/7 attaché. For better *and* worse, I could not go anywhere without his company.

Gorée Island is the site from which most of the slaves in the area were shipped out to foreign lands. I had not realized the extent of slave trafficking that had also been practiced by European and Arab states. In contrast to that earlier dark time, the sounds and picturesque scenery of present-day Gorée have the feeling of a relaxed Caribbean island. It's quite lovely.

Lake Rose is a weird anomaly where the Paris-Dakar Rally has its final stage. It is supposedly the saltiest lake anywhere, whose micro-organisms give off a reddish tint when struck by the right sunlight. Locals harvest the salt. Tourists come to relax by the lake and attempt to swim. The problem is the salt makes them so buoyant that swimming is difficult. It is funny to watch them try, though. Lying on their backs, it looked as if they were sitting on top of a platform.

My one adventure outside of the Dakar area was a trip to St. Louis, the quaint old capital port city with its crumbling New-Orleans-esque architecture and its nearby Djoudj National Park. Iba and I stayed with relatives of the family in Dakar.

Djoudj is primarily known for its skillions of birds. The park hosts over 1400 species, almost double the amount found in all the US. The most prominent members were the huge nesting white pelicans, the pink flamingos, and several kinds of cormorants and ducks. Other wildlife spotted during the boat ride there included giant lizards, crocodiles, a python, large amorous land turtles, and relatives to the wild boar-type thing in the Lion King.

In some parts of St. Louis, the giant pelicans come into town for a visit, pick a spot and call it their own, which sometimes includes the middle of a street. It was like they were daring you to cross their line in the sand. They stood their ground as if asking, "Why on earth do YOU think you have a right to walk down this street, punk?" Standing up, they came to at least my chest and didn't look like they had any intention of fighting fair. I didn't see anyone challenge them.

Avoiding the wrath of the pelicans, Iba and I returned to Dakar. In addition to day-life, nightlife was also a part of my Senegal adventure. Things in Dakar were apparently more active than usual because it was the week before the beginning of Ramadan, when Muslims must fast and give up many of life's vices for several weeks. One night we attended a house party hosted by one of Myrtille's friends. The evening had a slightly American feel to it when the party was busted by the police for "not having a proper permit." The twist was that A) no one was drinking alcohol, and B) the police confiscated the amplifier, insisting on a substantial sum (read bribe) to have it returned.

Another night I attended a 'Senegalese Soiree' at a dance club. Here, around 3 a.m. they turned off the music and brought out a drum group. As they pounded out African beats, men and women, generally one at a time, would run out onto the dance floor as if possessed by the rhythms. Many would wildly kick their legs up high in movements reminiscent of exaggerated double-dutch jump roping. I can't say I had ever seen anything quite like it. My attaché Iba was disappointed there was not the "string-of-pearls"-type, mostly nude dancers, that apparently often appear at this kind of soiree.

The time soon came for me to get back to the States to wash my clothes, apply for grad school, etc. I had not lived in Columbia, South Carolina for any length of time for over nine years. I was excited about having all my mail coming to one address, and most of my stuff under one roof.

I've returned to the good ol' US of A, the current hotbed (no pun intended) of the world's gossip. Before returning, I gained some international perspective, hearing my country (particularly its president) being disgraced in Japanese, Malay, Greek, French, Danish, Norwegian, Spanish, Arabic, Wolof, Portuguese, and the Queen's English. It is amazing how similar "Monica Lewinsky" can sound in all of these languages.

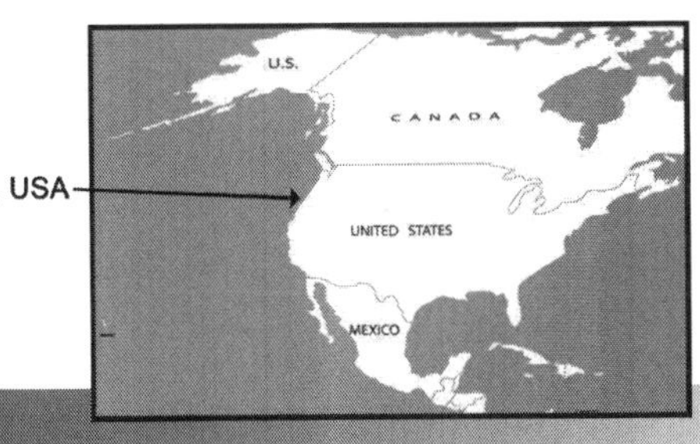

CHAPTER 13

The Krishna Bike, the Frenchman and the Comfort Biker

Rollin' in the USA

Oregon is far, at least from South Carolina. This was one of the biggest lessons learned by Christophe, who joined me on this expedition. Christophe came to Columbia, South Carolina—my home town—to work on his English and to experience life in the United States. We had been friends since my high school year abroad in France. He was now on his way to becoming a relatively famous actor in France, but I knew him more from back when we were rabble-rousers, doing our best (or not) trying to not get kicked out of biology class.

I had been dreaming about this bike trip since college, and it worked out his visit came as my plans were finally heading towards reality. 8,500 miles, 24 states, and three weeks later, I think we also safely covered the "see a bit of America" part of Christophe's goals.

Having already driven cross-country a few times, it was fun to have Christophe's fresh view on all things American. He was blown away by the expansive desert scenery and other wide landscapes out West that Americans like me might sometimes take for granted. On the way out, he was not at first convinced it was in our best interest to drive overnight through Kansas and Nebraska.

"I know you have done this before, so maybe you don't appreciate it as much as I might," he said.

"Christophe," I retorted, "Ooookay, but try to imagine over ten hours of corn, corn, wheat and corn."

After the first few hours of said scenery he got the idea and relented, "Yes, yes, you are right, let's just drive. Go."

Overnight we drove.

He was amazed at all the wildlife we encountered, and rightfully so. Animals were a big part of our trip. We managed to see deer, a bear, elk, whales, sea lions, rabbits, harbor seals, spotted seals, coyotes, tons of not-always-identified birds, a raccoon, chipmunks, more elk, squirrels, tons o' bison, Gary my old roommate from Alaska, plus a beaver and armadillos (in the road kill-only category). Along the way out, we stopped to see some of America's premier parks: the Badlands, Mt. Rushmore, Mt. Crazy Horse, Jewel Cave, Yellowstone, Lassen Volcanic National Park (California) and Mt. Rainier National Park. These served as opening acts for the main attraction of this Odyssey: the Oregon Coast.

The third critical player in this testosterone-dominated trip was my Dad. We met him at the Seattle airport, where a hired van drove us and our gear to the little podunk town of Raymonde on the southern Washington coast. We had planned a ten day southbound trip averaging around 50 miles (80 kilometers) per day and this town is where we were to begin the cycling portion of our trip.

Our threesome was quite a sight when we hit the road the next day. Christophe named my two-wheeled transport "The Krishna Bike" because of its caution-sign-orange color and Zen-like qualities. Christophe's bike and gear had been pooled together from various parts of our garage. His stuff was held onto the back of the bike through an infinitely complex series of straps, plastic bags and bungee cords. My dad had a good set of panniers (bike bags) but this advantage was overcome by his misconception of frugal packing. At the end of the first day he shipped 20 pounds (9 kgs) of excess baggage to the end of the road, including a seemingly lead-filled bag of reading and writing materials. I should have been wary earlier when he was disappointed that I refused to bring my laptop on the trip.

Biking the Oregon coast is extremely rewarding. Throughout the trip, much of the coastline was so spectacular it would be difficult to point out on a day by day basis which parts were the best. The rugged coastline is incredibly scenic and for the most part sparsely populated. There were countless breathtaking vistas of giant beaches, sweeping sand dunes and rocky outcrops. It was not unusual to hear sea lions barking, their sounds drifting above the serenade of the ocean spray. In a place renowned for terrible weather, we came out okay, with little rain during the whole trip.

Our first few days had their rocky moments as we worked out various bike and body-related problems. Between my dad and Christophe, I lost track of how many flat tires we fixed. On one such occasion on the second day, Dad was out in front trying to get a head start on us when Christophe got a flat while exiting Astoria, the city after crossing the mouth of the Columbia River into Oregon. Thrilled at having mailed off half his load plus having re-souped up his distraught bike at a shop in town, Dad plowed ahead, oblivious that we had stopped. We never saw him again until around sunset when he pulled up in a taxi at the overlook where we were paused to watch the waves below rolling in under the gorgeous setting sun. We had somehow managed to pass him, and he had searched the coast before finding us here.

In the taxi-come-bike-ambulance with him was Phil, a guy with a flat who we had tried to help a few miles back. Apparently our patch work was not enough to stop all the leaks he had. Phil was the only cyclist we met along the way who seemed worse prepared than we were. He was planning on trying to get to San Francisco in something like five days. Other savvy cyclists pointed out to him it would take two weeks minimum. "Oh," was all he responded. He was darn lucky to have my Dad come by and pick him up because he would have been stuck in no-man's land in the dark with no bike tools.

That night, incidentally, defined our future lodging patterns. My Dad, while up for the biking, was less than thrilled about camping and not-so-subtly vowed to stay in hotels the rest of the way. "I am not sleeping on the ground again," I believe is how he worded it. But Christophe and I were set on sticking to the original plan of camping. Thus, the following night, Dad grabbed a motel while Christophe and I headed to a beautiful beachside campground. I used local smoked salmon to make killer pasta over a fire as the sun set. We ran into a number of bikers there from the previous night's campground. We ended up seeing many of these same people over and over throughout the trip, which created a moving community-type feel.

Something else we continued to encounter were the ubiquitous delicious blackberries lining the roads and campgrounds. They had a way of showing up in various dessert incarnations of the many fantastic "everything homemade"-type cafes in which we stopped for many a re-energizing meal.

Day Four featured Dad, the now self-proclaimed "Comfort Biker," getting a jump by grabbing a ride half the way to the next night's stop. This was a 70-mile day for Christophe and I, so at the end of it we were glad to cave in and buy into this 'comfort' concept, taking refuge in the nice hotel my dad had settled into before we arrived. Don't let anyone kid you: a jacuzzi at the end of a hard day's biking is not a bad thing.

Christophe along the Oregon coastline

Day Five was tough. There was a cold fog bank, tangible headwinds, and arduous hills. In the plus column were the scenery and good opportunities for seeing seals and sea lions. It was a 60-mile day and we were all pretty beat up by the end of it. I was impressed at how my Dad had slogged through it, beating us into "camp." The next morning, though, he got a slow start and ended up renting a car to finish the day. We called this day Dune Day since much of the day we rode alongside massive sand dunes.It was only a short day to Bandon, the site of our long-awaited day off. Bandon was good at generating belly-laugh-worthy humor. The snickering began as we entered town when Christophe revealed that "Bandon" means "Erection" in French, leading to an endless array of related jokes. The second source of comedy drove up just as Christophe and I were a couple miles from town: Dad pulled up beside us, honking the horn and hailing us from a gigantic moving truck.

Concerned about the sketchy weather and his body aches, my father had decided to hang up his bicycle wheels for a set of four tires for awhile to play the role of backup vehicle. Unfortunately, there was only one vehicle available in the Greater Bandon Area for one-way rental. Showing our guardian angel's sense of humor, our new "sag wagon" was an enormous 26-foot

(7.8m) U-Haul truck, big enough to move a medium-sized family and ironically emblazoned with a picture of cyclists on the side.

Dad was not used to driving a stick shift and this monster vehicle was particularly cranky. We decided to take our humongous new ride for a joyride around the quaint little town. We were already having a good time, laughing at the hilarity of cruising around in this obnoxious loud vehicle. As Dad wrestled to get used to the gears, at one point the lurching motion repeatedly slammed our heads into the back of the cab window, causing our laughter to ratchet up to unabashed, uncontrollable, snorting levels with tears running down our faces.

For the last day of our bike trip, we rolled into Jedediah Smith Redwoods State Park just outside of Crescent City, California. What a grand finale! Despite the gorgeous scenery throughout the trip, the redwoods at the end marked me more than anything else. I had dreamed of them since I was a kid. Some of these awe-inspiring icons of American culture are over 2000 years old and taller than the Statue of Liberty. Their neighboring cousins, Giant Sequoias, are sometimes over 3000 years old and have diameters over 30 feet (10 meters)! You can look at them and think about them growing in that exact same spot since before the time of Christ, as the world and humanity evolved around them. They have an incredible energy. I couldn't help but go up to these elder statesmen and give them a hug.

The experience of this trip was often so pleasurable I didn't want it to end. I thought about turning left once we got to California and riding my bike all the way back to South Carolina instead of driving. One day…

This time, though, we switched back to motorized transport for the return trip home, stopping in California wine country, San Francisco, and Las Vegas on the way back from Crescent City.

I couldn't believe how much Vegas had changed in the four years since I last visited. We stayed in a gigantic hotel (New York, New York) which was on the site of a hotel that I watched being imploded in the middle of the night the last time I was there. Christophe walked around with his mouth agape looking at the bright craziness of Las Vegas, muttering all the English similes he could think of for the word "unbelievable." The climax came when he looked up to see the 1/3 replicas of the Eiffel Tower and the Arc de Triomphe under construction at the soon-to-be-new Paris Hotel. He smacked his forehead saying, "I can't believe it!" Christophe and I ended up wandering down the Strip until 4 a.m. or so when the lucky foreigner ended the night as a winner on the slots.

As the starting date for business school rapidly approached, many friends were wondering if indeed this would be the end of their nomad protagonist, Vacation Boy. All right, all right, I was probably the only one fretting about this. Everyone else, more likely, was just thinking, "When is this guy going to settle down and get a real job?" This could be it folks. I was committing to three years of this school thing, followed by…gulp…perhaps …perspiring palms…a career?? Is it warm in here?

But before jumping back into school, though, I ducked off for a look at Ecuador...

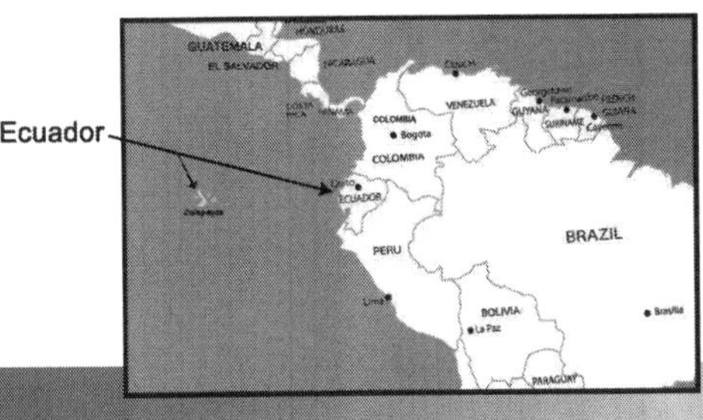

CHAPTER 14

How Not to Make a Great First Impression

Jungles and boobies of Ecuador and the Galapagos Islands

My first-ever visit to South America began with a social disaster. My initial destination was the Magic Bean, a popular restaurant/hotel in Quito, Ecuador, owned and run by a guy from Columbia, South Carolina (my home town). I arrived in Quito on a late night flight—something I dreaded. Luckily, exiting the airport was pleasantly void of hassles and I bus bee-lined it through town to my evening's destination without incident—at least until I arrived. I had never met Bill, the Magic Bean's owner, but I came bearing gifts from his family. To liven things up, I walked in and pepper sprayed his main office.

I'll admit to having been more than a tad nervous about walking through this sketchy Quito neighborhood late at night on the way in from the airport carrying my full travel bag. It is for that reason I had taken the safety latch off my bear-grade pepper spray, which I had originally bought in Alaska. Only a little bit discharged onto the floor when I accidentally bumped the canister trigger, but I was certain this was still going to mean trouble. Sure enough, soon the two office guys were trying to remain casual while coughing, crying and waving their arms trying to clear the air. They ended up having to evacuate the area and you could even hear people several stories up the open main staircase coughing from the vapors. The staff was good-natured about it, but I was completely traumatized by the situation I had inflicted. At least they'll remember me, right?

Once I got through that catastrophe, the rest of my trip went quite well. Ecuador is great, and I highly recommend it. The people are mellow and the scenery is fantastic. Contrary to my expectations, people were not constantly trying to rip me off like they tended to do in places like Morocco, or even as close by as Guatemala. While causing hardship for the country and bringing on a rise in crime, the recently floated currency had fallen to a third of its value of just a few years ago. The result for the traveler with a harder currency was unbelievably low prices. The one thing that was not working in my favor was the weather on the mainland. Ecuador is right on the equator, and the middle of winter means rainy season. Although I did not get hit with much rain, I was only able to see the tops of the snow-capped, towering volcanoes via postcards.

My first outing was a jungle trip into the upper reaches of the Amazon Basin. The more accessible Rio Napo areas are said to have been severely impacted by colonization and oil exploitation, leaving mostly secondary forest to visit with less-than-abundant wildlife. I think going there would have been depressing. Instead, I splurged for the first time on a multi-day comfy tour along the Aguarico River. In the limited timeframe I had to work with, this tour was the only way I could access the remote, pristine rainforest of the Cuyabeno Wildlife Preserve, which I so badly wanted to visit. Getting there required a flight from Quito, followed by a one and a half-hour bus ride, followed by a three-hour boat ride down river—and that was just to the starting point.

My group consisted of two older gringo couples, our guide, and occasionally some extra staff members here or there. Our first day into the wilds included a stop at a Cofan (indigenous tribe) village interpretation center. It was a house replica set up across the river from the actual village. I liked this system since we were able to get a taste of their culture without stepping all over it. Maricelo was our charming Cofan guide. His feet, size, and mannerisms reminded me of the cute Ewoks in *Return of the Jedi.* The coolest part was the blowgun demonstration. I got to try it and was impressed with its accuracy. I nailed the post across the hut on my first try. Walking in the nearby woods, Marcelio talked about the medicinal uses for the various trees and roots. He also talked about their ongoing struggle to maintain their culture, including how they had recently moved to escape the encroaching development of the city of Lago Agrio.

Later we hiked a couple hours to a lake where we were to spend most of the next day. At sunset we traversed the lake in a dugout canoe to the cushy camp on the opposite shore. After dinner, we headed out in the dark in a canoe with a serious spotlight. We were treated to sightings of a boa constrictor, a number of bats, including a big one (dog-faced something or other) with radar that even picks up fish—its preferred prey—in the water, and a tropical screech owl. Screaming howler monkeys off in the distance sounded like an eerie jet engine. A bushmaster viper swam right by us. As if the boggy mud trails weren't enough to appreciate the rubber boots we had been issued, wearing them apparently helps avoid accidental encounters with this snake whose bite, among other unpleasantries, can cause you to bleed from your pores until you die. Sweet.

The next day we tried our hand at fishing for piranhas. This is a fish which horror movies have trained most of us to avoid at all cost. The technique to catch them is anything but subtle. You hook a piece of raw meat on a cane pole line, slap it in the water and then shake the end of the pole to draw attention to it. We caught five piranhas and two other fish in probably no more than 20 minutes. If only it were that easy to catch Alaskan salmon!

You would think seeing these voracious fish pounce on the bait would be enough to deter any sane person from swimming in basically the same place ten minutes later, but it didn't. Ken (a fellow gringo in the boat) and I jumped in, making liberal use of a Get Out of Death Free card. In hindsight I have no idea why we did it. I don't think I was even drunk. Despite the guide's mentions of electric eels and other dangerous yuckies, Ken was even crazy enough to dive down 15 feet in the black water and touch the bottom. It gave me the willies just thinking about it.

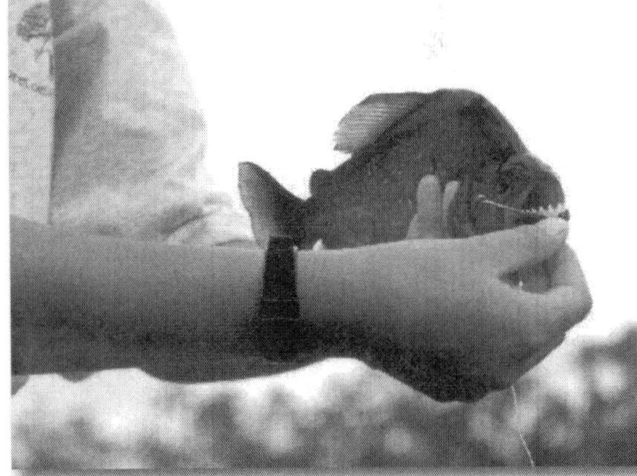

Our home base was a three-story floating mini-motel. We struck out from there in a dugout canoe to investigate a magnificent calm little alluvial path which quietly carried us for several hours back to the Aguarico River. It felt like the Disney Jungle Cruise minus the hippo, although we did have a comparable fright when a giant fish violently surged from its spot in the reeds, effectively stopping all heartbeats within a 20-foot radius. OK, at least mine froze.

We saw countless tropical birds including a bunch of blue & gold macaws, but the most extraordinary was the anhinga, a snakebird. To escape us, it jumped from its perch on a branch, plunged in the river and swam under water to safety. Didn't it know it was a BIRD?

The final day took us to the Lagarto River, which forms Ecuador's border with Peru. Before turning up the river we had to stop at a border checkpoint. Ecuadorians can sleep soundly at night knowing their country is well guarded by five 17-year-olds and two somewhat vicious scrawny dogs. The military types said our tour company's boat was one of the only ones they ever saw at the border. Along the Lagarto, we saw several types of monkeys, tons of birds and a rolling, tarpon-like, black paiche fish. The destination of our trip was a lagoon where we got to swim with rare pink river dolphins.

Once back to civilization I headed south of Quito to check out a wild 4x4 competition. A course had been sculpted from a cow pasture/marsh. Spectators lined the course to watch these noisy jeeps get beat to hell while their drivers got trounced with mud. The festive scene was energized with thumping Latin disco music while the young and old drank plenty of beer to further warm things over. Classic moments included spectators and a rolling hotdog stand fleeing from jeeps that decided to recklessly swerve into the crowd to get around colleagues who had gotten stuck in several feet of mud and water on the course.

During the gaps in action, especially while waiting for the third and final round, patience grew thin and pranksters grew thick. A number of people got shoved or carried and dropped into water bogs while mud fights broke out all along the course. I'd be shocked if none of the spectators or racers was seriously injured out there in all the mayhem.

Riding public busses tends to be a common denominator of my travels. Bus rides inevitably have their moments of color that, despite the inherent hassles, make it all seem worthwhile. On the bus ride back to Quito, someone in the back shouted "funda!" ("bag!"). But you didn't need Spanish to realize the driver's assistant was scrambling to find his barf bag supply.

On that same bus ride, in addition to the usual folderol, we passengers were given the extra bonus of a near-death experience. The Pan-American Highway is sometimes two lanes, sometimes four. Some creative drivers take advantage of a few extra lanes they invent themselves. The yellow line in the middle is treated as a suggestion rather than a steadfast legal demarcation. My bus driver preferred driving on the opposite side even when he didn't "need" to. Nonetheless, even this jaded veteran was surprised when a car coming at us in our lane (normal)—just when it was getting too close for comfort—cut over one lane further in our direction to swerve around a Delaware-sized pothole. A head-on crash seemed unavoidable. I started to duck and cover as if it would do any good. At the last second the oncoming car somehow managed to swerve out of the way, although our driver also had to swerve sharply to avoid him. Got lucky again I guess.

Sharks and Boobies of the Galapagos

Off to the Galapagos! Despite Darwin's incredible insight into the evolution of man, I imagined he never could have predicted seeing my 737 landing on Baltra, an island at the nexus of his ground breaking research on the natural world. From the airport we bussed to a ferry, ferried to a bus, and headed to Puerto Ayora, the somewhat sleepy port town of around 10,000 that is the biggest city in the Galapagos, and the place from which most tour boats leave. Also in Puerto Ayora is the Charles Darwin Center, which seemed to be an unending series of humping giant tortoises intent on preserving their species, or at least having a good time.

One giant tortoise taking a break from humping

Everyone talks about how amazing the Galapagos Islands are to the point I felt I needed to lower my expectations to avoid disappointment. It was an unnecessary effort. These islands meet and even exceed their lofty billing. I felt both humbled and extremely fortunate to be able to witness them in person.

The only way to visit the sights is by boat, and aside from this main island, people are not allowed to stay overnight on land. I was on a five-day plan, but I think most people stay at least eight. If I were to return and had the funds, I would do the same. My boat, *The Sea Man*, was a 16-passenger, 65 foot motor yacht. It, too, turned out to be better than expected. I was lucky enough to end up with a group of mostly younger Europeans who were intent on having a good time. We got along well. Most of us slept on deck at night, and were led onto the islands by our tour guide during the day.

Espanola was my favorite of the islands. As we pulled up to shore, sea lions were either playing in the water, or piled up on the various rocks and beaches sleeping soundly. They couldn't care less that we were there. Once on shore we had to be careful not to step on the marine iguanas, lava lizards and blue-footed boobies (a sleek, impressive fishing bird) that would make no particular effort to get off the path on which we humans were required to walk. Their emotions seemed to range from oblivious to curious about we the passing humanoids. Fear was not on that list.

Boobies are great. These birds are mellow, relaxed and personable. They make interesting noises not unlike the squeaky whistle of an air-filled plastic hammer toy. The males have a penchant for doing a curtsy-like bowing and wing-lifting movement to call to their mate. I call it the Booby Dance. They are also intense fishers, kamikaze-ing from 50 feet up, plunging 10 to 20 feet under the water, then hunting for the fish on the way back up.

The underwater world of the Galapagos was at least as intriguing as the above-water portion. One of my favorite moments of the trip was when a couple curious sea lions swam right up to me. I swam in circles with them. It was magical beyond words.

One other snorkel adventure is forever imprinted on my psyche. The water was murky and I was in the front of our snorkeling group as we crept along the inner wall of a crater. I saw a few bright yellow puffer fish, and a few other cool fishies, then—whammy—a huge hammerhead shark emerged from the darkness right in front of me. I'll admit I was not completely at ease about this fact...scared shitless would be a closer approximation.

Perhaps fortunately, this beast faded back into obscurity before I could get a photo off. Yes, we did see some other neat stuff along that wall, but after the hammerhead it felt like it was all just killing time, like watching a fishing bobber on a lake, until the next possible shark sighting. Our guide told us to wait in this one spot for a while because we would almost certainly see another hammerhead. Staring down into the darkness—knowing anything down there could see me much better than I could see it—this did not strike me as terribly comforting. The group got cold before the next shark decided to come and scare us out of our wits, so we piled onto the zodiac to head back to the boat.

On the way back to *The Sea Man*, a telltale dorsal fin approached us from nearby, cutting steadily through the surface. In the real world, this situation would have incited a panicked escape attempt.

In the Galapagos, however, our guide says, "it's coming this way... quick, jump in!" And crazy as it sounds, we did just that. Plunging in the water, I could see the fin approaching as the *dum-dum, dum-dum* of the *Jaws* theme song reverberated in my head. Out of the murky underwater darkness, glided silently the anticipated monster of the deep connected to that dorsal fin...accompanied by another hammerhead, and another. I was mostly ready for the first (which was at least eight feet long), surprised by the second, and frightened by the third, because I was wondering how many more of them might be part of this hunting party. I could clearly see their eyes in the side of the hammer less than five feet away from me. They continued on without incident unless you count the fact that my heart had stopped beating. Nothing like Nature to remind you of your mortal status on this planet.

A hammerhead shark WAY too close for comfort

In the end I was touched by the gentle, intriguing animals of the Galapagos. I also felt a tinge of guilt being one of the relatively few members of the human population fortunate enough to experience this special environment in person, while also fully aware that every additional visitor, myself included, in some way brings an incremental adverse effect to the fragile ecosystem we are there to see.

I attended business school to try and galvanize my varied experience and create a clean slate from which to springboard to a "real career". As part of my Masters program in International Business, I spent a year and a half at the main campus in South Carolina and a year and a half studying and later working in China. Following are a few of my adventures as a student in China.

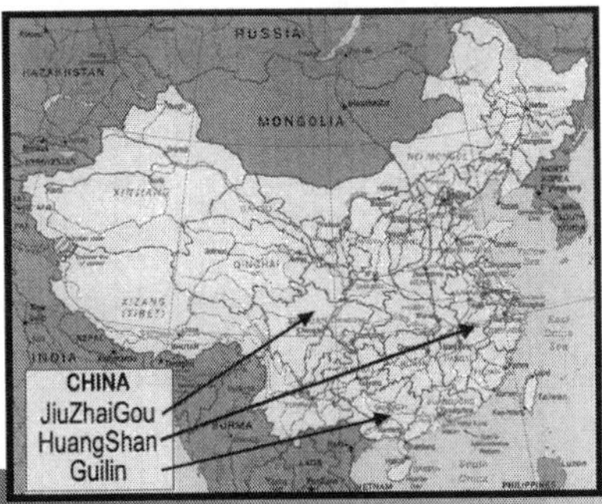

CHAPTER 15

The High Speed Chinese Bus Chase

A Visit to Yellow Mountain

As I often seem to end up traveling on my own, it was a nice change to have company for my first foray into Southwest China. I was joined by dear friends Nolan and Juliana. Along the way we saw untold amounts of scenic beauty, met many wonderful (and a few extremely not-so-wonderful) people, ate numerous unidentifiable yet tasty dishes and—on a personal note—got suckered worse than I have ever been in my entire life.

We started out from Hangzhou on a Friday right after class, dawdling our way through the rice-field-embellished countryside towards Huang Shan Mountain. We took our time, trying to avoid hitting this Chinese tourism behemoth on a weekend. The leisurely time was well spent, mostly figuring out how to make our way up a scenic, calm river towards Thousand Islands Lake and then onto Huang Shan. Complicating our task was following a map that was an artist's creative rendition of the terrain. Even in a drug-laced drunken stupor, said artist would never have guessed that someone would try and navigate this rural area using his drawing.

After hiking a couple hours into one mountain-wedged river valley, the road dwindled away. We continued by hiring a fisherman with one of those cool quintessentially Chinese thatch-arched-roof, small wooden boats to take us an hour up the river to what looked to be a more visited area. Once we checked out the pretty but possibly fake waterfall, we negotiated our way onto a friendly boat that was headed a couple hours upriver, exactly to where we wanted to go.

Arriving at this intermediary destination, the kind captain walked us to the bicycle taxis, which were there to take passengers to the bus station. On the way, we passed a toilet that was as frightening as any I have witnessed to date. The hole in the floor wasn't even all the way inside the door. I suppose at least the view was good.

Next ensued a faux James Bond-like chase scene where Juliana and I pretended to be fleeing Nolan in red three-wheeled bicycle taxis all the way to the bus station along narrow cobblestone streets. The chase theme was good preparation for the insanity to come.

We caught a 5:40 a.m. working man's boat across Thousand Island Lake. This almost five-hour ride was by far and away the best $1.50 cruise I had ever been on. Within 30 minutes we got past all the stupid, cheesy-themed islands I had visited here previously on a sightseeing boat tour. The sun soon rose above the horizon, although never became too insistent. The islands on either side grew higher and higher as they eventually transformed into riverbanks. Villages cropped up from time to time and the boat would stop to let a few people on or off. The scenery was fantastic to the point that we were wondering if our later destinations of Huang Shan and Guilin could compete. This was the calm before the storm.

Arriving at our final port, we began a series of bus rides that eventually led to a real wild high-speed chase. Approaching the end of our beautiful ride from some gritty transportation hub to a city near Huang Shan called Taiping, our once friendly bus lady began changing into a pushy, stay-in-my-recommended-hotel-and-take-my-overpriced-ride-to-the-tram lady. Her transformation did not surprise me entirely since I'd observed her interactions with other passengers earlier in the ride and felt she oddly resembled a conglomeration of people I had seen snap on a dime before. It turns out all those previous Jeckyll and Hydes had nothing on this loony bin shoe-in.

When we reached the end of the ride, everyone else got off, but the woman kept pestering us to continue on with them to some hotel. Not believing her insistence that there were "no more trams up the mountain that day," I slipped out of the bus to check out other options.

I found a taxi driver who said he'd already made a run that day and would not even need to pay the $2.50 gate fee for the park. The bus lady fumed when I returned to the bus, grabbed Juliana & Nolan and bolted. She followed us out of the parking lot, around the corner and down the block, unleashing her full wrath on our poor new cab driver. From what I could gather, the best offer she had for us was to get back in her bus so we could pay significantly more than what the new cabby was offering for the same service. Such a deal! I might have gleaned more information had she not been screaming all this at us in some obscure dialect at the volume of a Mötley Crüe concert.

After some persuading, our new driver finally pulled away, leaving the woman ranting on the sidewalk. Here, you would think all was well and good, but isn't that how classic chase scenes often start? Not even ten minutes out of town, the bus we had been on came racing up behind us and we could see the crazy lady screaming and waving her fist. Never seen this one before. We couldn't help but laugh in stunned amazement. Nolan started taking digital pictures, including some of the license plate just in case.

The advancing bus passed us on this two-lane highway and tried to cut us off, but our driver got around them when they stopped. They caught up again, though, and after braking and weaving back and forth a few times to slow us, they finally stopped, this time blocking the road in both directions. The psycho lady's fire hose of fury flowed more at the driver than us. Her ability to persist in screaming was impressive and funny to both us and passersby. I recorded a peppy bit of audio to accompany Nolan's photos. The best I could gather is she wanted to either drive us for her original excessive price or have the cabby pay her off. Somehow we were not drawn in by either option. Nearby road workers came by to listen in, giving us empathetic smiles.

The cabby seemed to be in no huge hurry to call the police or to drive off, so here in the middle of nowhere we gave up and got out and started walking. As expected, the comedy snowballed when we started asking a passing motorcycle cab to give us a ride. The two previous vehicles came rushing up before we could work out a price, so we started walking again and told him to catch up with us. He ended up becoming part of the caravan following us down the road.

Eventually, a real bus going to our tram destination came by, so we decided to jump on. The cabby, however, managed to park and run up, blocking Nolan before he could get on the bus. We ended up in a silly shoving match that ended in us almost tickling the guy to pull Nolan past him. Nolan gave the guy $1.25 for having brought us this far and the banshee woman standing nearby seemed to smile. Who knows what the full story on that circus was. Luckily we escaped before getting further wrapped up in it because we just barely caught the last tram up the mountain. But we did make it!

The payoff for surviving the bus ordeal was climbing up one of the most scenic landscapes in China. We felt a huge sense of accomplishment as the tram rode up the mountain like a low-flying jet dropping in and out of the clouds. Seeing the reddish craggy rocks poking out of the pine forest made us certain we had made the right decision to stay at the top instead of entertaining cheaper options at the bottom amongst the thieves.

Huang Shan, literally "Yellow Mountain", is a mixture of heaven, hell and Dr. Seuss. It is to Chinese landscape paintings what Stevie Wonder is to elevator music. You know the dreamy visions of mysterious mountain peaks engulfed in mist and odd-shaped pine trees? This is the place.

We discovered the next morning that what they don't show you in those images are the hordes of tourists being herded about by their flag-bearing and bullhorn-blaring tour group leaders. As if the latter was not enough of an annoyance in this otherwise natural place, from 8 a.m. to 5:30 p.m. the administration (whom we suspected was led by a leftover Cultural Revolution Red Guard) deemed it important to ruin the peace of the place with a stupid welcoming public safety announcement booming incessantly from loudspeakers in Chinese and English. "WATCH YOUR STEP" "DON'T LIGHT FIRES" etc. Ugh!

We had the fortune to escape the masses and the loudspeaker by stumbling across a brand new, breathtaking trail. The only walking paths in the Huang Shan area, remarkably, are made with well-laid rectangular stone steps—LOTS of them. When you see the size and quantity of these stones and think that people probably hauled them all up the mountain on foot, you feel the impressiveness with each incredible step.

The new path we found seemed to take the man-made trail concept to an extreme. The trail laughed at gravity as its numerous sketchy staircases—appearing to be supported by little more than air—wrapped around sheer rock faces, the bottom of which often disappeared into the swirling clouds. The fog perpetually shifted around, offering teasing glimpses of the tremendous landscape surrounding us. The mist dancing through valleys of precipitous spires and oddly shaped pine trees made me repeatedly pause in reverence to this otherworldly beauty.

To say we did not cross some parts of that new trail with feelings of trepidation would have me covering up the truth worse than Bill Clinton on a bad day in court. It was in our moments of knee-shaking fear that we found an unusually deep source of admiration for the people who had built this path. As the trail threaded its way back to its point of departure, we had the serendipity of running into those very workers. To meet and talk with them was amazing. These friendly men said it took a total of 100 or so people 18 months to complete this trail. They were the last to finish up their work and they were moving on to the next work site, lugging their tools and belongings, which were suspended on both ends of a pole balanced on their necks. Impressive people doing impressive work.

After this experience, much of the rest of our time on Huang Shan seemed anti-climactic. We checked out a few more areas, including one atop a bald rock where artists were doing their best to capture the beauty before them, taking breaks when the mountains became re-smothered in the fog. Before long, the Disney-like crowds, the annoying announcements and the mountaintop prices had taken their toll on us, though, so we decided to flee to lower ground earlier than expected.

Most every Chinese landscape scroll painting that is not of Huang Shan inevitably is of the "karsts," literally "big jutting up limestone mountains," in the area around Guilin, our next stop on the trip. Cormorant fishermen ply the waters of the placid river on bamboo rafts, weaving through the majestic karsts. Rice fields occupy much of the arable land. After stopping in Guilin's foreigner paradise of Yangshuo to soak up the relaxed pastoral ambiance for a few days, we bussed several days before finally arriving in Guizhou Province.

Pulling into the Miao indigenous people's town of Xijiang, our bus ran over a puppy. The bus stopped. What followed was pretty dramatic, as the solemn boy who apparently owned the dog threw the disfigured carcass down on the ground in front of the driver. As a crowd began to gather, a grandfatherly type quietly interceded to negotiate with the driver for some kind of compensation for the loss. We speculated what was going to be showing up on that family's dinner plate that evening (see notes about Guizhou cooking below).

Dead puppy negotiation

Our own dining experience was also interesting. We ate at an outdoor "café" down by the river across the rice fields from town. The chicken we ordered was carried in live from the village. The cook seemed to not even notice we were there as he wandered out of the kitchen with knife and chicken in hand and proceeded to kill and de-plume the bird right beside us. While I can't say the butchering improved my appetite, like back in the Dominican Republic, I thought it healthy to face the reality of my carnivorous habits.

Not even counting the latter experience, the people of Guizhou and Sichuan are somewhat sadistic with their cuisine. As you walk into an eating establishment, the cooks immediately begin chopping up fiery chilies, knowing they go in every dish. The first question the server asks is, "hot, or not hot?" but in this region a better translation would be, "very hot, or chewable fire?" On top of the chilies, they love to sneak in an evil spice, called huajiao. It starts out almost with a menthol flavor before taking over your whole mouth, making your tongue tingle to the point of feeling numb. Unpleasant. One of our first new Chinese sentences there, in fact, was, "please don't put huajiao in anything."

Locals are known to eat certain medicines to prep their stomachs before taking on notorious hell-bent eateries. Our only precautionary measure was to try our best to avoid eating dog butt. In one Guizhou town this was not as easy as you'd think. Every restaurant seemed to prominently display a canine derriere (back end out), which had already been de-furred and de-pawed, but not de-tailed. Juliana, our resident pseudo-vegetarian and designated animal lover, was so horrified by this scene that even she was mostly happy when we were able come up with a duck's-everything-but-actual-meat hotpot (its bill and webbed feet bobbed about ominously).

Once we arrived at Chengdu, the capital of Sichuan, it was time for Juliana to return to the U.S. to dive headlong into her PhD program, but Nolan and I still had a week of trouble to get into before our classes started. After resting a day, we headed north to Jiuzhaigou National Park on a frigid, smoke-filled, sleepless overnight bus. At 3 a.m. it pulled into the "town," a spread out strip of hotels and shops, which were all completely shut down until a saner hour. A group of us were dumped ingloriously under a streetlight where we chatted and shuffled about to stay warm. Finally, due to my lack of sleep, using every layer I could find, I laid down on the street exhausted to take a nap.

Eventually the town murmured to life and we began our hike up into the park. Here, the beautiful towering mountains were out staged by the star attraction: amazingly clear, blue and green water which formed endless combinations of crystalline pools and waterfalls. The storybook atmosphere—enhanced by the diverse wildflowers, mushrooms, thick moss and forests which surrounded the colorful water in its various forms—was perfectly surmised by Nolan's name for this park, "Fairyland."

The gnomes of Fairyland were the smiling indigenous people, the Zang, whose Tibetan-like traditional colorful dress was as beautiful as any I have seen. When not helping run the park they could be seen tending their farms, goats, sheep and furry yaks. The cool fresh air combined with a bit of altitude and the unnaturally comfortable beds of our wooden Zang guesthouse resulted in a couple nights' sleep so deep it was perhaps dangerous.

After all the clean air and open spaces, it was mentally taxing to return to smog-suffocated Chengdu. Other than making the obligatory visit to observe the insanely cute residents of the Giant Panda Research Center, to celebrate the end of our voyage and my three-month anniversary in China, Nolan and I went for a massage and—as mentioned at the intro—got suckered big-time. Literally. At the conclusion of a fantastic two-hour (one hour of which was just feet!) $8 massage, the masseur, for a grand finale, put some kind of heated glass domes on our backs that sucked the skin way up into them. It felt pretty uncomfortable both when he put them on and thereafter, not to mention the scary giant disco hickeys they left behind. At least it made for an interesting souvenir to take home.

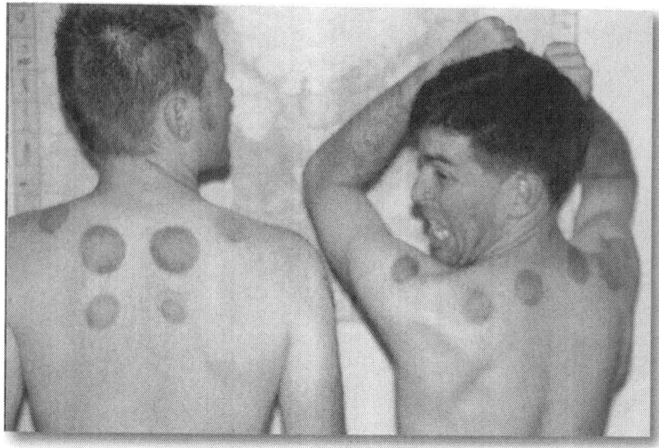

Ever been suckered this bad?

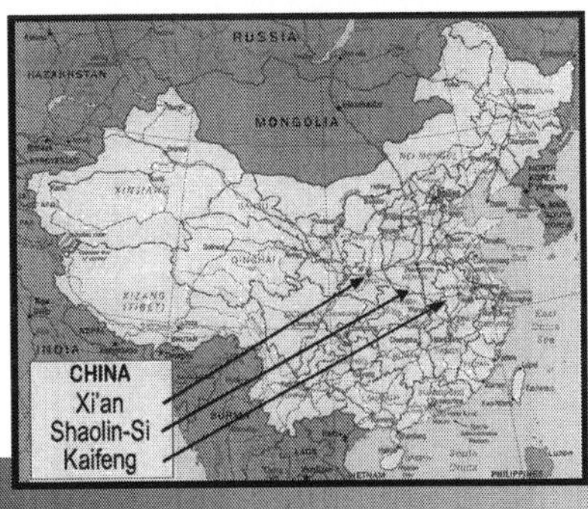

CHAPTER 16

"Making Coats with Kittens?" (My Chinese Needs Improvement!)

While life as a student in Hangzhou provided plenty of intrigue and challenges, leaving town to travel around China accelerated the pace of new experiences I encountered. For my first solo outing in China I took advantage of a week's vacation from school. I wanted to see more of what the country had to offer and what better way to get a lay of the land than to visit five of the former hubs of Chinese civilization.

My "Ancient Capitals Tour" got off to a good start, finding a bus leaving right after class from Hangzhou straight to Nanjing (ancient capitals one and two). My guidebook, although published just months before, was almost useless for finding cheap to midrange hotels. Chinese law used to require foreigners to stay in approved places, which were high-end hotels or a few university dorms. A recent change in the law now allowed foreigners to stay almost anywhere, but guidebooks had yet to catch up. I think my mother would be glad to know I passed up a $7 room in a brothel for a $12 room at a reasonably nice hotel.

I started my sightseeing tour at the unsubtly named *Rape of Nanjing Memorial.* I had heard about this World War II tragedy and had always been bothered that some Japanese still refute this massacre took place. It is hard to imagine how this city ever recovered physically and emotionally after having at least 20,000 of its women raped and 300,000 of its people butchered in the Japanese campaign of terror. The section that struck me most in this sea of bleak memorabilia were the photos they had of a prisoner getting his head chopped off with a sword. Two Japanese generals were having some kind of competition, each averaging over 100 decapitations a day. Another photo I could not walk away from showed a group of prisoners that were about to be mowed down by a machine gun. While most of them stared at the ground with grim expressions, one of them was looking up at the camera and smiling almost peacefully. I wonder what he was thinking.

The place left me angry about how awful humans can be to other humans. As I was walking down the street back to town, a few small children burst out of shop in the midst of a water pistol fight. Having just exited the memorial, their innocent play evoked a different, chilling image.

I left Nanjing, one of China's so-called "Three Furnaces" (a nod to its oppressive summer heat) jammed in a sardine can. The girl across from me admitted it was about as slow and unpleasant a train as one can get on. I dared not complain. I scored a window seat by two girls and a mother—all non-smokers. It's nice having good neighbors when you know you've got nine hours of sitting ahead of you. And I was the lightweight on this long-haul people conveyer. All three of my seatmates were to be on this clunker all night and then some. I am thankful I was able to reserve a seat since the aisle was crammed full of people standing for lord knows how many hours.

Outside the window, a collection of Chinese friends had come to the platform to see off one of their classmates. Onlookers couldn't help but smile seeing this pack of unabashedly sobbing young men. They driveled to the point of comedy.

The scenery outside the train on the way to Kaifeng was dull in comparison to the intrigue generated inside, a stage for high drama with the station stops providing the performance climaxes. I would have needed a degree in several local dialects, not to mention scam artistry, to fully catch the nuances of everything taking place. At one stop, a woman was suddenly throttling a guy right behind me while he screamed back at her, trying to push her off. A few minutes later I spotted her smiling and wandering outside the train with a couple of her cohorts. They were seat scammers, grabbing empty seats and then charging boarding passengers for the seats when they had no intention of using them.

You know you are in an iffy place when even the woman across the aisle with a counterfeit train ticket has her money concealed in her stocking below the shoe buckle. When the fearsome ticket checker banshee came screeching through, many people—including that woman and a guy sitting next to me—made quick exits for the opposite door. She nailed my one innocent seatmate with a suspicious "cargo tax" for having large boxes as part of her luggage.

All in all things were going pretty good (if you don't count the nearby barfing kid) until the Kitten Guy climbed on board. Amongst everything going on, *this* was over the top. An old bad-toothed smiley guy starts pushing his way through the crowded aisle with burlap bags half-full of what were clearly (by the sounds and movements) squirming kittens. Everybody started yelling at him to take them elsewhere as he started shoving the kitten bags under the seats. People nearby were covering up their noses from the stench. Eventually he gave in and moved them further down the aisle where the passengers didn't make as big a stink about it.

The Kitten Guy and his partner unloading their "merchandise" from the train

Due to a Chinese language intonation error, I was unnecessarily further horrified by the scene. I asked the girl across from me what these guys would be doing with the cats. She told me it gets cold in the North, so people use them to make linings for coats. It turns out she had dozed off and had missed seeing Kitten Guy come aboard. With my tone error, she thought I was asking what people do with "wool" (mao2) rather than "cats" (mao1). It was pretty funny when we sorted that one out. I still have no idea what the cat guy planned to do with his cargo, but I am certainly not eating in any restaurant near where he got off.

Eventually I reached my next destination, the third ancient capitol of my journey, Kaifeng. Surrounded by ancient fortified walls, Kaifeng is a great town to wander around. It is one of those places where busses do not play the Goliath role they do in other bigger cities. Here they slowly and meekly dodged their way through the rivers of bicycles.

Taking advantage of the cooler air, locals emerge at night to gather under streetlights for games of Chinese chess and lively conversation. I was a little disappointed in myself for not being brave enough to try the cicada-nymph skewers at the night market.

Passing a wedding dress rental shop, I realized I had never seen something like that before, but thought it was a great idea. Seeing those frocks drying on the rack under the streetlight made me think of all the excitement, hopes and dreams that must pass through those dresses throughout their apparel career.

July 4th, 2000 – Independence Day from Hell

I went into this day with the premonition that it would suck, and I wasn't let down. I started the day with a head cold, which worked in cahoots with the rainy weather, to make me miserable. I hardly had any cold medicine with me because who catches a cold in the middle of summer?

My goal for the day was to check out Shaolin Si temple, the birthplace of kung fu. Sounds cool, right? I had no problem with the first bus out of Kaifeng, but my interactions in Zhengzhou hinted of what was to come. Shaolin is a monstrously popular tourist destination and is fully exploited as such. People hound you by the train station, trying to get you to ride in their vehicles. Once I found and boarded the actual public bus to Dongfeng, two passengers battled to become my best friend, wanting to know if I was interested in studying Kung fu in Shaolin. I wasn't. Both guys mysteriously disappeared before the bus pulled out.

Once to Dongfeng, a young guy convinced me to take his public-looking bus, offering the standard fare to Shaolin Si. Who would have thought something as benign as this would end up with me pinned in a gift stand with three guys yelling at me? But let's rewind. I got on the bus and it did the standard infuriating several laps through town trying to round people up. This was par for the course, and I was used to this sort of thing by now. The thing that bugged me was stopping after that in the middle of nowhere to wait for busses getting to the end of their route, from whom we would pick up riders continuing in our same direction. Two busses, many "five-more-minutes" assurances and another 30 minutes later we finally got going again. The wait time had come close to an hour by now and I was sick of their shenanigans.

When it then became clear that they were dropping us off not at the actual temple they said they would, but rather two kilometers away from it, I snatched my money back and pushed my way off the bus. The three bus guys were less than pleased. With my Chinese not yet as good as it could be, there was a lot I didn't fully comprehend of our ensuing heated conversation. They walked me over to a gift stand so I could see the poster of the monastery. The ladies working there tried to help, explaining that this was the place to see that site. In return, I tried to explain that these clowns, who by now had blocked my exit, were liars for saying they were going all the way to the monastery when in fact we were two kilometers away.

Shaolin-Si Temple

The guys were not about to let me by and at least one spit out some menacing sounding invective which might have been threats. I was asking for it, but I was fed up. Having at least gotten something off my chest, I gave them the 40 cents and left. The driver was nice enough to follow me down and point out the sign saying their bus was not allowed down the road to the temple. Why didn't they just explain that when I first got on? Anyway, crisis averted we both parted smiling.

The actual Shaolin temple felt spiritually vacant. Now, it is all about the money. Monks at this revered temple first developed martial arts as a way to exercise between meditations. I had read that Shaolin had lost touch with its roots long ago, mostly because of the post-revolutionary government's discouragement of both martial arts and religion. The kung fu side was revived only when the recent popularity of kung fu movies brought tourist-shaped dollar signs to the eyes of the government. The locals reminded me of a bunch of carpetbaggers coming in to make money off a ghost town.

The true remnants of the ancestors of the art had the biggest impression on me. In one of the temples, you could see the depressed spots in the bricks where monks had stood for centuries practicing the katas. There was also a neat garden of vertical car-sized brick pagodas, which served as gravestones for the masters of years past.

Most interesting of all was a conversation I had with four French guys who were in Shaolin training in kung fu. I met them under a temple in a dark cool basement full off large Buddha sculptures. They smelled of the morning's workout. For having lived in Shaolin two years already, they seemed fairly cynical about this sport they were dedicating their life to. Their consensus was that especially in the last three years, what little was left from the original Shaolin, the defensive meditative art of old had been overrun with a fighting style resembling a combination of kick boxing and big showy movements not truly intended for defense.

But there seemed to still be some salvaging factors. A bunch of youths train in the Kung fu schools that have sprung up around the temple. On my way out, it was refreshing to see the kids working out diligently in their colorful outfits.

I walked back to the public bus area past a sea of drivers trying to tell me there were no more busses to Luoyang (capital #4). There was, in fact, a bus waiting to leave and as we pulled out, I thought to myself "yay, we are going!, but how long will this last?" It turns out the answer was "not even five minutes." Once out to the main road, they stopped and asked us to switch to another waiting bus, since there were too few of us. I made sure Bus A Lady talked to Bus B Lady and confirmed with Bus B lady that I would not need to pay again. Lady B said no problem, but I never felt at ease until I got off the bus, especially since later I saw her in full flaming fury ripping some poor old sap a new one for reasons I will never know. I figured travel days like this one help you better appreciate when everything goes well. It turns out, perhaps there are no busses going to Luoyang, because there's nothing to see there. Ancient capital or not, the world has moved on, and so did I. I continued my capital tour to ancient capital number five, Xian.

Once finally to Xian, I went on a sightseeing rampage. The highlight, naturally, was the Terracotta Warriors, one of the ultimate sights to behold in China and a big impetus in making me want to visit Xian. Walking the gift vendor gauntlet on the way into this Wonder of the World, I could have sworn my name was "One Dollar" by the way the hoards of vendors were shouting it at me.

But then I was inside. Almost holding my breath in anticipation entering into "Vault 2", the scene I beheld ...was something I think only an archeologist could get excited about. You are mainly looking at an airplane-hangar-sized field of dirt with much of it still an unexcavated work-in-progress.

One thing that did catch my eye was the fact that everyone was walking around with cameras in their hand. My guidebook had mentioned you were not allowed to take pictures. Signs on every wall indicating photography was prohibited reinforced this idea. I finally asked a guy who was shouldering a giant tripod what the deal was. He said the rule was completely disregarded and no one working there seemed to care. I thought it weird anyway that they would not permit photos in a place they are billing as the 8th Wonder of the World.

The Terracotta Warriors were not discovered until 1974 when a farmer was digging a well. They were originally constructed as the guardians of the still unexcavated tomb of Qin Shi Huang (259 BC – 210 BC), the emperor whose impressive resume lines include things like unifying China as one nation for the first time, plus building the Great Wall, the Grand Canal, a massive national road system, and his own tomb here, which alone took almost 30 years.

Vault 1 steals the show and is what the fuss is all about. The hundreds of ceramic sculptures—all unique—have amazing lifelike detail, making it seem they might start marching forward at any moment. They are all standing or kneeling in rows, gripping the air in one position or another. Their weapons are missing apparently having been stolen when the mausoleum was pillaged during a peasant rebellion soon after Qin Shi Huang's death.

They have recently added an exhibition hall to house the two amazing half-size, bronze, horse-drawn carriages which were not found (at the same site) until 1987. I find it intriguing discoveries as amazing as the terracotta warriors or these chariots can be made at this point in history. You are left feeling China has some major unknown untapped reserves of hardcore tourism buried underground all over the place. This theory was further bolstered the following day when visiting the Famen Si temple.

Two Kiwis from my hostel and I headed off in the countryside in pursuit of this cool sounding temple. It was hay-transporting season in Fufeng, a farm town 120 kilometers from Xian located in an area full of scenic red clay hills carved out to form houses. Apparently, up to 80 million Chinese live in this kind of cave house. We saw numerous trailers stacked up so high with hay that from the back you could not see the small tractors pulling them. We had such a good time on our ride through the countryside that seeing the temple itself became icing on the cake.

Famen Si has an interesting history. It has long held an important religious status since it was known for having finger bones of Buddha that had been brought from India. A pagoda had been built to house them. During the Tang dynasty (600-900 A.D.) these bones were worshiped even by the emperors. At one point, every 30 years the artifacts were marched across the country to visit the Imperial Court. The emperors and their followers bestowed a bunch of nice goodies to the bones and these gifts were carried back to Famen Si and buried in the crypt. Later, the area fell into disuse and the main temple was destroyed. Tales of the Tang Dynasty treasures and the bones became a local legend. In the 1900's a new pagoda was built in the original location. In 1981, this pagoda collapsed, breaching the ancient crypt below it. Most of the treasures were preserved in perfect condition. Now you can see the large bone digits (if they are indeed human it must have been one big Buddha) and all the Tang-era wonders. They would not allow pictures, and I do not know enough words to adequately describe the beauty of this treasure trove of gold, silver, bronze, pearl and silk items. Amazing.

CHAPTER 17

The Off-Genre Superhero Track Meet

Near the end of the semester, our Chinese university held a mandatory official all-school track & field meet. They take that stuff seriously! We did not. Recognizing the ridiculousness of it after being required to go one day just to practice marching in for the Opening Ceremonies, we decided that the rest of the competition would be much more enjoyable if we wore costumes. It was. I was Aqua Boy. Classmates Nolan, English Richard and Finnish Aki all joined me in our subtle protest, assembling creative, off-genre superhero outfits.

Aki (my quiet Finnish roommate) had been silently poo pooing the costume idea right until we were about to leave. Then suddenly inspired, he assembled a genius costume I can only describe as looking something like a lumberjack thief with a huge bulge in his crotch area. Aided by having come through with this brilliant, last-minute outfit, Aki delighted the crowd with his long jump performance.

We all got clobbered by the Chinese students who looked like they had been training for years for this day. I was in the long jump and 800-meter events. I still accomplished my goal of beating at least one guy in the 800 while wearing Aqua Boy's mask, snorkel and rain poncho.

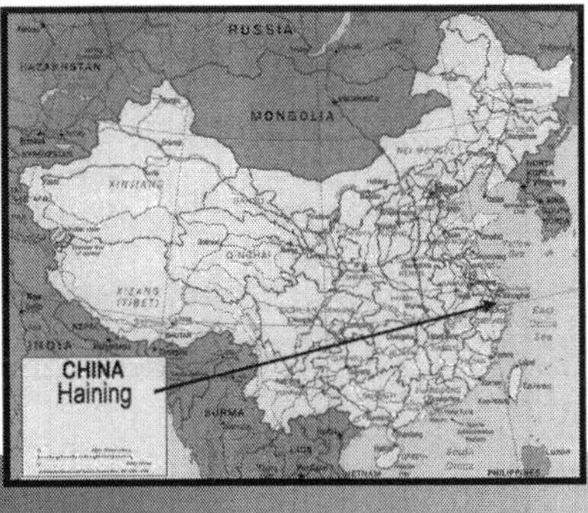

CHAPTER 18

Chasing Bore Tides

My lamb-skewer-loving Finnish roommate Aki and I made a bike trip across the tea-field-covered mountains around Hangzhou and down to the sizable Qiantang River to check out the famous bore tide we had heard so much about. We joined the amassing crowd by the riverfront to wait and see what Mother Nature had in store for us.

A bore tide occurs during a rising high tide where a large vertical tidal shift is pinched into a channel, causing a wave to form. In this region near Hangzhou, the wave is spectacular enough on its peak day of the year that the event is covered live by the national news.

In later hindsight, the bore tide coming up the river looked like some of the 2011 Japanese tsunami footage. In the moment, however, we felt completely safe perched behind a five-meter (15-ft) retaining wall…until the moment we didn't feel safe at all.

The wave turned towards us unexpectedly, like a dragon rearing an angry head. We began running in a panic but it was already too late. The wave crashed into then over the wall, arching like a liquid rainbow over the top of us and all the surrounding screaming spectators. We scrambled into the busy road behind us to escape, but before most of us could hardly budge, the imposing wall of water crashed straight down, soaking us through to the skin.

It was a frightening wake up call to the strength Mother Nature can kick up when she wants to. Every year, despite its publicity/notoriety, up to 100 people are killed in China by this monthly event. Now I knew why.

After seeing that dramatic alluvial display, I wanted more. I felt compelled to check out the area where this bore tide is at its most extreme… near Haining, a town much closer to the mouth of the river.

Aki ran a leather jacket company in Finland and traveled often to Haining—"The Leather Capital of China"—for business. Nolan and I went with him to visit the factory with which he worked most, plus make a side trip to see the bore tide come in. The family that ran the factory decided to make an outing of it, treating us to taxis, park entrances, lunch and a mighty wild ride.

They decided we should see the wave from three spots. We got a late start, so when we arrived at the first viewpoint, the wave had already passed. What ensued was a white-knuckled backseat thrashing as our driver barreled down a winding country road at 70 MPH, at times flying by forlorn, mostly-alive sheep dangling from the backs of bicycles and motorcycles.

We made it to *"The"* famous place for viewing the tide with plenty of time. Here mobs of people nibbled on snacks and sipped tea as they waited for the wave to roll past. Not that it wasn't amazing there, but compared to the untamed torrent that spilled up the river near Hangzhou, this mile-wide, straight wave seemed orderly and calm.

Our near-death taxi roller coaster ride to get to viewpoint #3 removed any sense of a lull in our day. The spectacle at viewpoint #3 was gripping. In this lesser-known spot, the wave smashes into an L in the river. First the wave roars past you, then rushes up a retaining wall, sending people fleeing, then it reverses, lurching back downstream arching up into ferocious 10-foot waves spilling over the side of the retaining wall (sending more people running) as it rumbles back toward the sea over the incoming tide. Witnessing the grandeur of Mum Nature throwing her weight around to this magnitude, I found myself shouting aloud in amazement.

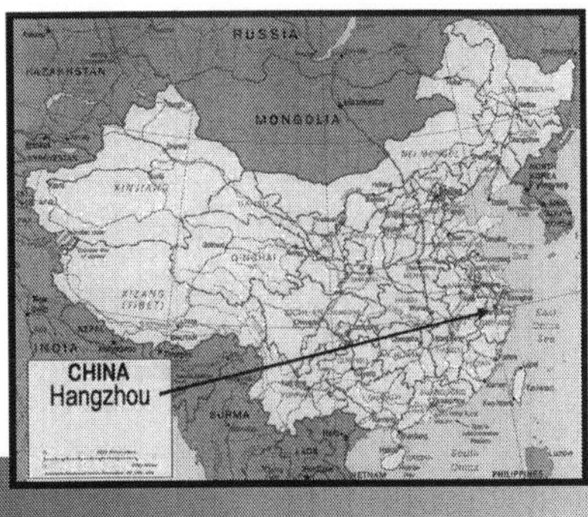

CHAPTER 19

The First Halloween in Hangzhou

Costumes Required

Halloween is one of my favorite holidays, and I thought it would be fun to share this experience with my fellow students in China. Likeminded classmate & roommate Nolan and I began a series of weekly planning meetings that started with the foreign students, then spread to involve many Chinese within and beyond the university.

We had at least 20 Chinese students show up for our main preparation meeting. Half the effort went into explaining to them what "Halloween" is. The energy in the room swelled as the students shifted from trying to grasp the concept we were after to generating their own ideas.

A documentary film crew would have had some rich footage covering Nolan's and my party preparation activities. One choice scene was when we put our rarely-used suits on and traveled to the West Lake Beer Company to solicit them to be our beverage sponsor. Originally, they had requested we have someone from our school's Communist Youth League accompany us there, but eventually accepted our program's administrator as a reasonable alternative.

The guys at the company were nice yet said they had never participated in anything like this before. This was a beer company! Aghast at their lack of marketing zeal, we tried to offer helpful ways to promote their brand at the party, but they hardly seemed concerned. When we asked if they had branded goods like T-shirts we could give away as part of the costume contest, they sheepishly lowered their eyes and apologized, "We wore them all for a softball game uniform."

It finally came down to the numbers. Our administrator almost fell out of his chair when I asked for 100 large bottles. Before he could recover and back pedal our request to something considerably more modest, the beer guys responded quickly with a 72-bottle offer and the deal was done. They even lent us their car and driver to get us home. Big high fives all around.

Next was the fundraiser. This consisted of Nolan in a toga and me in a flasher's outfit going door to door to the rooms of the foreign students. Nolan put together a catchy number on guitar called, "Bless the Lord and the Money in Your Pocket." He sang it while I threw in random backup vocals. At an appropriate point in the song I flashed the prospective donor, exposing the Kleenex box strapped strategically on my waist, which had a sign on it saying, "Come on…100 kuai ($12), please, please, please it will be fun" …priceless footage for the documentary.

We were not exactly buried in donations. As a matter of fact, I think we netted 17 kuai ($2.04) TOTAL on our first run and caused one of our quiet Korean classmates to run down the hall laughing in terror before slamming her door behind her. Once the foreign students better understood what we were up to, however, the funds flowed in.

Next we were off to find a fog machine. Who would have thought in a town like Hangzhou there would be a street lined with fog machine vendors? I never would have believed it if I hadn't seen it myself. I was shocked to find even one. In one store run by guys that looked like Italian speaker salesmen, they threw on their disco lights while demonstrating their fog machine, to give us the full party effect as the fog billowed out onto the street. Where's that film crew when you need them?

Then as Saturday came, so did the party. Aside from local party-goers we had a few special guests from out of town. A Japanese friend of mine, Kaori, came over to take a break from Tokyo life and join in the Halloween festivities, and a fellow business school alumni couple also came down from Shanghai to party.

Due to the creative inspiration of the Chinese students, the decorations were amazing! We built a spooky black tunnel as an entrance into the room. Once inside there were tombstones, a pumpkin-head man riding the costume-contest-prize bicycle, and smoke from the now infamous fog machine. The bar was covered with candles, cool watermelons cut like jack-o-lanterns, spider webs and live goldfish with giant weird eyes. Ghosts and decorative plastic pumpkins hung from disco lights. Little white horror images speckled the black curtains which surrounded most of the room and the air-conditioning towers were transformed into scary robots. We had *Dracula* and some Chinese horror movie silently running on a giant screen. My favorite decoration came about at the last minute: big artistic lettering saying, "Halloween in Hangzhou 2000."

I figured if we were going to be showing people their first-ever Halloween party (especially after all the pep talks I had given them about costume ideas), I'd damn well better come up with an appropriately extreme costume. I went with Big Momma—the plus-plus-sized black woman in the Martin Lawrence film. I thought it ironic that the first article of clothing I ever had tailor-made ended up being an oversized dress. I couldn't find anything big enough in stores, and the custom made dress only cost about $8. The key to my costume, however, was the engineering under the dress. I worked out a double-fleece jacket brassiere sling and a harness that allowed the giant booty package I created to bounce around with gusto. The outfit was rounded out with a flowered bonnet, a convincing borrowed hairpiece, face paint, oversized (aluminum foil) earrings, white gloves and some house slippers. Big Momma was ready to roll, and the effect was better than I had ever hoped for. At the sight of Big Momma, students, guards and teachers alike shrieked with delighted laughter and applauded.

Once people figured out who I was, a number of administrators and other people started coming up and asked worriedly, "When is the party going to start?" Seeing as how it was already 7:20, the room was packed, and the music and disco lights were going, I was a little unsettled to know they didn't feel the party had started. I finally got the hint that I needed to make an announcement. I also realized that the freshly delivered beer was not being served, so that seemed to be as good an excuse as any to make a declaration. I asked a Chinese friend to fill in any remaining culturally-necessary expressions to make sure we had a legitimate party going. And boy, was it ever.

One of our party stipulations was you had to have a costume to enter. Two real uniformed security guards were placed by the entrance to regulate traffic flow and costume standards. Official capacity only allowed 100 in the room at one time. As a result, at some point during the first hour we had a line of over 100 people waiting to get in. Eventually Nolan somehow convinced the administrators that there weren't too many inside so as to get another batch of people in the mix.

In addition to the attendance, we made a number of other miscalculations about the evening. The first was we assumed that like most Chinese parties, it would start slow and need to be carefully nurtured if it was to go anywhere. Wrong. Once Music Coordinator Nolan got back from changing into the perennial Halloween favorite—Satan—he put on dance music and the place started jumping. We had never seen anything like it in China. We threw out the first planned live music set to let the momentum ride.

Completely contrary to expectations, the four people working the bar got mobbed and we had to send people out on repeated beer runs for at least another 30 big bottles.

The games we set up were the bane of our existence much of the night. They were intended to be value-added fun, particularly for those who were not crazy about dancing, but ended up being an organizational disaster. First of all, the setup ran way behind schedule. We needed potable water for "Bobbing for Apples," and the boiling water I had to use was not cool enough until at least an hour after the party started. The darts and balloons game may have never gotten completely set up. Fortune Telling worked at some point (I think).

Nolan and I had envisioned a point system where you could draw for a possible prize once you collected enough points from doing the activities. While we had ironed out the idea beautifully in our heads, its practical implementation never fully materialized since the requisite components were scattered all over the room during the afternoon's preparations, and during the party few of the people who transiently helped run the games ever understood the frighteningly popular concept.

While I spent a lot of time trying to bring together all the pieces, I honestly don't know if the drawing for prizes ever took place. I know we ran out of the 250+ points I had printed up within the first 30 minutes. While it was a confusing mess, it was obvious the Chinese were enamored with the idea. They enjoyed playing through whatever it was we had set up.

Touch the Yuckies was the worst. This was the traditional diversion where you stick your hand into various boxes with nasty-feeling stuff inside. Nolan had devised an ambitious slot machine-like concept where there were several cards in each box and you could get one point for participating, but two if you ended up with matching shapes from each box. Unfortunately when it was finally ready to roll, poor non-Chinese-speaking Richard from England was in charge of explaining it under the thundering music. Once the Chinese students figured out among themselves that they could get points by jamming their hands into the box and pulling out cards, a chaotic feeding frenzy scene reminiscent of Jurassic Park ensued where the Touch the Yuckies table and Richard were pushed up against the wall until the game was finally obliterated. One of the funniest images of the evening for me was one of a peeved Richard—foil from his costume dangling from his face—pointing a finger menacingly at one of the students that had been pushing up against the table, phrasing something along the lines of "Back the F*** up!"

Nolan started out the live music set, playing guitar with the Chinese rock band he had put together. I joined them on ukulele for the last few songs. My favorite was a rousing rendition of monster "Head, Shoulders, Knees and Toes." Big Momma got everybody out on the dance floor to teach them the song and get them to do the hand motions together. It was a blast.

The mike-driven events ended with the much awaited costume contest. To encourage costume creativity, we had bought a new bike ($25) to offer as the grand prize. Our beer-negotiating administrator was in charge of selecting a group of finalists. He failed to understand, however, that he was not supposed to include the organizers in the contest. The winner was to be decided by applause. I would have won the stupid bike had I not finally insisted on being disqualified. The next two top contenders were impossible to sort out at first due to an equally rowdy crowd response, but a winner thankfully eventually emerged before we all went deaf.

We were psyched the party was a raging success. Many of the students told us it was the best party they had ever been to. Hopefully Halloween will return to Hangzhou in the future.

We went out for an after-party, but obviously the Halloween scene in Hangzhou on the 28th of October was not all that. Locals had no idea what we were up to. Big Momma had to wait for the real Halloween night (Oct 31st) in Shanghai for her encore. Kahori's flight back to Japan was to leave from Shanghai November 1st, so I went there to join her for a night on the town before she left.

The hotel staff looked a bit perplexed as Big Momma and Kaori, as a self-created character "Ghost Girl," headed out on the town. The cab driver gave us a smiling "thumbs up" as he drove us off to Rojam, one of the biggest, most happening clubs in Shanghai. This was all about going out for pure fun, without the responsibilities of running a party.

When we walked in, the Rojam dance floor was packed, but not where Big Momma and Ghost Girl started throwing down. A hole opened up and people circled around cheering and clapping. Just like out of a Saturday Night Fever scene, Kaori and I had our own spot on the dance floor as people crowded up to the balconies overhead to check us out. It is hard to describe how much fun it was.

We had arrived just in time for the costume contest. When they started soliciting entrants I was pushed up on the stage pretty quickly. Big Momma put her booty to work to get some bank, and bank she got. Crowd applause landed 1000 kuai ($120) in my hand in prize money. It was quite the rush. The best thing was being able to get back out and dance some more. Not being born with Big Momma's curves, it brought a fun new dynamic to dancing. I also loved seeing the delight on the people's faces around me. Everybody kept trying to pat me on the butt or boobs. I fear what would happen if a true Big Momma ever went out on a dance floor here to shake it around.

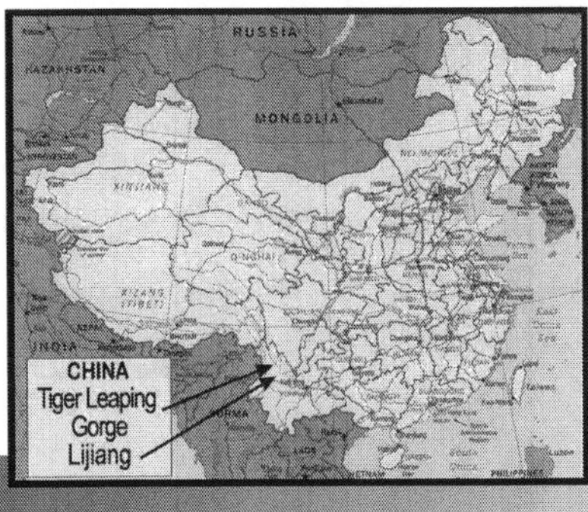

CHAPTER 20

Mom Says I Shouldn't Have Gone to the Tiger Leaping Gorge

The pace of change in China never ceased to amaze me and it almost derailed the start of my trip to Yunnan. I was already running late when I collapsed in the back of a taxi only to hear, "You are leaving from the new airport, right?"

"What new airport?"

When you buy a ticket for a plane, you generally think it is going to leave from the airport for which you bought the ticket, yes?

I had heard rumor that a new airport was being considered but had no idea that it would be constructed and ready this fast. It was an extra hour away and I would have never made it in time. After making some panicked calls as the minutes ticked away, the cabbie and I learned that some flights had already shifted to the new airport, but the rest (including mine) would not be switched over until the following day. Whew!

I flew straight to Kunming, the capital of Yunnan, a province in southern China. Arriving at this shiny metropolis, I was overjoyed to see the bright blue sky filled with puffy clouds—a sight I had not seen in many moons. It felt like it had been miserably rainy and cold in Hangzhou since before the time of rice.

Kunming is a city that had modernized faster than its inhabitants. As passengers departed the jet, the cleaning crew came pulling up along the tarmac on their bicycles. On the way into town, I saw horse carts pulling onto the double-level highway and goats being herded along the road shoulder.

Not much of city guy, I skipped out of town northwest to the small higher-altitude town of Dali. It was darn cold and dark when

I arrived, but after life in the construction-obsessed Hangzhou, unbelievably quiet. You could almost hear the stars.

From there I played tourist up to the antique gem Lijiang, a city that has been awarded UNESCO's World Heritage Site status. Lijiang's charming rows of wooden, tiled-roof houses are interwoven by clear canals and narrow cobblestone streets.

I spent New Year's in this quaint, quiet place in the company of a cute quirky young couple from Beijing whom I had bumped into earlier on the ride up to Dali and who would eventually become longtime friends. It was unusual for Chinese nationals to travel long distances for fun. Many were not allowed to leave their home area without special permission. So it was not a huge surprise to once again bump into this fun, unique couple at the one bar/restaurant in town that seemed to be open New Year's Eve.

In a traditional Chinese village like Lijiang, people were focused on preparations for the Chinese New Year while the Western calendar's January first New Year went virtually unnoticed. I, however, was intent on celebrating the Western one, and I was happy for some company. Undeterred by the village's dearth of party fervor, my new friends and I made a strong, albeit lonely, quest to whoop it up around town when the New Year was rung in. And thanks to the tradition shared by a former girlfriend, we even incorporated a customary Colombian-style celebratory run around the block carrying a suitcase (to encourage luck in travel during the year) just after the silent bells tolled. Puzzled people who crossed us in the quiet streets were visibly surprised to see us celebrating, but seemed to put two and two together that it was for New Year's.

I wanted to start the new millennium with something extraordinary and thus became obsessed with getting deep into the renowned Tiger Leaping Gorge by nightfall on New Year's Day. I got a late start, which certainly didn't help things. It was already after 1 p.m. by the time I reached Qiaotou, the gritty bustling town that serves as the entry point for the gorge.

I could never seem to get what felt like adequate information on the 50 kilometer-long "upper" trail, but figured I had enough to go for it. That said, I could not help but be impressed at how the Internet can be an amazing resource. On it, I had found a description that allowed me to cut up a driveway, sort of through someone's garden and down a ladder to avoid paying the Tiger Leaping Gorge entrance fee (which was disproportionally high for foreigners, a practice I am not a fan of). It felt like a magic trick when it actually worked.

As the trail rose above the river, wrapped around the mountain to the left and into the beginning of the gorge, menacing clouds began flowing over the mountains behind me. The dark cottony sheets chasing me became blocked by the impressive rocky, snow-dusted peaks forming the opposite side of the gorge.

The smart (but highly neglected) voice in me said "Turn Back." I identified a separate, eternally optimistic inner voice I now call my Ego. This alternate self ignored the wind (which had progressively gained force since the morning), gathered opinions of locals that indicated, "Nah, it won't rain" and deduced that I should go for it while I still could. Luckily the locals were correct about the rain since this area is considered extremely dangerous under wet conditions.

A couple hours in I crossed the first hikers coming the opposite way. They turned out to be the only non-locals I would pass on the trails for the three days I hiked in the gorge. They were optimistic that I could make it to the Halfway Guesthouse by nightfall and said that it should be easy to find even if it did get dark because the trails were clear. They ended up being wrong on both counts, but it sounded great when they said it.

Things would have been fine had I not lost the path while coming over the highest peak on the trail. Trail navigation was complicated by the fact that numerous goat trails crisscrossed the main hiking trail, which was virtually never marked with signs anyway.

Dropping down the backside of the summit, I thought I was on course, but then the trail became smaller and smaller to the point that I was starting to bushwhack. This was not good, particularly because I was barely on pace to get to my destination before nightfall. The sparse semblance of a trail then evaporated into what looked like a field of marijuana (which there was rumored to be plenty of hidden in this part of the country), provoking emotions ranging from 1) Fear of potential protective farmers or their booby traps to 2) Excitement of 'Wow that's a lot of marijuana!' (Incidentally, I picked a couple leaves which some "experts" later determined was not the real stuff.)

I backtracked and managed to scramble through the brush back to the top, but could still not find a better alternative path from the one I first descended. After several aborted attempts, I decided to get to the bottom via the only means that seemed certain—the steep path taken by the power lines. This was by no means an easy option. While the area had been somewhat cleared, or at least chopped down at one point, Mother Nature had retorted with angry thorny plants as a quick replacement. I was getting pretty beat up by all the brambles. For footing, where there wasn't tree shrapnel, there were mostly slippery dirt precipices.

As the light dimmed and my fatigue increased, a reoccurring image appeared of my mother scolding me, saying, "Don't put yourself in these kinds of dangerous situations!" I gave myself some mental raps on the knuckles, too, since I had decided to rely on this New Year's experience to foretell the rest of the year, and here I was doing something stupid already. (Stupid with two O's.)

I finally found a substantive path a ways down the steep power line track that led me in the right direction. I was worn out when I arrived at the town of Bendiwan. I don't know what those guys I met earlier on the trail were thinking when they suggested the guest house would be easy to find in the dark. The electricity was out and the houses blended into the side of the mountain, making the town virtually invisible. The trail branched off in several directions and there were no signs of any sort. Not what I was hoping for, particularly since I was completely exhausted. Like a blind man trying to navigate by the only means available to me, I headed toward the sounds of people and dogs in the homes below me. Fortunately, I crossed helpful young locals who pointed me in the direction of the guesthouse.

I amused the three Australians staying there when I stumbled in out of the dark and collapsed. They had been there relaxing for most of the day and were leisurely about to start dinner. Nice timing. Some hot vegetable soup did wonders for recharging a body that had been running on Oreos and pistachios. It turned out to be a cozy evening of candle lit conversation and a welcomed rest at the end of a real long day.

After a clear lesson that my body was no longer the start-on-a-dime health machine it once was, I took it a lot easier the second day. I felt saddled with the reality that I would have to take care of my body and get real exercise if I wanted to do outings like this one without killing myself.

The next day I took an hour detour straight down to the river from the point where the high path meets the low one. While nervous about the fierce wind and the fast moving clouds, it was not bad enough to stop me from going down. The views were fantastic. Finally reaching the bottom of the gorge, I fulfilled my obsession of touching the water of the renowned Yangzi River. This detour was one of the highlights of my three days in the gorge.

My not-so-distant destination for the day, Walnut Grove, was an attractive village perched above rice terraces which dropped down to the river. I stayed at Dan's Place. With the guidebook suggesting Satellite TV and "Magic Pancakes" on the menu, why go anyplace else, right?

In reality, the pancakes tasted pretty lousy and there was no electricity to run the TV because of the heavy winds. But these details were of little consequence to the group of foreigners assembled there that night who were out to have a good time regardless. We all ended up around the kitchen fire fervently imbibing much of Dan's alcohol reserves.

My journal entry on this third day of the year was titled, "A Day from Hell." As I made my way out of the sparsely populated back side of the gorge, the path direction was again not always clear. Thank goodness my Guardian Angel strategically placed people at each fork in the trail where I was about to head very much the wrong way. Maybe he was working overtime to make up for taking the day off when I started this trip. Or, perhaps he knew what was in store for me the rest of the day and figured I would need a break.

I finally found the Yangzi ferry crossing that put me on the outskirts of the town where busses left for Lijiang. I was annoyed to have a guy from the boat dock follow me the entire way in an attempt to receive some kind of commission. I don't like people following me. I also didn't trust the information he was telling me regarding bus times since it ran contrary to that of my guidebook and that which I had found on the Internet. He kept suggesting I would need to stay in the town that night.

When we finally got to the place from which the bus supposedly left, there was no sign of it. Since it was not even 1 p.m., I did not buy the "There are no more busses today" routine for even a second. I did not like the attitude of the hotel people in the town and was not about to stay there—bus or not.

At this point I had already hiked five hours, yet still took off with the blind optimism that I would find a Lijiang-bound bus somewhere up the road. Although this tactic usually works, this time the locals might have been right. I will never be sure since I started out on the wrong road and a bus could have easily passed while I was off course.

I started walking towards Lijiang knowing full well that I could never walk the full 90 kilometers. I was determined to catch a ride on any transportation available and/or stay in some assumed-to-exist village along the way. Things started out OK with me getting a brief ride on the rock pile cargo trailer pulled behind a Mad Max vintage tractor.

Then, however, I walked a lonely couple hours up through a scattered hillside village without having a single car pass in either direction. I bought a silly-looking straw hat to defend against the unrelenting sun. Around 4 p.m. I had yet to eat anything that day and was pretty darn hungry. With no food to be had, I popped a multi-vitamin to at least boost my nutrient level. I knew that you are supposed have something in your stomach when you take these, but I had done this before and it never seemed to bother me. Until now.

About 20 minutes later my stomach started feeling queasy. Just when I started feeling decidedly *ungood*, the first vehicle to pass in my direction all day stopped for me. While I was extremely fortunate the two friendly guys in the truck were happy to offer me the extra seat in the cab, their cigarettes and loud, bad music certainly did not help my physical disposition. I strategically asked to have the window seat. It wasn't long before we pulled over for the first in a series of puke breaks. The guys were very kind considering the state of their new passenger. The driver even offered to let me drive, thinking the road was making me sick rather than something self-inflicted.

While the snow-capped mountain scenery was fabulous, I would have appreciated seeing it in the non-double, swirling version. We stopped to fix a flat tire (them) and upchuck (me) right when the temperature began to plummet. We were at the beginning of a slippery ice-covered mountain pass that seemed to last several eternities. Eventually we made it down the far side and back to an appreciably warmer Lijiang.

After an intense nap I forced myself to forage for food since I had not yet eaten. I will be eternally indebted to the hostel (Sakura's) owner and her husband, who came up with a scrumptious chicken soup and fresh strawberries dinner which brought me back to life.

After running myself into the ground, it seemed like a wise move to lay low for a day. This recovery day also allowed me to see the Naixi Ancient Music Concert. Just seeing some of the old musicians being helped onto the stage and hearing them tune up assured me that I had made the right decision to stick around. The 20-or-so-piece orchestra consisted mostly of *really* old guys that looked like they had shuffled straight out of some Chinese storybook. The MC had a bad habit of talking—so bad that in the 90-minute concert he probably talked more than the musicians played. As a result, the older men often dozed off in between tunes.

The percussive music was both melodic and fascinating. In one sense, it looked like a living funeral. Above the stage was a collection of photos of musicians from the group who had already died. It made you survey the group to guess who might be the next picture on the wall. I am not sure I would want to be an orchestra member with that in mind.

I met this gentleman the second day, coming the opposite way on the trail. We stopped and chatted, taking a break.

When I first began learning Chinese, I envisioned "success" with the language as arriving to the point where I could meet a regular Chinese person on a bus and chat with them about their day in their language.

Even at the time I met this gentleman, I remember reflecting on the fact that me talking with him meant that that I had achieved that very goal and it gave me a tangible sense of accomplishment.

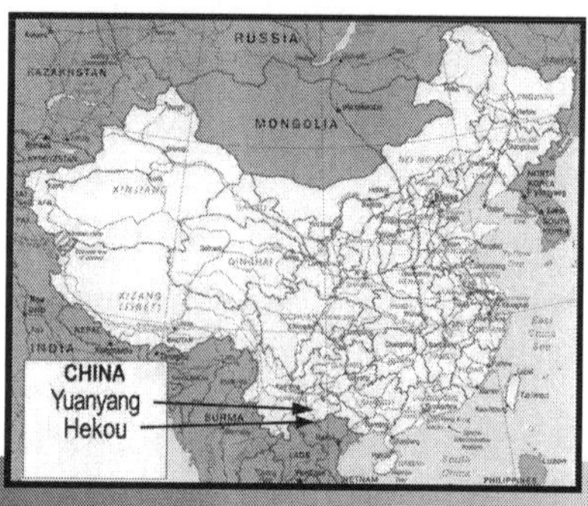

CHAPTER 21

Racing the Slow Red River

More Adventures in Southwest China

After my New Year's fun in and around Lijiang, exotic Southeast Asia beckoned. Even before boarding the bus in Kunming's southbound bus station, the shapes of people's faces began taking on more Vietnamese characteristics. Jaw lines became more slender, cheeks bones rose higher. Once on the bus, other tangible signs of lowering latitudes whizzed by outside the window, including a notable increase in banana plants. My southern soul rejoiced at the tropical flora, the rising temperatures, and the news that it was now snowing in Beijing and over much of the rest of China, which was steadily retreating in the rear-view mirror.

The areas close to China's southern border with Vietnam had been off limits for travel even up into the 1990's because of a border war between the countries. Luckily, the situation had since improved as it was a fascinating area to visit, and I am sure the inhabitants were happy to no longer be on war footing.

By the time I reached the small hilltop town of Yuanyang there were no busses heading onward to my overoptimistic destination, the Vietnam border. Everyone in this region seemed to extremely underestimate travel times. When I was quoted any transport time from one to four hours, I learned I needed to add one to two hours to that estimate. Any time quoted

over five hours meant adding an extra three to four hours before you'd be even close to arriving. If you were in a hurry to get anywhere down here, you were in the wrong place.

I was anxious to get to Vietnam as my time to spend there was ticking away, but staying in vibrant Yuanyang was an excellent decision/happenstance as it turned out to be a highlight of my two-month trip. The town was bustling with colorful minority people in amazingly varied traditional dress. The town reminded me of the cantina scene in *Star Wars.* While its people were fascinating, the primary attraction of Yuanyang is what the people of this region and their descendants have built: the breathtaking rice terraces which surround the town.

These rice fields were as extreme as any I have seen, serrating 3000 or more vertical feet of mountainsides at times. As it was winter, instead of green growing rice, the topo-map-like curving contour layers were illuminated by the sun reflecting off the exposed water filling the empty fields, which were gripped in place by unusually sturdily constructed walls. Hay-thatched adobe houses, joyful ducks, water buffalo and black pot-bellied pigs interspersed throughout further livened the landscape.

Numerous men could be seen along the side of the road with meter-long bamboo tube bongs. I have no idea what they were smoking in them. Some of the men looked to just be using them to smoke their cigarettes. In the town a man had a bong rental stand where men would casually settle in for a puff.

The question as to why the minority Hani people's rich blue costume includes a straw mat hanging from their backs was answered when I saw them using the mats to support big rocks, piles of bricks and other heavy loads.

A side thought: if the US ever wanted to communicate any urgent news or political agenda to China it should use NBA basketball side-court banners since that seems to be the only thing I saw regularly on TV from the States.

The next day was noted in my journal as "Racing the (slow) Red River Day," although it was previously intended to be "Entry into Vietnam Day."

My morning started at 6:30 a.m. when I was told that the bus to Hekou, the town on the border with Vietnam, did not show up. I hoofed it down to the main road by the Red River before the sun rose above the mountains to see what other transport I could find. Little did I know that after a mishmash of transportation modes later (including a lot by foot), I would still be by the same river and still in China when the sun set.

From the truck that could not get out of second gear to the one with the bucket of spilling pork parts, my twelve and a half hour journey to the border eventually wore me out. The pork parts adventure was in the back of my second or third pickup truck ride of the day. The guy next to me was valiantly but unsuccessfully struggling to stabilize his plastic-bag-covered, overflowing bucket of pig guts. I became familiar with the bucket's contents not through casual speculation alone. As the road was plenty rough, some of the bloody mess sloshed out onto my pants and the floor of the truck, leaving jello-ey pieces of pig liver jiggling on the truck bed.

Ultimately, the docile Red River water I saw in Yuanyang this morning probably beat me across the border into Vietnam by a wide margin. Hanging out with locals in a variety of podunk villages along the way made for an interesting day, but in terms of moving on to Vietnam, my bad luck wasn't over. When I finally reached Hekou, not only was the border closed for the day, but I was told the following day was to be the opening ceremonies for a new border crossing bridge. I would have to wait through the opening ceremonies, then cross midday when the new bridge between Hekou and Lao Cai (Vietnam) opened for traffic.

While still the night before the big event, the ambiance in town had an excited, almost Christmas Eve feel to it as everyone prepared. It was fun to feel their energy. To commemorate the event, the town's prostitutes seemed to be out in full. Dodging them at every turn, I passed by the new bridge entry while looking for a place to eat. A military band was there practicing the Chinese national anthem over and over with some flag raisers. The band was almost drowned out by the sounds of the nearby bulldozers and a work crew tearing down the cement barricades that previously blocked the bridge entry.

I ducked into a new fast food place close by to grab some ice cream. I might have been their first customer since they were not officially opening until the next day. The manager took a break from training the squeaky new staff to bring me some free fries and onion rings to ask how I liked the taste. She ended up refusing to take money for the ice cream, too. You don't see that every day. Not in China.

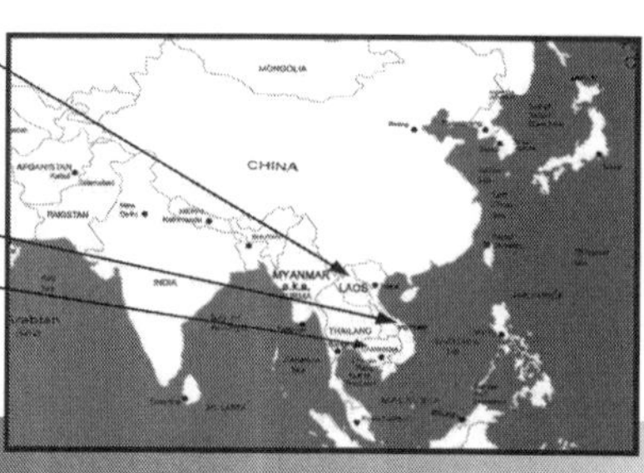

CHAPTER 22

My Son and Angkor What?

The Southeast Asia Road Trip Continues

Despite all my efforts to get into Vietnam earlier than now, I embraced the opportunity to be one the first people to enter via the new bridge crossing. While waiting the next morning, I took advantage of the time to explore this Chinese border town's exotic market, which featured goodies like fuzzy rodents of unknown origins, snakes (mostly for making elixirs), a nurse-shark-like freshwater fish, and fried dog's head. I'm not sure if/how one was supposed to eat all these or whether some were destined to be pets.

I showed up at the appointed hour to be one of the first to cross the new bridge, but was let down when the customs officers on the new bridge said they were not yet ready to handle foreigners and redirected me to cross via the old bridge. Oh well, so much for helping to make history.

Nothing says marketplace delicacy like dried(?) pig face. right?

I crossed the old bridge just as officials from both sides approached the midpoint of the new bridge to do the classic Official Hand Shaking Thing. As part of the celebration, in what struck me as a wildly reckless act of border security, citizens of both countries were allowed to freely cross the border for the day with no checks of their papers. Clearly a well-received idea, I was lucky to get across, through customs, and out of town just ahead of the deluge of Chinese pouring across the new bridge.

Vietnam (at last)

Vietnam's border city and countryside looked noticeably poorer than their Chinese counterparts across the river. While Chinese rely on busses or passenger vehicles for most transportation, Vietnam had an entrenched and growing motorcycle culture. I got my first taste right across the border, hiring a moto-taxi driver to run me out to visit a mountain minority people's village for the afternoon.

That night I took an overnight train to Vietnam's capital, Hanoi. The train company wasn't kidding when they called my choice of accommodations a "hard sleeper." I have slept on softer granite. My hip bones were bruised in the morning from sleeping on my side. Neither the millimeter-thin straw mat nor the top rack's 2.5-foot clearance did anything to increase the comfort level, but I somehow managed to get a decent night's rest.

The train was different from any I had ridden before. Foreigners are sequestered to certain cars and are forced to pay five times the locals' price for this privilege. All the cars had a heavy-duty metal grate across each window, which was

supplemented by a metal shield that pulled down outside the grate. It made you wonder what you were heading in to, particularly if you noticed the dents in the shields.

In the middle of the night I wandered into another world, entering the grimy dining car next door. Here inside the train, the cook was boiling water over an open fire for instant noodle dishes. Most of the room's dim lighting came from the flickering fire.

In the morning, blinking and rubbing my eyes, I walked off the train ready to see what Hanoi had to offer. To start my visit off right, I motorcycled straight to Ho Chi Min's Mausoleum to see the glass-encased man himself. He looks amazingly good for a dead guy. Apparently they send his body back to Russia once a year for routine maintenance.

The highlight of my visit to Hanoi turned out to be a "water puppet show". I still don't know how it works. It originated in the 11th century when farmers used the unused rice fields to do these performances. How to describe it? The action was accompanied by a lively musical ensemble, which played traditional instruments and sang the story lines. The stage floor is a deep pool of dark water with a curtain as a backdrop. The puppets enter along the water surface and move around at a distance that would be too far to be reached by hands from behind the curtain. There are no strings controlling them from above. For most of the performance I thought the puppeteers were swimming out under the puppets to operate them and I was testing to see if I could hold my breath as long as them. But when the show was over and the puppeteers came out, they were only wet up to their waists. I was dumbfounded since the movements looked to be far too complex and rapid to be controlled remotely through the water. I felt both silly and refreshed that I couldn't figure out how an art form this old worked. And they don't tell you.

As a rule, Vacation Boy does not do package tours, and my trip to the oddly named Perfume Pagoda confirmed why. I don't like being herded around with big noisy groups of people that you inevitably spend half your time waiting for. More concretely, I wish one of my neighbors on this tour bus could have found a better way to air his personal grievances than via his Mekong Death Farts, which nearly caused me to smash out a window to escape.

Despite the bus tour drawbacks, the trip was interesting because of the inherent beauty of the destination and the scenic journey to get there. The karst (steep limestone) mountains resembling those of Guilin, China are fronted by flooded rice paddies which could only be reached by boat.

I noticed many dogs in this part of Vietnam caged in a way that looked suspiciously like produce. Here, when people ask along with the tune "How Much is that Doggie in the Window?" you could guess that they are looking for a price by the pound.

Vietnam was a lot bigger than I first imagined. My first-ever 24-hour bus ride took me down the coast to Hoi An, which is only halfway down the coast. This city's Japanese and Chinese influenced antique architecture helped it land UNESCO World Heritage Site status.

It was in this city close to a beautiful beach and home to some excellent, cheap tailors that I re-bumped into the crew from the San Francisco School of Art (not to be confused with the OTHER San Francisco fine arts school). I first encountered them at a temple in Hanoi. They were hard to miss. Those in the group not hauling around a John Muir-class giant hooded camera were each still weighed down with more camera equipment than offered by most well stocked camera stores. They were on a five-week class trip lead by their instructor, the renowned photographer Linda Connor.

As a closet photo junkie, I was irresistibly drawn to them and their curious gear, and apparently I was not the only one. They talked about the scene they caused coming through customs apparently to the dismay of Vietnamese customs officials, especially when the photographers had understandably refused to have their boxes of rare 8x10-inch size negative film run through Vietnamese X-ray machines. The group set up darkroom tents in the airport so the agents could open the boxes without ruining the film, taking them well over an hour to search through everything.

Linda had remembered me and my endless questions in Hanoi, and was kind enough to invite me to join them for dinner. She also invited me to accompany them the following day for their photo excursion to the Cham ruins of My Son (that's really the name of the place—did anybody skim down here just to see if I had a kid they hadn't heard about?).

While I had been thinking about taking a day to relax by the beach, I could not pass up her offer. My Son was one of southeast Asia's great religious centers from the 4th to 13th centuries, but was later retaken by nature. It was rediscovered by the French in the early 1900s. Giant U.S.-inflicted bomb craters riddle the grounds, a testament to the site's more tumultuous recent history. During the Vietnam War, the Viet Kong used it as a base camp and the U.S. went after them.

On the day we visited, the peaceful ruins were overtaken by invaders of the photographic sort. I did what I could to learn by observing the photo students while they—as my sister's biologist husband would say—"did their behaviors." It was a lot to try and take in. Feeling like a wooden-spear-toting barbarian coming up against an armored tank division, at least I now know better why my photos will never compare favorably next to those found in books and magazines—the preserve of pros that actually know what they are doing. Still, they were a fun group to hang out with, breaking up my typical routine.

Unfortunately, the Perfume Pagoda trip would not be my last package tour in Vietnam. In Vietnam it is standard practice for foreigners to be overcharged several times the going rate. Cafes/travel agencies sell tours and transport packages at rates that come out cheaper than it would cost you to do it on your own, especially since often there is little to no public transportation to get to tourism sites. In a decidedly non-English environment where travel via regular public transportation can be confusing, way overcrowded, and arduously slow—package tours are too hard a formula to resist.

After several strong recommendations from travelers, the Mekong Delta became my next must-see destination. You could feel the pace of life slow down, the hammock count increase, and the temperature rise as the tour van (yes, I went there via a package tour) made its way into this most southeastern section of Vietnam, pulling away from the frenetic polluted rat trap of Saigon (Ho Chi Min City). I am not a tremendous fan of the cold, so here in early January it was a truly joyous moment when I finally needed to change into shorts because of the heat. Summer was BACK ...Yes!

Tet, the Vietnamese lunar New Year, was right around the corner and apparently it is considered lucky to marry just before Tet. On the way down to the Mekong Delta, we passed at least 20 wedding processions heading in the other direction. A ceremony is held at the bride's parent's home, followed by another party at the groom's home, where the bride would then live.

The other main Tet-related activity was plant acquisition. Plants were being sold like Christmas trees in numerous temporary stands along the roads. The most interesting sighting of this was at night in Cantho, the province's capital. I'd never seen anything like it. It's considered good luck to buy a plant before Tet, and shopping for them here became a cruising scene. In the center of town by the river, the road had been taken over by a giant plant market. While a few people were diligent about making a plant purchase, many more in the continuously circulating crowd seemed to hardly even look at the flora, much less inquire about the prices. They were much more interested in

the *fauna*. A Ho Chi Min statue under renovation benevolently saluted, seeming to condone the gregarious activity below. It was a unique social occasion for young and old alike to spend with friends and family, and I felt lucky to just witness it. Think how additionally lucky I would have been if I'd bought a plant, too.

The Mekong River starts in the Tibetan Plateau and weaves through five more countries before belching into the South China Sea. One of the other highlights of visiting the delta was getting out on the river itself. Images of the *Apocalypse Now* gunboat riding up the river are inescapable if you watched the movie the week before you left on your trip (like I did).

The people along the small tributaries were incredibly friendly. It was hygienically painful to watch them carry out their daily riparian activities of bathing, washing clothes & food, and using the bathroom in the same water, knowing how many people had done the same for hundreds and hundreds of miles upstream.

The busy floating markets were also fascinating. Buyers and sellers were all afloat in various dark wooden crafts conducting business as if they were in a regular farmer's market on land. Merchants at the

Floating market

floating market would indicate which produce they were selling by hoisting them up on a mast. Not surprisingly, the plant boat received a particularly warm reception that day.

Easter Day was my Day of Death. The series of events that took place this day somehow felt spiritually linked to the e-mail I received the night before about my Great-Aunt Bessie passing away unexpectedly. Receiving this grave news from home mentally transported me out of my foreign Internet café surroundings, back to the U.S., flipping through my mental memories of her. Aunt Bessie was from a family of seven sisters and two brothers who grew up on a bare bones farm near Arkadelphia, Arkansas. I always remembered that there were seven sisters from their stories about having only one dress each and swapping amongst themselves every day so that they would have a different dress to wear for each day of the week. Aunt Bessie, like her sisters, had a cow-sounding name (Elsie, Ocie, Bertha...) and shockingly huge biceps which they attributed to hauling water out of a well throughout their childhood. I found myself mentally comparing the rural poverty they experienced as children with the Asian scenes passing before me.

Images of Aunt Bessie echoed in my mind as I headed out in the morning in Saigon with a visit to the chilling War Remnants Museum (toned down from the original name: the American War Crimes Museum), which graphically outlines various atrocities committed by US troops in Vietnam. I found it odd that of all the military hardware displayed, none of it was North Vietnamese. It was as if the US was just invading and brutalizing the peasants unopposed. There was also precious little about protests against the war in the U.S., and nothing whatsoever about South Vietnamese resisting the North. The grizzly photos made US soldiers out to be ruthless monsters. I am not saying that the US acted like chivalrous Boy Scouts there, but

Grizzly images from Ho Chi Minh City's War Remnants Museum

I would have appreciated even a modicum of balance to the presentation. I guess you have to win the war if you want to write the history any differently.

From Saigon, to save some time I flew straight to north-central Cambodia. My motorbike taxi ride arrival from the airport into the calm dusty village of Siem Reap was disturbing. Approaching one of the world's great monuments from the back of a motorbike with the wind and exotic scenes rushing by, I had been in a buoyant mood. That joyous feeling was erased by the scene that unfolded before me. Near one intersection, people were gathered around a truck stopped awkwardly across the road.

The police were making chalk tracings to document the fatalities. A trail began behind the truck, starting with a shoe and leading to a lifeless boy who lay quietly looking my way from under the truck with his skull cracked open like an egg and his young brain flowing out onto the orange dirt road. Further forward was another body silhouette under the truck carriage and the crushed moped they had been riding. More gruesome than anything I had ever witnessed, the magnitude of the horror left me sensing that the rest of what I would do that day would feel insignificant and small.

Not knowing what else to do, though, I proceeded to look for a place to stay. Along the way Death's hand waved at me yet again. I stopped to watch a funeral procession primarily made up of school children. The coffin was on an elaborately decorated float with orange-clad monks riding alongside. I thought about Aunt Bessie and hoped that all these connections to death did not somehow have to do with her spirit being unable to rest peacefully.

The reason for going to Siem Reap was to see the renowned Angkor Wat. If you are unintelligent and unfamiliar with the world's great treasures like me, you are thinking, "Angkor *What?*" That was pretty much my exact initial reaction as I had honestly never heard of Angkor Wat before I started planning this trip and decided it might be fun to cut through Cambodia. It turns out this expansive collection of Khmer ruins represents one of the greatest empires of all time, once spanning from Vietnam to Burma. It makes me wonder what else important I am missing out on this planet.

Angkor Wat is a complex of many temples spread out over 200 square kilometers. There are about 30 main sites in various states of renovation and reclamation from where the jungle had overwhelmed the structures. Most independent travelers like me hire a motorcycle driver to run you around for the day ($6-12). I explored temple ruins literally from dawn to dusk. Fun, steep staircases abounded—the kind you need to scale on all fours. It makes for a good workout in the oppressive heat.

While Angkor's elaborate ruins and the areas where trees are pushing up through the structures is described as mind blowing, throughout my visit I could not stop my thoughts from drifting back to the child's mind I saw earlier spilled out onto the dusty road. The horrific image accompanied me wherever I went.

My favorite part of the visit was following a group of young Buddhist pilgrims wandering through the site. Their bright orange robes seemed to perfectly complement the surroundings. Seeing the contrast of them in traditional garb using a modern video camera and taking pictures of each other made me grin at the technology time warp.

In the late afternoon en route to one location a ways outside the main collection of sites, I was able to answer the oft-asked question: "What happens if you get a flat tire in The Middle of Nowhere, Cambodia?"—you walk. I enjoyed the hour of rural scenery and friendly people, but was still glad to be able to hitch a ride in a Japanese tourist's comfy hired car to cover the rough last couple miles to the site I was heading to. My moto driver was somehow able to patch the flat and catch up with me in time to meet me there by sunset.

While people suggested I would need three to five days to do Angkor Wat justice, I had a hunch I might be able to get my fill by the second day. I had a couple fantastic days there, but at the end I was right that was satiated for visiting ruins for some time to come.

I was also hopeful I was through with death's cameos. Within a week, however, it would brush by me once more in Laos. After an overnight bus ride through Thailand, I found myself on a bus in the company of three American guys heading up to the highlands near the China border. I was on my way to do a UNESCO sponsored trek up to a remote mountain village and they were off for some fun in the sun. On my return I coincidentally bumped into them again. Only now there were two instead of three of them. The visibly rattled pair recounted how up in the highlands their buddy had O.D.'ed on opium and how they had spent a harrowing hour in the back of a bumping pickup truck trying to do CPR on him while transporting him to a hospital, all to no avail.

Still not released from my memories of the child on the road in Siem Reap, Aunt Bessie's recent passing and the images from the museum in Saigon, the news of the death of this fellow traveler I had only met a few days earlier was more than enough of a reminder of how fleeting life can be. I just hoped I could escape this cloud without becoming part of it.

Not that I am afraid of death. At least I would like to hope I am not. I have a habit that every time right before a flight takes off (something which seems to be a frequent occurrence for me), right when the engines engage I pause to reflect on the question, "Would I be upset if this plane crashes?" I feel that I have been so fortunate to see and experience the things I have up to now, it would be selfish of me to be disappointed to not live longer. Additionally, if I can avoid it I don't want to be stressed out when I die. You can't stop a plummeting plane so it would be much better to accept it, relax and appreciate everything you have experienced rather than fret about that which will not be.

Going through this regular meditative gut check exercise sometimes leaves me answering, "Yes, I would be upset" but that is usually if I left things off in a state I would regret, such as an unresolved argument with my mother. Not that I encourage death, but reminding myself it can be just one truck bumper or a blocked artery or plane crash away, I enjoy life's blessings every day that much more as I feel I am already in the bonus round.

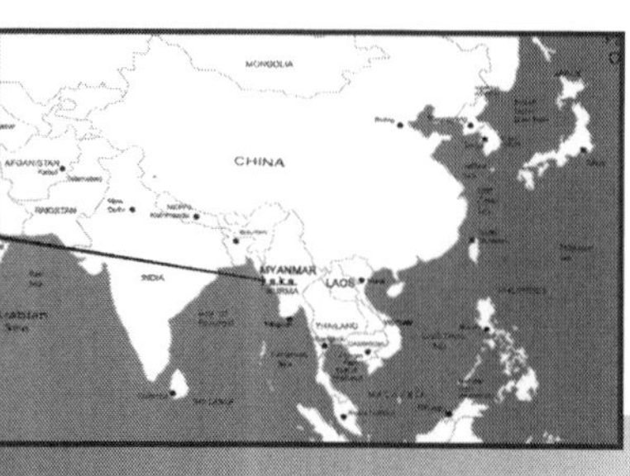

CHAPTER 23

A Father's Perspective on Travel with Vacation Boy

Myanmar and the Burma Road to China

Written by Dr. Jon I. Sattler

For some masochistic reason, my son wanted to travel the Burma Road from Myanmar into China. He was moving from his university in Hangzhou, China to a school in Beijing but had a break in between which he, of course, intended to fill with travel and for some reason had become obsessed with seeing this obscure corner of the globe. Little information existed regarding travel in that remote area and frankly, I was apprehensive about traveling in this country run by a heavy-handed military dictatorship, venturing down a road described as, "tends to disintegrate during the subtropical humid wet season." However, I wasn't about to let him head into this tropical abyss alone. Using the guise of helping him move up to his new apartment afforded me the rationale to visit Asia again and dive into this adventure with him. In pursuit of the Burma Road, we stumbled upon the unexpected delight of Myanmar (Burma). What a wonderful find it turned out to be—isolated, bustling, friendly, charming, visually compelling and unspoiled by rampant tourism.

I should explain that my son and I are not exactly compatible travelers. I am retired and like a modicum of comfort. He, on the other hand, is a student (albeit graduate student) who could best be described as an 'extreme traveler'. He likes to get close to Mother Earth and manages to find a way to be coated by her from hiking, biking, sleeping or whatever. His philosophy is that unless you travel on the most difficult form of transportation available and find absolutely everything yourself, you haven't fully experienced what an area has to offer. Which is why it took us six weeks to come to an agreement as to where to go and what to do in Myanmar. My reflex was to find an English speaking guide, rent an air-conditioned car, and stay at the best hotels we could find. I found I could even put together a grand tour for eight days and seven nights with air fares, ground transportation, hotels and sightseeing fees for under $800 per person. Lots of luck when you're with 'Vacation Boy.' "Are you kidding me, Dad? I can go for months on that kind of money!" he would say, insisting we travel by bus or train. Hence we became FITs—foreign independent travelers.

Myanmar is the modern name given to Burma by the ruling military junta. However, most folks one encounters there refer to themselves as Burmese. Myanmar was virtually sealed off from the outside world in 1962 when a dictatorial regime took control of the government and economy. In 1988 there was a popular uprising and national elections were held. The military, however, refused to relinquish power and remained in control at the time of our journey.

The Myanmar government prefers to corral foreigners into package tours through a select set of tourist sites. Large tracts of the country are off limits to foreigners, although there is still plenty to take away from the areas which are permitted. In Myanmar, it is not surprising to see foreigners in the touristy areas; however, it is rare to see Americans. Most visitors are Asian or European.

The military dictatorship's take on the "People's Desire"

It took most of our visit to fully get used to the currency circus that greets the foreign visitor to Myanmar. It starts right when you arrive at the Yangon airport (currently the only approved way for foreigners to enter the country). Clearing passport control, we were greeted by a sign declaring we were required to purchase 300 FECs (Foreign Exchange Certificates) for $300. FECs, which we immediately began referring to as "feces," are issued by the Myanmar Foreign Trade Bank as a second currency "for the convenience of tourists visiting Myanmar". Ha. This Monopoly-like monetary system is one of the government's less subtle ways of obtaining hard currency. The more ubiquitous domestic currency is the *kyat* (pronounced 'chat'). The black market exchange rate of kyat for FECs fluctuates daily, remaining about 30% below the value of actual US dollars. "Officially" foreigners are not allowed to obtain kyat. In practice, if foreigners were truly unable to convert Feces or US dollars into kyat, we would soon starve and rot, particularly outside of well-tread tourist establishments.

The black-market is a signature of the entrepreneurial spirit growing in Myanmar, especially in the tourism sector. Private hotels, restaurants and transportation are encroaching upon the Ministry of Tourism's offerings.

One immediate example right at the airport were the English speaking guides who would offer their services, included with the price of a cheaper non-government taxi. Once they had you as a captive audience, they made a convincing sales pitch for a tour of the city that was hard to resist. Unfortunately for them, the young man and his driver who approached us had no idea they were going to get caught in the first showdown between the Comfort Traveler and the Backpack Kid, namely to find a hotel for the 'right price'. The Boy's travel instinct would have led him to stay in a rock bottom-priced hotel, likely with a shared bathroom and a fan. I am a wuss and need my comfort and my air. This resulted in our unsuspecting guides hauling us from hotel to hotel in search of a non-existent 'holy grail' of hotel rooms that would have fully satisfied our differing definitions of "value."

Finally, when my son's fatigue factor kicked in I pounced on the Guest Care Hotel. For 20 bucks we got a private hot shower, mini-bar, satellite TV, air conditioning, complimentary breakfast and a view of Yangon's major attraction, the Shwedagon Pagoda. I was delighted to get this much for so little, and the Backpack Kid even conceded that if we were going to pay that much at least he could get his news fix watching CNN, which was blocked in China.

Over the course of the trip, I developed a Dirty Fingernail Scale that related to the level of dirt we were exposed to because of the condition of the roads, the form of transportation, the sleeping accommodations, the type of food & the tools to eat it with, and the availability to wash hands and body. The best score was zero, meaning no dirt under the nails and clean hands, to the worst score of ten, indicating constant grime in the nails with dust in the cracks of the skin and perhaps a smudge of grease or oil on the dorsum for good measure—usually only seen when camping. Traveling through Burma we stayed right at seven to nine during the day with a clean up at night to a two or three.

5 a.m. came early, but it was the time we had to pop out of bed to be able to see the sun rise over Shwedagon Pagoda. We climbed the hill to the pagoda in that tranquil time of day when the air is cool and the sky is lit with a pink-orange glow before the sun shows its yellow globe.

With shoes in hand (like many places of worship in Asia you must remove your shoes to enter), we ascended to the level of the central golden stupa. Throughout Southeast Asia the Buddhist places of worship are called pagodas. The Burmese word equivalent of this term is paya, literally meaning 'holy one' and can refer to people, deities, and places associated with religion. They have two basic architectural forms: stupas and temples. A stupa is a doorless, spire-shaped building often painted gold or white that has no prayer chambers. They may contain 'relics'—either objects taken from Buddha himself (especially pieces of bone, teeth or hair) or religious objects blessed by a famous Burmese Buddhist master. Temples come in many shapes and sizes with interior spaces containing multitudinous forms of Buddha, designed for contemplation and prayer.

Shwedagon pagoda has a 300 foot tall central golden stupa. The base is painted gold and halfway up the paint is replaced with pure wafer thin gold leaf that gleams in the sun making the structure a brilliant beacon. Above the gold-leaf the gold becomes plates measuring 30 square centimeters each. The crown is decorated with gold and silver bells topped by a vane encased in gold and studded with 1,100 diamonds and precious stones. The pièce de resistance is a golden sphere mounted with a single 76 carat diamond. The central stupa is surrounded by temples, bells, monuments and pavilions and smaller stupas. These are arranged along a cool smooth marble floor that encircles the central stupa and provides an smorgasbord of religious and tourist activity. Shaved head monks, men in brown and burgundy robes and nuns in pink robes, are seen in clusters or conducting services throughout the complex. One tall American looking monk, who certainly could have made basketball's Final Four, was circling the central stupa with prayer beads in his hand. A family had brought a meal of some kind, which they offered then sat in front of the temple and consumed it.

Worship here takes many forms. Women can be seen lighting candles, decorating Buddha sculptures or carvings with flowers and anointing him with a ritualistic triple washing, passing over him with small amounts of water from shallow cups, symbolically purifying him. Flowers decorate icons as a form of adoration. Artisans of the region are famous for their weaving. As a form of worship, samples of their weaving are placed on the progressively higher tiers of the stupa, the highest honor being given to those at the top. This placement is conducted by a group of individuals who resemble mountain climbers, complete with belaying ropes. A major difference being they climb barefooted and without safety clamps. It is a bit frightful to watch these devotees go at it with great fervor up the surface of this man-made monolith.

Having been around the world I have had the opportunity to observe man's incredible talent to create edifices to God. To this list I now add Shwedagon Pagoda as another joyous and lyrical ode to the Creator. It is a unique celebration of the splendor of man's creativity that is worth traveling to the other side of the world to admire.

That afternoon we flew from Yangon to Heho. This is the arrival terminal for the Taunggyi region. Taunggyi is the capitol for the Shan State in the eastern part of Myanmar.

Jon negotiated gallantly for a fair taxi price to the hotel I had insisted on, called the Hu Pin Hotel at Lake Inlay. Once the driver had caved in to Vacation Boy's hard core bargaining, he delivered us some 20 miles later to the Hu Pin Hotel in Nyaung Shwe, a town at the northern end of the lake. Who could have known this was one of *two* Hu Pin Hotels on the lake? The second hotel—our hotel—being another 20 miles away. The driver and Jon almost came to blows when Jon insisted the driver intentionally took us to the wrong hotel. I suggested we compromise and sweeten the pot for the driver, who upon accepting the deal, took us to our real destination, the Hu Pin Resort in Khaung. This Hu Pin Resort was perched over the western edge of the picturesque Lake Inlay, surrounded by hazy blue mountains. As the driver unloaded our bags he shook my hand, then shook his head and scowled at my son. Then he went over and shook Jon's hand and kissed it in a gesture of absolution, smiling. This man was only one of the many beautiful people we had the pleasure to meet in our adventure.

Bright and early the following morning we were up and at 'em to see the magnificent trove of treasures that were ours to behold in life on Lake Inlay. We were picked up by a guide in a long-tailed boat at the dock by our hotel. As we departed a phantom like figure wearing a dark blue outfit appeared from out of nowhere insisting we pay a lake entrance fee. Luckily I had a few FECs on me that covered the $6 fee, for which we were properly receipted.

Then it was off to the market. The main floating market was not open this day so our guide took us to a local village market. What an experience! Wandering through the scene of fish mongers with live fish, a barber with hand clippers, foods of every shape and description and products sold in plant leaf packaging were villagers often decked out with traditional face decoration. The Burmese protect their skin with a white powder, made from the branches of a tree

similar to sandalwood that serves as a sunscreen and beauty lotion all in one.

Halfway down the western side of the lake we visited the fascinating floating village of the Inthas. Bamboo houses on bamboo stilts were intermingled with larger beautiful wood-frame houses in this village, which was situated completely over water. Intermingled between the houses were floating gardens made from water hyacinth and loam from the lake floor. These were anchored to the lake bottom via long bamboo poles. The gardens produce tomatoes, legumes, a variety of vegetables and flowers.

Born and raised on the water, even mere babies have mastered their people's unique way of rowing with their legs. Young children row boats about the lake as easily as an American child might ride a tricycle on a sidewalk.

Lake Inlay is only 12 feet deep throughout its 40 mile length, allowing a unique form of fishing. The fishermen submerge conical baskets down to the grassy bottom of the lake. Then through a hole in the top of the basket they jig using a harpoon like device to spear fish. We saw a lot of jigging going on but not too many fish being caught. It has been going on for hundreds of years so they must catch something, sometime.

What do Buddhist monks do all day? When we stopped at the Nga Pha Kyaung monastery we found a most unusual answer for at least a select few of them: they train cats to jump through hoops. After seeing them demonstrate this ability we asked the obvious question, "Why?" A smiling monk adept with the English language replied, "It keeps me from getting bored."

The next day at 4 a.m. we took our pre-ordered taxi to Schwenyaung to meet the 5 a.m. Bagan-bound bus coming from Taunggyi. My argument that we could sleep in and catch a flight to Bagan and get there in one hour fell on deaf ears. Jon insisted we needed to be close to 'the people' to be able to get the real feeling for life in Myanmar.

The Nga Pha Kyaung monastery

Thus began, what I have come to call, Torture Bus Trip #1. Huddled around an open fire in the dew drenched darkness, we were fortunate to make friends with a traveling Irish lassie. A series of buses, pick-ups and trucks stopped on their way west, but the bus to Bagan was unmarked. Had it not been for the fact this woman's guide stayed with her until she got on the right bus, we might still be sitting there today.

The bus seats were designed to accommodate petite Asian frames, different from my own, with space between the rows far less than airline seating on its worst day. The seats themselves were basically a wooden plank for your bottom and another to put your back against. Since there was no luggage compartment, we had that stowed under our feet. So like that, off we went for our scheduled seven-hour journey. The fact that it took eleven hours was just a slight oversight by the ticket salesman.

My son was right, however, that the bus ride had a life of its own. Our scenery began with incredible mountainous ranges that provided sheer cliffs and hairpin turns, then descending onto the arid Meiktila plain with its lakes and toddy palms. We also experienced thrill a minute two-way traffic on a one lane road, the battalion of military troops that forced us off the road to let them pass, and the various pit stops. You could stop the bus anytime by shouting out you had to use the bathroom. By 3 p.m. we had missed our ETA by three hours and there were some hungry, slightly irritated folks. So we mutinied for a lunch break.

No matter how bad the road, a hot shower cures everything. We stayed at the Thande Hotel in old Bagan, nestled in the archaeological zone along the banks of the Ayeyarwady River. Our new Irish travel buddy joined us to catch the sun setting over the river and then on to a traditional Burmese feast and the consumption of a bottle of some seriously smooth rum. We almost forgot the bus ride.

The following morning, we didn't shake out of the rack quite so early. The fermented sugarcane squeezings had taken their toll on our ability to rise and shine. Something from somewhere deep inside my son, however, decided we should see Bagan by bicycle. Not a respectable 21-speed lightweight street bicycle mind you, but a straight-geared conveyance of antiquity. King Anawrahta surely did not construct those hundreds of payas around the archaeological zone to serve as a training zone for the Olympics. Nevertheless, Olympic-grade training we did as we covered 33 miles riding the perimeter then through the archaeological zone, climbing 200 feet up various payas, and walking probably another ten miles in, around, over and through payas. How does the saying go? "Only mad men and Englishmen go out in the noonday sun"? I guess that shows where we fit in, since we were out there baking and we're definitely not English.

On our odyssey through Bagan we stopped at the river jetty for a welcomed lunch break. We watched villagers on the Ayeyarwady loading, or I should say overloading, boats headed north against the downstream current. The current was so swift as to make the boats appear to almost be standing still.

Later, while Jon climbed over the Dhammayangyi Temple, a gold covered stupa displaying the finest brickwork in Bagan, I sat in the shade of a cafe getting my ego fed by the locals who couldn't believe I was 56 years old. They kept insisting I was a much younger man.

Of the hundreds of payas to talk about, we ended the day with one of the best: Mingalazedi (Blessing Stupa). This one was a favorite because it was officially the last paya I had to climb. We scaled its steep staircase to see the magnificent sunset. To the east, the amber rays illuminated the ochre colored Bagan Plain, with the gold, white and red spires of pahtos and stupas prickling from it. In the opposite direction the sun sank behind a low mountain range casting a long shadow over the river.

Vacation Boy's Father, author of this chapter

We were up with the birds and off to what I had determined

was a compromise between a one hour flight, a two day luxury cruise or another adventurous "seven hour" bus ride: we took the narrow-gauge train to Mandalay. This form of locomotion was sheer comfort. We had a first class ticket that allowed us two seats facing each other with a table between us. Passing through a large desert plain, replete with tall palms and oases, we drank in the ambiance of the country-side. The temperature was 60 Fahrenheit and felt good, albeit a little dusty. Among the visual treats we enjoyed were ox carts, goat herders, coconut trees with ladders tied to them for gathering the coconuts, train bridges where the construction of the bridge was underway right below us, children running alongside the train begging for people to throw out money, vendors carrying clay pots of water with a common cup, a variety of edibles from rice cakes to steamed crabs, breathtaking panoramas and lakes of lotus flowers.

As we made our last stop before Mandalay, we experienced an incredible piece of one-upmanship. A Mandalay taxi driver jumped on the train and offered his services. Not only did he have a cab but he could give you a tour of the city. We tend to shy from these aggressive fellows and shooed him away, only to find him waiting for us when we got off the train. As he was an affable guy, we wound up going with him, which I think he regretted after my son did his bartering dance.

Mandalay was the last Myanmar Empire capital to fall before the British took over in 1857. Now this second largest city in modern Myanmar sprawls with busy streets, a lively cultural scene and a rich history. The nightly ritual of finding a room yielded a gem of a hotel for $17 a night at the Royal City Hotel. Everything you'd expect in a pricey hotel and breakfast to boot.

One comment about Burmese dining: there are no menus. The only question you are asked is what you want in your curry; mutton, fish, chicken or shrimp. Then they serve a gambler's choice of vegeta-bles in small bowls and depending on how your stomach seems to be feeling, you try a little of each of the mystery vegetables. Occasionally there are some that can't be eaten, but not often.

We were bent on trying to find an Internet connection, unavail-able until now, to let our friends know we were about to embark on the Burma Road, and when to send out a search party if we didn't make contact. The only place Internet was available was in the pricey Sedona Hotel which slammed us a whole US$2 for each 1 kb of e-mail. Pretty cheeky considering once we got to China the price dropped to $1 for a whole hour on the Internet. The search for an Internet fix did, however, lead us to our first Western meal in several weeks. It was a European hotel with an Italian restaurant. The food was cooked Burmese style, but it was good.

We didn't dally after dinner because we wanted to be on time for the Moustache Brothers a-nyeint show. An a-nyeint show is a form of old school theater that combines dance, music opera, comedy and drama into a sort of vaudeville show. Lu Maw was the greeter, house manager, announcer, producer, director, techie, business administrator, public relations man and general 'go-fer' for the Moustache Brothers. He referred to himself as 'the boss' or as the Americans had taught him, 'the top banana'. He and his family, less his brother, put on a wonderful performance. Lu Maw's brother was jailed five years ago for telling a joke about the government. He had two more years on his sentence.

We set out bright and early the next morning to explore Mandalay and the environs. We sat in the back of a flat bed pick-up for 18 miles south to the Ma Ha Ganda Yon Monastery in Amarapura. It's an odd place in as much as they have made a tourist attraction of the Buddhist monks getting their daily rice donations. Normally a monk would have to go into the street to beg for rice from a family, but at this monastery they have it down to a socialistic science. Here they take monetary contributions and buy huge vats of rice that are handed out to all the monks in the monastery at one time. A little ways down the road from the monastery is the interesting two-mile long wooden U Bein Bridge that spans Taungthaman Lake and leads to a small island where there is quaint village and, of course, a paya. The bridge culture is an interesting study unto itself with a mix of tourists and villagers traveling back and forth, vendors hustling their wares, and the village life below.

Monks lined up for rice

Back in town that evening when we realized the sun was fading, we made a mad dash for Mandalay Hill, which is located outside the northeast corner of Fort Mandalay and its destroyed palace. The palace compound was surrounded by an imposing wall and moat that have been restored. The ancient palace was destroyed by bombs and fire in 1945 when the allies drove the Japanese out of the fort.

The Hill itself is over a thousand feet high and can be climbed on foot. Time was short and we were beginning to tire, so we elected to take a truck-taxi. Even when you get to the end of the road, you're not there yet. There is still an elevator and stairs that ascend to the top. The effort is worth it. The panorama offers a grand view of Mandalay; the near-by old race course, the moat and palace wall and a scattering of payas throughout the countryside. Throngs of fellow sun worshipers gathered to bid the sun farewell for the day.

We walked down the hill, passing climbers agonizing on their way up. It took us a good 25 minutes to climb down. I wouldn't want to guess the time to climb up if you did the whole thing on foot. On the way down we picked up an English speaking monk whose mission was to teach Buddhism to English speaking people. Having an interest in Buddhism, it was an enlightening refresher course to have him walk with us. He told us how he was sponsored by his village, and his mother donated 3000 kyat (~US$8)/month to help support him in the monastery. He accompanied us down to the Kuthodaw Paya at the base of the hill where 729 small temples each hold a marble slab that contain the Buddhist scripture written in Pali, the ancient Indian language used in the Buddhist writings.

Bidding our spiritual mentor a good night we headed back to the hotel. After being sidetracked by some shopping, we got in so late that the hotel kitchen was closed. They said they could send out for beer, soda and noodles. We lucked out by taking them up on their offer as it was probably one of the best meals we had in Burma. Then it was off to bed in high anticipation of our adventure on the Burma Road.

The Burma Road

Built by the Chinese as a military supply route in 1937-8, the Burma Road is a highway 700 miles long stretching through southeast Asia from the railhead at Lashio, Myanmar to Kunming, China. It was used by the Allies during WWII. Supplies for China landed in Yangon and shipped by rail to Lashio. From there they were transported by truck across rugged mountain terrain. After the war, the road fell into disuse. Not much is written about the road in travel literature. That which is written, however, gives one the idea it is not a road to be traveled lightly.

My son, an extreme traveler, likes to put himself in positions of questionable safety and hardship. He gets excited about the thought of journeying over a road that disappears in the wet season and 200 miles of it is described as bumpy hard-cobbled road. Lucky for me I was able to at least talk him out of taking the rougher back roads through tectonically unstable regions engulfed by jungle.

Well before we left Jon insisted it wasn't worth going to Burma unless travelled on this road. My initial attempts to see if this was even possible were met with cold and emphatic "No's" from the Myanmar Embassy in Washington. Subsequently, just about everyone I talked to said tourists were not allowed to travel past Lashio going east. Gradually, I was able to work through a California-based company, who worked through a tour company in Yangon to arrange a packaged tour from Mandalay to Lashio to the China border at Muse with a car, an English speaking guide and possibly a border pass into China.

It is hard to get into Burma but even harder to get out. The border pass was the greatest obstacle still awaiting us. We had to apply three weeks ahead of time. The government had to have a fixed itinerary and assurance we had no concern with political affairs. E-mails flew back and forth but that didn't change the fact that when I departed for Yangon I had no idea if we would be able to get out of the country across the border or not. Even after we met the tour company representative in Yangon, an exceptionally nice man named Mr. Min Din, we still didn't have the pass confirmed. He would have to notify us as we traveled toward Mandalay. Finally two days before we were to head for the border we got a fax from Mr Min Din to pick up our guide in Mandalay and start our journey to China: the pass had been okayed.

Then there was our licensed tour guide, Mr Sai Moon Sein, who I think was instructed to scare the stuff out of us so we wouldn't ever think about doing this again. He made disquieting statements like, "This is not the right tour for foreigners," or, "I was surprised you got a pass, they don't like Americans in Yangon." As we approached the military guard stations he'd say, "Don't say anything." As we settled in for the night in Lashio we heard, "They want us to call them in Yangon and make sure we got this far," "It will probably take most of the day to talk to the guards at a military check-point," and "It depends on what kind of mood they're in as to whether they will let you cross the border or not."

That said, Mr. Sein wound up being an informative helpful guide. Even with his concerted efforts, though, it seemed like we would never get out of Mandalay. We stopped to get immigration papers copied, to get the drivers clearance to leave down the road towards Lashio, to get his supply of pepper-vine-leaf-wrapped betel nut and to do other administrative chores I wasn't clear about.

Not far out of town we hit our first military checkpoint. There were military and then there were car check points. The latter seemed more like passing through a tollbooth than anything else, but we were stopped all the same. The military stops were a little more threatening. They had us get out of the car and went through luggage, albeit cursorily.

Our hired driver's car looked more like a demolition derby has-been than "an air-conditioned car." He could really drive it, but not in the good sense. We theorized he was an opium runner on the side. Fortunately Mr. Sein noticed Jon and me turning green in the back seat as the driver careened down the hairpin curves on the wrong side of the road. Mr. Sein made him slow down and keep more to his side of the road.

Much to Vacation Boy's chagrin the road was extremely well paved and we rode along smoothly. Roughly100 miles north-east of Mandalay and about 2600 feet higher we came across an old British hill station called Maymyo. This was the cool retreat for the hot season in Mandalay. Old Tudor-style mansions have been maintained, reflecting the colonial influence. The faces of the townsfolk reflect the Indians and Nepalese who assisted the British in their conquests, then stayed to raise families.

As we climbed into higher elevations the roads began to twist and turn. Coming out of one river bed up the side of a mountain we noted traffic backed up for miles. Our nonplussed driver casually switched to the wrong side of the road and proceeded forward to the scene of the problem. A grossly overloaded truck had been making a hairpin turn when its transmission fell out. The truck was incapacitated and the road was blocked. There were no towing services, so the only thing that could be done was to repair the truck where it stood. Mr Sein said this happened regularly. Luckily there was a slight gap between the truck and the edge of the mountain through which vehicles the size of our car could get over with a running start. It was touch and go for a minute then we were free to be on our merry way, passing up to a mile or more of huge trucks that looked like they might literally be stuck there for days.

As we continued down the road we came to the town of Hsipaw where we visited the Shan Palace, home of the last royal family who were vanquished in the 1962 military takeover. It turns out the last Shan Princess was an American who now lives in Colorado. She wrote a memoir, *Twilight over Burma: My Life as a Shan Princess.*

The sun was already heading for the horizon when a few miles short of our destination of Lashio, Mr. Sein detoured to catch a Hindi celebration before we could call it a day. Off we went through a dusty nightmare. After what seemed like 20 miles of blinding dust, rocky projections, and heavy duty pot holes we came upon one big party. Hindus from across Myanmar had come to celebrate 'the Feast of the Bleeding Rock'. The event is commemorated with three days of what appears to be a giant fair and market with religious side shows and lots of people having a good time. One thing that fascinated me was their free kitchen. Some 3000 worshipers were served two meals a day for free and the food looked pretty good. There were also multiple reed-like huts with hay on the floor where families could stay. All of this was free to those who came to worship, supplied by rich donors.

We finally had to pull ourselves away from the festivities and head for our own supper and night's rest. One comment about Burmese dining: there are no menus. The only question you are asked is what you want in your curry; mutton, fish, chicken or shrimp. Then they serve a gambler's choice of vegetables in small bowls and depending on how your stomach seems to be feeling, you try a little of each of the mystery vegetables. Occasionally there are some that can't be eaten, but not often.

We had to get up at 5 a.m. to get to the minority Dai village before they left for the market in Lashio. One of the main reasons Jon had wanted to come this way was to see some of the various minority groups known to live in this part of the world. While somehow a bit disappointed the trip had otherwise gone so well, Jon put forward that we needed to at least see one of the minority people in the area to make this trip on the Burma Road complete. In his resourcefulness, Mr. Sein found a guide that took us and our trusty car out to one of these minority villages.

We passed villagers on their way to market carrying all kinds of goods: food, bundles of fronds for roofs and many additional unidentifiable things. When we arrived at the village, a haze of the morning dew mixed with smoke from the houses framed a cozy, picturesque, agriculturally-based community.

The villagers of this minority group decorate themselves ornately in silver jewelry and expand their earlobes with coils of silver. They also have black teeth and gums from chewing betel nuts and this appearance is thought to be attractive in this culture. We encountered several families on our visit. Through translation, one group of small children who were alone told us their parents were gone for several months working on the opium farms on the border with China. They can make enough money to feed a family for a year by opium farming only three months.

Lashio was a stark contrast to the minority village. Modern looking stores and goods were present everywhere. The toll road from Lashio to Muse was quite good, apparently funded by the opium kings of the region. It was finally time for our encounter with the border guards and anxious moments as we waited to see if they would let us cross. All our paperwork was stamped approvingly, and with our bags on our backs we walked the last few feet into a communist country.

Don't ask me why an American would feel more comfortable here than in Myanmar, but I did. For one thing, when we crossed the border into China the Dirty Fingernail Scale soon dropped to a four or five during the day getting close to one at night. The Chinese portion of the Burma Road did not require a packaged tour or elaborate border paperwork (aside from our China visa). We were totally free to do what we wanted. As long as we kept shelling out Yuan, we were welcome anywhere.

I looked for the tallest most ostentatious-looking hotel to celebrate our arrival into China. I couldn't have done better: the Jingcheng Hotel. Ten years in the making, the spacious and luxuriously marble infused hotel had opened a month earlier as if in anticipation of our arrival. Ruili has the best and worst of conditions as a result of being a border town. The city is the main conduit for Burmese heroin entering China. This accounts for its high incidence of AIDS and addiction. Commercial sex is available in open storefronts where one supposedly has tea with a group of ladies then steps into the backroom with the lady of choice. This, however, is only a small part of this humming city with its paved roads, tidy storefronts, and karaoke clubs with their music pouring out into the street. We made our reservation for what was to become Torture Bus #2.

The next morning after a gourmet breakfast we set out to find a Dai village to be able to see the traditionally dressed minority people on this side of the border. We hired a car and the driver took us down the well-paved road west of town. Along the way signs would say Burma 50 meters, pointing out into a field. This piqued our curiosity and we asked the guide where the border was. He said we were basically riding on it. There is a standing joke in Ruili that when a Chinaman marries a Burmese girl, she sleeps in Burma and he sleeps in China. Another story is told that you feed a chicken in China and you get an egg in Burma. The border is apparently something foreigners have to worry about, not the locals.

The Dai village felt like a hoax. There may have been Dai living there but they had long ago given up their customary dress. Everyone there dressed like contemporary Chinese. The driver explained that minority distinctions became moot as individuals obtained wealth.

We were scheduled to take a seven-hour mini-bus ride to Baoshan. This bus had all the comforts of a moving van. People who boarded brought all their possessions with them. The top was loaded with large plastic containers that looked like harvested crops. There were also the chickens on the roof and the rabbits nuzzled between us on the floor. I was given the seat by the door. If I could stretch my legs, that spot would have been an advantage. Unfortunately, there was so much luggage piled in the aisle it didn't help. I was OK with almost everything except the six-foot cross saws sitting on the floor. I knew if we rolled over, one of those things was going to decapitate me.

Two hours north we stopped in Mangshi to deliver the harvest. Along the road I had struck up a conversation with an alternative medicine drug rep, using a hand held language convertor. It was very handy. I never did figure why he and his boss and the boss's girlfriend were traveling by bus. Jon didn't find it at all unusual.

As the sun began to drop out of the sky we came upon a tunnel being built, and beyond it a massive highway was being constructed. For now the road became the rough cobbled road Vacation Boy had been looking for. We traveled along parallel to the construction all the way into Baoshan. You could see most of the workers were living in a mobile shanty town right on the construction site which moved as the road was completed. By night fall I was a bit weary and happy to find a nice hotel with Internet service and fine accommodations. It wound up being our second choice as Jon was originally intent on staying in a flop house close to the bus station where he had stayed before.

The morning bus rides to Kunming began around 7 a.m. No matter the size of the bus, the characters within instill it with an interesting life of its own. The passengers on this run were no exception. The old man sitting behind my son in the front of the bus got sucked into a con game when we had a potty stop. A charlatan appeared from nowhere and in minutes had a crowd gathered round him. He was pulling a variation of the pea under the walnut routine using a coin under large discs. He would throw the coin under a disc then cover it with his foot then have his mark guess which disc the coin was under. The old man insisted he didn't intend to bet, but he just happened to have his money in his hand when he pointed to the empty disc. When the hustler took his money the old man kicked up a ruckus. A young couple to whom he was complaining told him to shut up, he should have kept his money in his pocket.

We literally rattled up and down the Gaoligong Mountains across high ridges and descended into the green fields of rice and sugar cane en route to Xiaguan. The man across from me kept hitting my bag with the pumpkin seeds he was spitting on the floor. At the potty stop I moved it out of his range only to have the cute young woman then sitting on it start puking from bus sickness. Luckily she missed my bag and instead deposited it in the stairwell in front of me. Jon tells me this is a regular, if not expected, occurrence on Chinese bus travel. Woman and children seem to be most susceptible.

We made Xiaguan around noon and grabbed lunch to take with us on the next express bus from hell. We were early so we got the two seats behind the driver. We kept one of us posted to watch the seats while the other gathered food for the journey. I ran into a language problem getting in the men's room and proceeded with my business while the female attendant ran out the door. I apologized profusely to her, hoping she would understand I couldn't wait.

The last leg of the Burma Road is a super highway, indistinguishable from any in the States, including toll booths. But the risk to life and limb was slightly greater if you had our bus driver. He would pass on outside curves going uphill, drift all over the road and take curves at speeds that would roll most cars. It might be the tires are more rubbery, who knows. It didn't help my confidence to pass six accidents on the way from Xiaguan to Kunming. Death options were easy to visualize especially in places where you could see evidence of where a vehicle had plunged through the railing and down a 300 foot cliff. Our maniacal driver didn't even slow down as we went by.

Thanks to our guardian angels, we made it to Kunming, the capital of Yunnan province. Historically it has been a supply depot during various conflicts. During the Cultural Revolution historic buildings perished at the hands of the Red Guard. Virtually all that remained was cleared when the city center was rebuilt in its current modern style to impress visitors attending the 1999 World Horticultural Expo. This was it, the end of the road. The dirty fingernail scale dropped to one during the day and zero at night. Some people (Vacation Boy) would say the city is too clean. Even I admit it is a bit sterile. It still has its measure of antiquity in areas surrounding the city but the city itself is modern with parks, colorful round-a-bouts and strikingly futuristic architecture in its office buildings.

I, for one, was glad to get back into the world of airplanes and cars and leave all the buses to my son. But I have to admit this was one fantastic trip. I'm ready to head off with him anywhere he gets a hankering to go. Well ... almost anywhere.

CHAPTER 24

Fixing a Bike Across South China

Riding the Chinese-Burma Border

After a year and a half of studying and working in China, I wanted to end my stay with a Big Hurrah kind of adventure and I was by no means disappointed with what followed.

THE CONCEPT: December's cold was starting to settle on Shanghai. The dual temptations of warmer temperatures and the remoteness of China's southern border with Myanmar (formerly Burma), beckoned me in a way that proved irresistible. My goal was to meander in a trajectory on the China side as close as possible to the border, using the People's Transportation—a bicycle.

Walking out of the countryside airport to the main road to catch a bus, I noticed life around me was moving at a much slower pace than the bustling financial hub I had vacated in the East. The nearby town Mangshi in southwestern Yunnan province served as my launch point.

I had $150 to get me through the week, which included the funds for purchasing the bicycle that would be my transport. While there were a number of bicycle vendors in town, I arrived already well-versed in the many ways Chinese bicycles break down and was wary of the cheaper ones. I spent close to $75 on my new steed—three times what I had paid for any previous bicycle. One store did have an export-quality bike priced as high as $120 and all I can say to anyone interested in doing a similar trip: *Bring enough money so you can buy the most expensive one you can find!*

I started the biking portion of my trip on my back in a bed with a man I had just met. I had never been certain about the distance I would be traveling, but knew I would have to cover some distance by bus if I was going to make it to my destination (Jinghong, principal city of tropical Xishuangbanna) in a week. When I saw "Jinghong: 913 km" posted in the bus station, I hoped it was a bad joke or referred to the triangular distance it would be if the bus passed up through and back down from the provincial capital Kunming. (It is sometimes faster to go WAY out of the way like that because of starkly different road conditions.) To this day I do not know the distance I ended up traveling, but that 913 kilometers might not have been far off the mark.

Oh yes, the man...The only bus going in the direction I wanted to go was a sleeper bus. These "bed busses" are unlike anything I have seen outside of China, but can be quite practical for traveling long distances. The reclined position is good at relieving spinal stress when rattling down rough roads, but the downside is they put two people per single bed-sized seat. Great if you are a couple, less fun if it's me and some farmer guy who smokes and snores. It wasn't bad, though, and seemed like an ironically cushy way to begin what was supposed to be a hardy biking adventure.

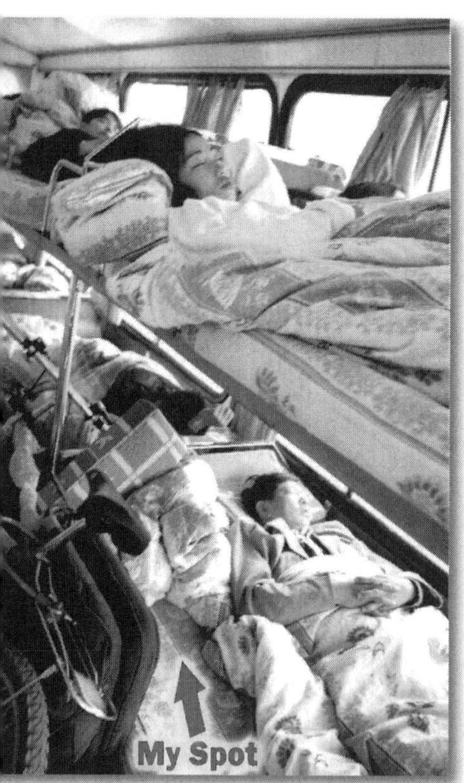

I took the bus for much of the first day. In hindsight this was a tremendously smart move, partly because I covered some mediocre terrain quickly, partly because my new bike had some mechanical wrinkles that would have left me stranded otherwise.

Blissfully clueless at the time, though, right after a village whose name sounded like "pizza", I strapped my backpack to the bike's back rack and off I went. After only three hours of pedaling, the whole crank arm fell off.

Luckily, I was entering the outskirts of my evening's destination, and I only walked a couple hundred yards before coming across a car repair shop. The completely grease-blackened mechanics would be the first of literally about 25 people who would work on my bike in the coming days as I gradually replaced most of its moving parts, some more than once.

On Day Three and several police checks later (being close to Myanmar there is illegal trafficking of many sorts in this area), I found myself biking up a perpetually uphill, isolated road with a bicycle whose pedal fell off every 50 yards. Reaching road rage levels of frustration, I even tried holding it on with my hand as I pedaled. Impossible.

I gave up and started walking, hoping a bus would get to me before I pushed the full five kilometers to the next town. Sure enough, half an hour later a minibus—which might have been the only vehicle coming through that day—rumbled up the dirt road. They stopped but only to tell me they had no room for me and my stuff. For a lightly loaded country bus like this one (but applicable to most anywhere in China), this made for an obvious mistruth, because when motivated, people always find ways to pack things onto busses that seem to have no apparent molecules of space left.

Not wanting to be bothered (for what probably seemed to them to be a short distance), these country folks weren't budging. Unfortunately, they did not have any tools that could help my plight either. As a last effort as they started pulling off, I whimpered out, "You mean you can't help me at all?"

It must have tweaked the right heartstrings. 40 meters up the road the bus slowed, then stopped. The now smiling Bus Guy jumped out to help me load my stuff. I overheard some passengers laughing and repeating my words to each other, saying it was too much to resist. Once the decision had been made to let me aboard, they welcomed me, helped support my bike, and peppered me with questions.

We never discussed price, but the fare would only be pennies for this relatively short distance. When we got to the town, I made a proposal: I would pay them whatever fare was due, or...I would sing them a song in English. Chinese love singing. Half the TV shows in China include some kind of live ballad singing. Curiosity killed the cats. So did my singing. Their faces lit up when I whipped out the ukulele hidden in my bag and began playing. However, somewhere between my being fatigued, out of practice and nervous, the rendition of Rocky Top I belted out was not one of my best ever. Suddenly they seemed to have a pressing engagement somewhere else. I had barely finished the first chorus when the driver said, "OK, that's fine, that's fine," motioning they needed to go.

They pulled off leaving me in a cloud of dust, and I did not realize until later, that these people had dealt me a twist of fate that forever altered my journey, all for the better. They dropped me in a place where I was able to both buy a tool from a car mechanic that helped with my pedal problem, and where I would have the lunch that changed my fate. During my meal, I asked some out-of-towners, and fellow diners, about where I could find villages of the minority cultures that supposedly lived in this area. One man, coincidentally of the native Lahu people, pointed to a place on my map he said should absolutely not be missed. I have grown wary of Chinese people's travel recommendations as they tend to find interest in things very different from what Westerners do, but somehow his words carried extra weight. Providing my mechanical steed would stay in enough of one piece, Mengka would be my destination.

I began the final ten kilometer approach to Mengka village off the "main" road as the sun was setting, casting a golden glow on the winter-dried rice terraces that surrounded me. I was exhilarated by the scenery and by the rattling rapid decent down this roughest of roads. Something about it felt right. When I stopped to ask an older man if I was still headed in the right direction, he nodded and then paused, asking innocently, "Are you from another country?" With Vacation Boy being the whitest of whities here deep in Asia, I found his question charming.

I could tell I had arrived somewhere special well before entering the village. The well-groomed fields and hedges, and the well-maintained fences were unusual in their precision. You could tell there were an unusually cultured people at work here. The exclamation point to that impression was the series of religious statues and guard huts that marked the entry to the village—I had never seen anything quite like it. They emanated a calming, old spirit.

Around the next bend I entered what felt like a live scene from a previous era. The houses were all large, beautiful, triangular thatch mushrooms whose roofs extended down to about two meters off the ground. The walls were wooden or bamboo and the construction was of unusually high quality. Chickens, pigs and ducks meandered about. Before I saw any people, I could hear the sounds of work and the laughter of children playing. Marvelous. I pulled up to a crossroads where I was surrounded by blinking onlookers. It was a sensation I

had never felt—like arriving in a new world. All I thought to do was ask, "Where should I go?"

The consensus of those around me seemed to be that I should continue on to the New Village. I did as they suggested, striking out for another mile in the now dusky light. It was only with a bit of trepidation that I did so, because in China, the "New" City is usually a modern concrete disaster with little resemblance to the older quainter original. For New Mengka, this was not the case. Yes, they had a cement schoolhouse, village office, and temple, but almost everything else was of traditional construction. I would later learn that to the best of everyone's knowledge the "New Village" had been founded some 200 years ago.

Mengka was an unusually happy, welcoming place. The Chief of the Village, Mr. Zhang, greeted me at the New Village's administrative office. "Chief of the Village" was a rotational position that was only held for a year by an individual. The administration building consisted of a few barren rooms in which a few people lived, an office, and the phone room. They decided to put me up in the phone room, which also had a couple beds. The phone, interestingly, was the only one in the village and was connected to the lower Old Village, and to another village five kilometers further up the mountain. It rang in all three places at once.

It was time for dinner and a meal was assembled for me to eat with the chief. Chief Zhang acted as my host and translator, because most people there could not speak Mandarin. I was the first foreigner to visit them in at least a generation.

I was exhausted from biking and had assumed they were going to do like most country villages: go to bed early. Not so. My jaw dropped when Zhang told me they usually didn't go to bed until 11 or 12 o'clock, astounding for a place with little electricity. Electricity had arrived about 10 years prior and TVs had appeared in a few households in only the last few years. As tired as I was, it was neat to see how groups wandered around the dark village to visit other friends and family, socializing until much later than I could stay awake that night.

I found it ironic that every now and then someone would start a sentence saying, "We are so poor so…", because these were some of the happiest and best adjusted people I had ever met. I wondered if they had not gained that impression by comparing their situation to the images seen on the recently arrived TVs.

Every home seemed to have a bunch of the stools you see here at the ready for when guests came by. They are designed so they can be stacked out of the way.

Rice was prepared in a communal fashion for much of the village, which reduced the drain on firewood and work by its inhabitants. The roofs all had a social window that let in light and also made it easy to chat with neighbors walking by.

They spent a lot of time cooking for their pigs. They have giant woks in their homes just for that purpose. They were amazingly talented at in-home fire management. Inside these wooden and thatch homes they always maintained coals in the fire pit. They seemed to raise and lower a flame as effortlessly as I could with a stove.

Chief Zhang playing on my bike with the local kids

I was on a relatively tight schedule to make it to Jinghong in time for my plane. I had intended to stay in Mengka one night and leave in the morning, but threw that plan out the social window soon after arriving. I had to stay in this special place at least two nights. I spent the next day checking out (and being checked out by) the village.

Chief Zhang was always smiling and kidding around with the others. At one meal, a troop of children gathered to stare at me eat. I offered to share my meal, but when he translated what I said into their local dialect, they all took off running. When asked what happened, Zhang said he told them I had said, "Get out of here before I hit you!" So much for my hopes of making a good impression.

The other way I blew it was by not being sufficiently hungry. The first night, it was fatigue that slowed my appetite. The next day at lunch it was a result of appetite sabotage. I had been invited to visit the house of Xiao. He offered me a substantial batch of spicy noodles as a late breakfast. Little did I know that lunch was going to be served right after I returned from the visit, and I could hardly eat a bite. More disappointed looks.

By the afternoon, I had learned my lesson. When I finally realized I was being invited in for tea or food wherever I went, I started to decline the food as politely as possible, telling them I had to save my appetite or the Village Chief was going to get mad at me for not being hungry. They seemed to accept my reasoning.

That afternoon I ventured up to the remote neighboring village of Manggong. In doing so I got to draw a road on my map that had not existed. On the way, a couple school girls accompanied me as far as a vista point so that I would take their picture. Whereas in many places people might solicit money to take their pictures, these girls wanted

to pay me to take their picture with the promise that I would send them copies of the photographs.

The indigenous group that inhabited Manggong gave off a different vibe than the warmth I felt from the people of Mengka. Walking through their village, it seemed they were five kilometers away in distance, but 500 years in social development. The village was quiet and dry, primitive and impoverished. The construction was of lower quality and the homes were less tidy. They did, however, have two cool totem poles in a small communal square. Of the people I saw, none of them spoke to me or even paid me much mind. The few people I did see were quietly occupied preparing thatch for roofs. If they looked up to see me, they looked down just as fast to go back to their work. I now understood better the confused looks I was given when I asked the folks in Mengka if they had social events with the people up here.

It was a relief to return back to happy Mengka. I cut through town and kept going to reinvestigate the Old Village. It was as magical as when I arrived the night before. Wandering around, I was invited into a dimly (sun) lit house where maybe 20 people were being served food. These men were helping to build a house. The exchange was that the future owner supplied the materials, fed them, and gave them cigarettes for their free labor. During certain phases of the construction, most of the community comes out to help as a social occasion, much like a barn raising party.

For me, the new construction evoked mixed feelings. All the new houses were more modern, switching away from thatch construction to aesthetically dull wooden frames and metal roofs. I understand why. They spend an inordinate amount of time preparing and re-roofing thatch on the traditional houses, which must be replaced regularly. Long term, it is cheaper and much more time efficient to have the modern structures, not to mention their "cosmopolitan" intangibles. But…but…did you see the magnificent thatched skyline of this village? If they continue at this pace, that will all be gone in ten years. They have something special there, and I hate to see it go. The new roofs will inherently change their social interaction, too. I tried as best as I could to explain how rare and special their village was in its traditional form… tourism was a possibility at their remote doorstep and they have the added advantage that they could preemptively and proactively control its impact and harness its benefits.

One of the house raising parties was going to take place the morning I left, but I absolutely had to get down the road if I was ever going to make it to Jinghong in time for my flight. I did get to see the pre-party where the frames for the walls were completed. The monks came over from the temple to hold a blessing séance. They ran a string around the future walls and brought its ends to their gathering in the middle of the site where they lit candles and incense and chanted for hours as people worked around them.

After a detour to a reasonable sized city for some critical bicycle repairs (mind you I am only mentioning a sprinkling of the actual bike-fixing stops I made), I headed up a beautiful valley to check out some recently discovered prehistoric paintings on cliff walls. I determined that, despite its absence on my map, there was a road

that would allow me to avoid doubling back. The downside was that people who told me about the "road" had been using the term loosely. Some places it was so washed out or mud laden I was unsure I could cross it even on foot. Worse was knowing it was getting dark, but not knowing how much further I had to go. I was glad to come out relatively unscathed (although covered in mud) and able to draw a new line on my map.

When I arrived exhausted at my destination, it had been pitch black for almost an hour. Mengsheng, the town that looked so pleasant on a map, turned out to feel like a Wild West town gone bad. The buildings of this dusty crossroads were all ugly, modern concrete structures. There was garbage everywhere, one of the two sides of the road had been clotted with junk to the point it no longer functioned as a road. As I passed open storefronts, I was reminded of a scene in a Batman movie where everyone's brains were being sucked out by cable boxes. Everyone's stares were locked onto their TVs. I suffered in my mosquito infested room until late into the night, serenaded by bad karaoke singers at the nearby brothel. Compared to Mengka, it felt like I had descended into Hell. It was amazing that two cities so close could be so spiritually far apart.

This woman is reading a scale. In my year and a half in China. I could never figure these out.

As the song goes, I still had a long way to go and a short time to get there. I bussed most of the day to be in position to visit the Menglun morning market. I arrived in a pickup truck full of vendors and their stuff as the sun was rising. Market highlights included yummy snacks being prepared right as I arrived such as flame-scorched pig and dog faces and seeing the hearts in the *very* recently butchered cow meat still beating and steaming in the chilly morning air.

My entire last day descending down to Jinghong was out-of-bounds as far as my map was concerned. "Rough" does not begin to describe the rutted out mud gullies I often had to push my bike

Mmmm, nothing says morning snack like blowtorched pig's face. Warm your hands, too!

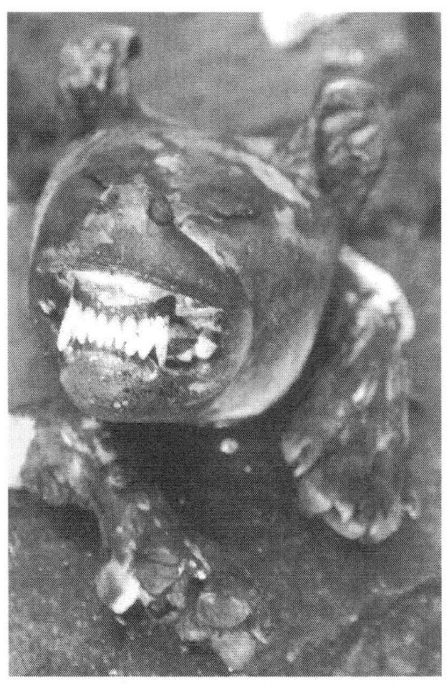

For whatever reason, here the dog head was always merchandised just with the paws.

through, but by now I knew the drill. Still, this would have been a good day to have brakes that worked. As one bit of modern irony, while struggling on this "road" way off the map in a place where I had not seen any humans in some time, my cell phone rang, shattering my pioneering adventurer complex. It was a travel agent confirming my flight out of Jinghong the following day. Modern traveling.

In the end, I made it to Jinghong with time and lots of mud to spare. Before flying off to Thailand the next morning (Christmas Day), my final task other than intensive bathing, was to sell my bike. It ended up going to the proprietor of the Forest Café for about $25 plus lunch, and my prayers that the mechanical gods smile more favorably on it in her hands.

Vacation Boy Retires (from being Vacation Boy)

Those who knew me well found the above proclamation dubious at best, but Vacation Boy had to go away for awhile: Jon got a J.O.B. Perhaps appropriately, it was a job that came to fruition during the course of a road trip.

I had already planned the trip before I was offered an interview for this position and it made more timing and logistical sense for me to "swing by" Chicago on my way to Denver. Thus, I made my way from Durham, North Carolina to Chicago for the job interview, over to Denver to pick up French friend Elodie flying in from France, down to Telluride and Taos for some skiing, over to the Grand Canyon for a four-day hike, then looped through other stunning but frigidly cold national parks like Bryce and Zion before ending in sunny Las Vegas, where my car blew up.

The journey was intended to be a round trip back to South Carolina with a turnaround point in Las Vegas. Coming out of the desert and into Las Vegas, my little Ford wagon had been acting sickly enough that I made it a priority to get it looked at before turning back East. I dropped off Elodie at my old Club Med friend Ray's house in Las Vegas and Ray jumped in the car with me to run down to a nearby auto shop before they closed.

After driving 4,464 miles across the country, including long stretches through desert Nowheresville, at block two of the four blocks to the auto store the motor started making dramatic, horrific clacking noises. The car limped into the auto parts store parking lot where I asked a knowledgeable car parts guy to come out and take a listen. I took it as a bad sign that when I started the engine, he immediately covered his ears shouting, "MAKE IT STOP!"

I had originally purchased this vehicle with the intent of using it through graduate school, then on until I got a decent job. Somehow the car sensed it had served its duty and was ready to move on to car afterlife. It did not require a litany of investigation to conclude that with a blown timing belt, the poor thing was done.

How could I complain? This extraordinarily cheap car literally delivered me to the end of my job-free existence before sputtering out. In fact, I was scrubbing some road grime off the motor waiting for the salvage guy to arrive at the exact moment when I received the call with the job offer on my cell phone. I accepted right there in the parking lot. I had already been contemplating trying to live car-free in Chicago anyway if I were to get the job, so this expedited the decision making process.

With her trip fully accomplished, Elodie skipped back to France while I became a House Guest From Hell at Ray's house. Within one day I packed and shipped everything I couldn't carry as I completely converted my road trip into an airborne, career-beginning quest. I flew to Chicago the next morning to find an apartment and then back South to truck my stuff up so as to be moved in and ready to start work within about a week.

The job was selling dental instruments around the Pacific Rim for a storied American company. Their headquarters and main factory were in Chicago, where I was to be based. I was responsible for growing sales in places like India, Taiwan, the Philippines and Hong Kong, and the position required significant travel to these countries and around the region. I wasn't exactly going to be collecting dust in the "Windy City," and thus came the birth of... ***Corporate Boy!***

Life was good. Who knew selling dental instruments could be so much fun? My challenge came in trying to figure out how to get quality and premium priced instruments into the hands of dentists in the developing countries that made up my territory. Friends and family who groaned at the idea of adding a new address in their book for me could at least take comfort in the fact that for the first time in my life I had signed a 12-month lease. I felt so domesticated!

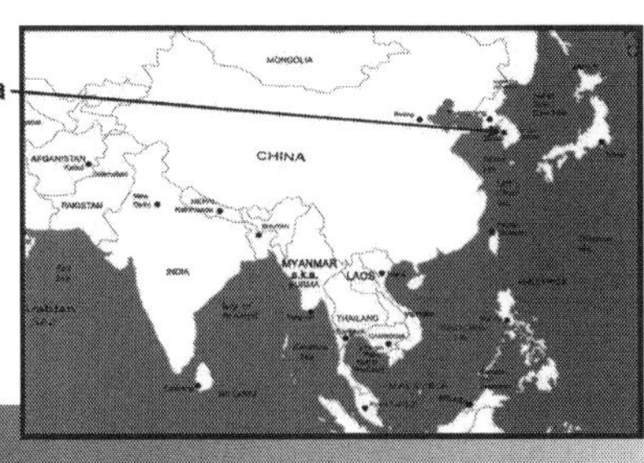

CHAPTER 25

Corporate Boy's Korean Christening

Three countries, three dental shows, and nine stitches on my head later, my international dental sales career was well under way. That's right, three dental shows. It is amazing how different the business for fixing the same part of your body can be from one country to another. Instruments that were hot in Thailand were two-day-old soup in Korea. Our dealer in Thailand was a Mom and Pop organization who invited us into their home like family, while talks with our bureaucratic Japanese dealer felt more like wrestling with an elephant's leg.

One highlight from my trip—other than getting my picture taken with Miss Universe—was spending an evening as a patient in a Korean hospital. We hadn't been in Korea five hours when my boss and I decided to play a game of squash. This, my lifetime squash debut, probably didn't last a full ten minutes. You would be surprised by how hard and unforgiving those walls can be when you run into them eyebrow first.

It didn't hurt all that bad, but it made for an embarrassing mess. The cut I incurred was kind of big. I thought I could walk it off and be fine, but my boss who had the perspective of being able to see the gash and the blood running down my face said," Um, no you're not."

My trip to the hospital was as interesting as any evening's entertainment could have been. My ambulance—a taxi whose driver spoke zero English—dropped off my guilt-filled boss and me at a building that was generally, but not overwhelmingly, hospital-looking.

The English fluency level didn't pick up much inside. I was aghast that the triage nurse casually walked up and removed my bandage to see what was awry...without wearing gloves! I didn't know if I should be more worried for them or for me. My operating room was hardly my own. There was a bubbly but pained young girl sitting at the foot of the same operating table getting her stubbed toe worked on, and other people were milling in and out. The friendly staff did not seem to mind me being insistent that they put some kind of cover over the fluid-stained table before I laid down on it.

A plastic surgeon came in to do the stitches—and that's all. He was all business. If I had not made an attempt at some idle conversation with this person who was about to perhaps permanently alter my facial complexion, I don't think he would have said anything other than "This is going to hurt." A model of efficiency, his nine stitches were done in less than ten minutes while speaking less than 50 words. He did great work, though. My father—also a plastic surgeon—later had the fun of making his son flinch while removing the sutures, and he was impressed by the quality of the stitching. I considered the incident to be the official christening to my new International Business career.

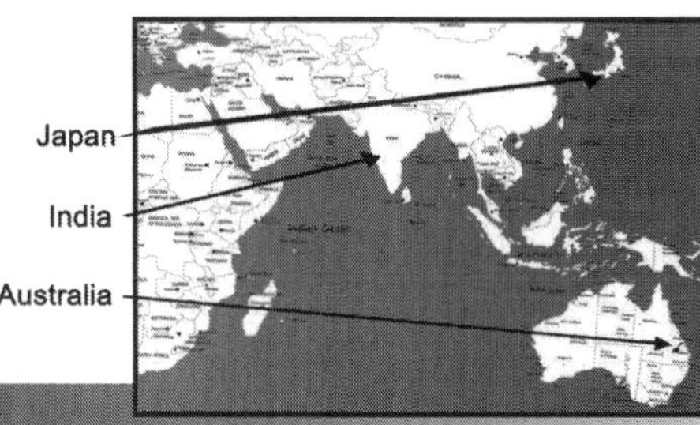

CHAPTER 26

Corporate Boy Goes Around the World in 30 Days

India

Dog fights outside my hotel window jarred me from sleep at 4 a.m. in Mangalore. Unable to fall back asleep, I took a few moments to collect my thoughts after a week in monsoon India. Mangalore, a verdant, coconut-tree clad city in the coastal south, was my first venture out of the financial capital, Bombay (now called Mumbai).

Much more angst provoking than the morning's dog fights was the previous day's landing at Mangalore's airport—apparently ranked as the most dangerous airport in the world. Nice of my host to wait and share that bit of trivia with me until we were on the final approach. The airport is positioned on a knoll and was initially constructed only for use by the helicopters of the British colonizers. Airline pilots have to use a special (rough) braking technique to stop on the abbreviated runway. If that were not enough, prior to our final approach we circled for a half-hour, waiting for a break in the monsoon clouds since there is no instrument landing option available there.

India is home to a mishmash of cultures and castes. There are those that are very rich and those with nothing. Since I was taking part in a dental conference secluded in the suburbs of Bombay, I was too removed from the pulse of the city for my taste. At one point

I realized I had not even stepped outside the hotel in over 72 hours.

Every day it seemed there was a new news report of a dramatic train accident. My curiosity about what Indian trains were like got the best of me. Going against all the advice I was given, on my last day there I took a commuter train into town. OK, I at least heeded the suggestion that if nothing else I should purchase a first class ticket—or so I thought. It was a tad embarrassing, but kinda funny that I ended up getting a second class fare by accident… and then caught by the train attendant for being in the wrong car. I had a train car full of Indian eyes on me as he wrote the ticket.

I have seen my share of dire poverty around the world, but India was one of the few places where poverty comes up and insistently taps you on the arm. Unsettling. Overall, though, I never felt a sense of danger throughout my two-week visit.

Two things hardly ever abated during my visit to Bombay: rain and traffic. Monsoon time is a joyous wet period of rejuvenation coupled with scores and scores of monsoon-related accidents. 11 million people jamming into a small peninsula inevitably elevates Bombay's traffic gridlock to epic proportions on a daily basis. The monsoon rains just add a few new twists. A mudslide here, submerged streets there...

Two other constant delights for my eyes and ears during my India visit were 1) the flowing colors of the beautiful traditional saris worn by the women and 2) unbelievably good and spicy food. Let me speak to the latter point to say we are not getting the real deal back in the States. I loved Indian food before, but wow the food in India is even more amazing. After one ridiculously succulent lamb dish, I swore to the restaurant staff I would not leave until they gave me the recipe. (I meant it!) It turned out one of the

Saris are worn even into the ocean

key ingredients was a meat tenderizer that came from a plant they grew themselves. Not only did they give me the recipe (or at least a foot-long list of ingredients (which I later bravely attempted to hunt down with an Indian friend in Chicago's Little India) but they also sent me home with a container of their home grown spice (which later burst in my suitcase, covering EVERYTHING).

Bombay introduced me to another amazing Indian custom. Actually, it's unique to Bombay—the dabawallahs. Run by one distinct cultural group, the dabawallahs—in addition to having a fun sounding name—have developed a supply chain for delivering lunches that baffles even corporate heavyweights in its efficiency. Basically, the dabawallahs pick up 300,000 or so literally home-cooked meals every day and deliver them in time for lunch to customers' loved ones working in the city. The process is then reversed and the used tins are returned to the home where they came from. Apparently there are only about four mistakes per million deliveries, making the system considerably more accurate than much-touted Six Sigma company processes.

Dabawallah at work

Before concluding my first-ever visit to India, I had one final adventure: a massage. When I heard that an 'Advartanum' was a local aromatic "powder" massage, I had visions of baby powder and fair maidens soothing the ills of the day. Instead, it turned out to be not one, but two guys scrubbing me down with oil and what felt like spiced sand. They say this type of massage is conducive to weight loss, but I have to think that comes more from the amount of old skin they scrape off. It was like a manual exfoliating car wash, yet was fun in its unusualness. I was impressed by the syncopation of their movements. It also begs the question, "Why have one masseur when you can have two?" Very good concept.

Japan Calling!

I was pinch-hitting in Japan, as this was not a country in my assigned sales territory. But I was happy to be back. I even got to take a day for myself to play. I met up with my old juggler friend, Brian, from my years as a college exchange student to Japan. We headed up to the mountains in his van, with a couple Canadians, to go rafting.

After my eyebrow incident in Korea, I imposed one and only one rule—"No Injuries!" Not more than ten minutes into our trip I broke the only rule we had. After a bad wipeout, I was thankful both to have not broken my arm and to have come out of the water breathing.

It was my first attempt at inflatable kayaks in white water. In the first big set of rapids I ate it hard, got whacked on some serious boulders, lost my paddle and got sloshed around underwater enough that I wasn't certain I was coming back up. Nothing like a good mortality check to get the blood flowing.

My biggest error in (Brian's) World of Kayaking was that I made the rookie mistake of letting go of the paddle. Somehow life seemed more important at the time. Brian and I trekked back upstream to find it wedged under a rock across the river in the middle of these same intrepid rapids. I have always known Brian to be a tad off-kilter, but it was here that I witnessed him in true psychotic yet extremely impressive form. Without a boat or anything, he bounded into these rapids that tried to eat me and swam through/across them like Tarzan, retrieving the paddle.

That was the ying, then came the yang. During the time it took us to retrieve the paddle and return to the boats, the river had risen several feet. In that timeframe, Brian's own paddle had washed away. This was the first time in his storied kayaking career (including appearing on an extreme adventure TV show going down monster rivers in Chile) that he'd lost a paddle. He was furious at himself and will be mortified that I am sharing this part of the story, but I have to so that I can tell you about two things:

1) Whereas I had enough trouble navigating through the rapids on my own, Brian ended up having to paddle for the both of us to get through the big hydraulics. My boat was tethered to his back. Somehow while my craft was pulling on him in one direction and the rapids were trying to tip him over and send him in 15 other directions, he managed to successfully guide us through the mess of beautiful boulders flying by. Impressive.

2) In fairy tale form, at the end of the day when Brian started calling around to find a place to purchase a replacement for that $300 paddle he had borrowed (and had been fuming about all day), he spoke to a store owner downriver who told him that the lost paddle had been turned in at his store. With the relief of finding the paddle and no permanent injuries, it was at last considered a perfect day.

Down Under in Australia

Entering the customs line at the Sydney airport, I overheard fellow arriving passengers joking with each other, saying they should each be able to go first because they had "come such a long way". This rings true for anyone who makes it to Australia, and it certainly felt apropos for me. Setting foot upon my sixth continent in order to work at my first major international trade show with this new career of mine, it certainly felt like I had come a long way.

That feeling was compounded by the fact that I was lucky enough to stay in an airplane-hangar-sized suite in the middle of everything. In case you ever find yourself in Sydney with more money than you know what to do with, write this down: Quay Grand Suites. The discreet hotel and its friendly Aussie staff are sandwiched between the harbor's main transportation hub Circle Cay and Sydney's lush Botanical Garden. I bet on a still night I could hear them singing at the Sydney Opera House, which I could see from the balcony. I sensed (correctly) this would be a one-time event, since the only reason I was staying there was because one of the company's top executives had come with me on this trip and had originally planned to bring his wife.

I had one day for jet lag detox and I intended to take full advantage of it, knowing it would be my only free day for the rest of my stay. I began my explorations by ferry. With the dramatic Bay Bridge stretching out across the water from the shiny downtown skyline, Sydney is spectacular. I heard myself saying "WOW" under my breath as the boat rounded the Opera House, sweeping the downtown area behind it as a backdrop.

On the way out to visit a spot by the ocean, the wind was ripping at full force, which tempered the blazing sun to the point of needing a light jacket. Watson's Bay forms one lip of the mouth of Sydney Harbor where it opens out to the sea. This is the gateway the British 7th Fleet first entered in the 1700's. As my tribute to also arriving in the

Commonwealth, I grabbed "takeaway" fish & chips and headed to a small coastal park to picnic, looking out across the harbor to the cityscape.

The peninsula formed by Watson's Bay has dynamic flora & fauna and a rugged coastline interspersed with beaches. Some of the local fauna could be spotted on the one official nude beach, called Lady's Bay Beach. Based on my observations, I think a better name would have been Johnsons' Beach. Definitely a male majority, if not monopoly.

I bussed along the coastline to the famous Bondi (pronounced…I still can't get it right…something like BON-dai) Beach. I had intended to try my hand at surfing, but the combination of the blustering cool wind and the small waves kept me on shore. There was, however, plenty for landlubbers to do, particularly this day because it was the day for the annual Festival of the Winds, a kite flying festival. This year the wind was plentiful to the point that many of the contestants dared not let their kites get off the ground.

Enjoying the nearby food and performances, I almost didn't make it to the beach at all. Most intriguing was a demonstration of a Brazilian dance/martial art called capoeira. Originating from that country's slave culture, capoeira evolved as a way to let off the steam at the end of the day while also surreptitiously training in combat. It is practiced to the beat of an African-sounding soundtrack, performed live with traditional instruments, and is meant to look like something between dancing and stumbling drunkenness while being unexpectedly lethal—things like headstands turn into wild-looking kicking motions. I had never seen anything like it. Apparently there are clubs for it in major cities around the world, including Chicago, which I went and tried for myself upon returning home. It's tough!

My day of adventure behind me, I moved onto the world of work, which in Australia was also an adventure. Even in this "English" speaking country, some things dentists would say were hard to comprehend. "Oh, that would be great for a wizzie!" referred to the utility of a certain instrument relating to the wisdom teeth. It also took me some time to realize that they use similar names to identify different instruments.

I also had my first dental consultation, with me as the consultant. A cabbie dropping me off at the convention center started asking me about some unpleasant dental symptoms he had been dealing with. (Not the kind of descriptions you want to hear first thing in the morning!) He persisted even when I insisted I was not a doctor and that any of my suggestions should be taken as seriously as a horoscope. But he insisted so I advised. After checking with a legit dentist later, it turns out the advice I gave the cabbie regarding his probable case of periodontal disease was correct.

In the mornings before heading to the expo, I tried jogging as the sun came up, in part to help work off the fabulous meals I'd been eating. My route seemed surreal, winding around the Opera House and through the Botanical Gardens, past beautiful wild parrots, ibises, cockatoos and a plethora of bats. On my last day I ran over the Bay Bridge and took a commuter ferry almost right back to my hotel.

My recommendation: If you ever have a chance to go to Sydney, just go. No, no, no. No questions, no buts...just go.

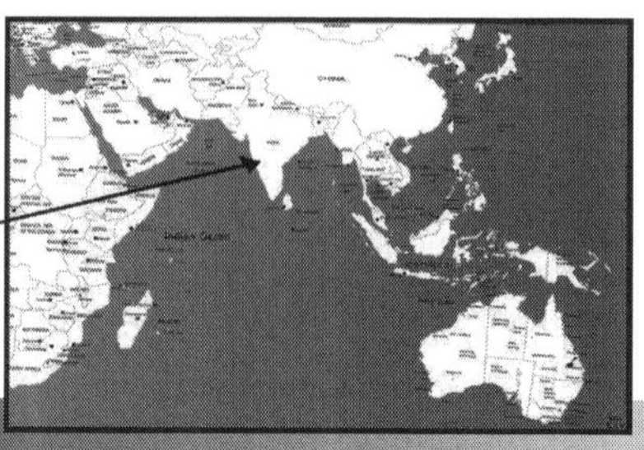

CHAPTER 27

"We're Not on a Pilgrimage; We're on a Business Trip!"

India Revisited

Nothing on my trip had been going exactly right until the Friday afternoon when I set foot on the beach of Palolem in Goa. While this was my third trip to India, I had more troubles on this trip than my prior two combined. First, my luggage (with my suit and all my samples) showed up four days late. Then, the conference which was the focal point of my trip was poorly attended. Then came the nationwide strike, etc., etc. Sigh. More on Palolem later, but first let me tell you how I got there.

This was to be my first real road trip in India: a big, two-week southern circle from Bangalore to the western coastal city of Mangalore up through Goa and then back. It was quite the road show. In addition to the conference, I visited nine different dental schools, giving presentations at most of them. For most of the journey I was accompanied by Samet, our Indian dealer's regional sales rep.

The road trip kickoff was an 11-hour drive which lasted until three in the morning. Even a simple road trip can uncover some interesting cultural differences. For one, our driver said a prayer before turning on the headlights the first time (way after it was too dark to safely see the road). This custom apparently has extended out from a certain candle-lighting ceremony. When he did turn on the headlights (finally), a separate interior purple light lit up the Ganesh—an elephant god—on the dashboard. Ganesh, "the Remover of Objects," is the god of choice for drivers. This selection makes sense considering the number of things that wander onto the road. Cows are considered "natural speed bumps" because when they meander onto the road, which they do frequently in their ever-slow motion, they get everyone to hit the brakes.

Night is the time everyone makes long road journeys in this region. In fact, while there are no busses going between Bangalore and Mangalore during the day, over 100 of them make the trip in each direction every night. This meant the later it got, the more of these fast-driving road hogs came barreling at us.

Our driver was a bit quirky for someone supposedly doing this for a living. He insisted we stop three, maybe four times for tea. He also had me move to the back seat because I made him too sleepy when I started dozing off next to him.

At the show, the scene was one I could only imagine in India. The following parties all had booths at the same show: us, former employees (and family) of our dealer who had been fired last year for embezzlement and fraud, two of our sub-dealers who were not allowed to purchase any more of our products because they hadn't paid our dealer in months, and one former employee of my company cum competitor—all in the space of about 12 booths. It was a den of iniquity if I have ever seen one.

Of course you can't work all the time, right? We were to stay one night at a town called Udupi, a renowned pilgrimage destination close to a dental school we were visiting. To my delight, our stop there coincided with the once-a-year Tesli Festival of 1000 Lights. Delighted, that is, until Samet decided he didn't want to stay, saying he wanted to head further up the road before the festival got under way. I relented but seriously regretted having to leave this unusual event. There were huge bulbous carts being decorated and lit for what looked to me an impressive processional. That, plus the elephants, plus the exotic sounding band, plus an unabating inflow of locals (and some cows) seemed to be setting the stage for an impressive event. Oh well, off we went for another dangerous lonely night's drive down the highway.

A float being prepared for the Tesli Festival under a full moon

A detour another day to check out the coastal town of Gokarn led to my favorite quote from the trip: "We're not on a pilgrimage; we're on a business trip!"

Gokarn is known as a pilgrimage destination because of one of its famous temples. Ignorant of the hazards that can arise from a casual visit to such a temple, I had inadvertently cast my associate into the hands of zealots.

I simply wanted a closer glimpse of the temple, famous for having a statue inside so marvelous it is said that one look at it will absolve you of all your sins. Not just one or two—ALL of them to date! Unfortunately, because of the bad behavior of those who came before, we foreigners are going to be stuck with our sins because we're no longer allowed inside. Indians, in contrast, are not only allowed, but even get roped inside—willing or not—for a price.

We both got pulled into the initial ceremony where the priest helps pray for the various members of your family and you end up with a red dot smudged on your forehead. Despite Samet's protests that we were in a hurry, the priest/guide managed to cart him off for a more involved, bare-chested ceremony inside. At the same time the priest insisted upon some princely sums for this privilege.

I thought Samet was going to be mad about all this since he had been hedging about going near the temple in the first place (he sensed something like this might happen, but didn't tell me until afterward). But in fact he was pleased to have done the ceremony, saying his wife was going to be thrilled. They had been trying to make it to this temple for some time to do this type of ceremony. He was only frustrated about the time we lost as a result, thus his quote above to the priests when initially trying to refuse their services.

Absolved sinner Samet and non-absolved sinner Vacation Boy, post-ceremony

I'll skip all the other little drudgeries so I can get to the part about how much better things were post-Palolem arrival once I sat down and mentally unplugged. Palolem is about all anyone could hope for in a laid back, coconut palm-lined, crescent of a beach. Palm-leaf shacks were tucked under the trees at the edge of the beach. The young, relaxed Reshma D'Silva owns Riva huts, the place I chose to call home this visit. My raised bungalow was located over a drum shop (which turned out to be fine) facing square out to the gorgeous beach and the waves crashing only 40 meters away.

While the long-haul backpackers that made up much of the area's population shied away from the premium $6 a night price tag for a beach front place, for me it was perfect beyond imagination. Heck, I had paid more than that in tax at many of the places I had been staying. I did feel a bit silly though, getting help lifting my huge suit- and-product-samples-laden roller suitcase up the rickety ladder. I also felt like a geek for sitting under the stars on my bungalow's porch typing these words as the surf crashed in front of me, but it sure was relaxing.

Palolem's beach has an interesting mix of sari-wearing women, cricket-playing boys, cows, happy dogs and a whole pile of backpackers. The foreigners here were more of the mellower earthy yoga crowd than the heavy partying sort, which have their own nesting grounds in other parts of the region. I had dinner with a group where the shortest voyage amongst them was eight months. The high end was two and a half years on the road. It's not that I haven't done my own fair share of traveling, but these kinds of mega trips still boggle my mind. How are they financing it? How can they stand being on the road THAT long? I guess I am too mainstream. Maybe if I can put enough money in the bank, my view on this will change. For their part, these guys couldn't fathom how I would pop into a place like this for the weekend during what was otherwise a business trip.

Corporate Boy actually working

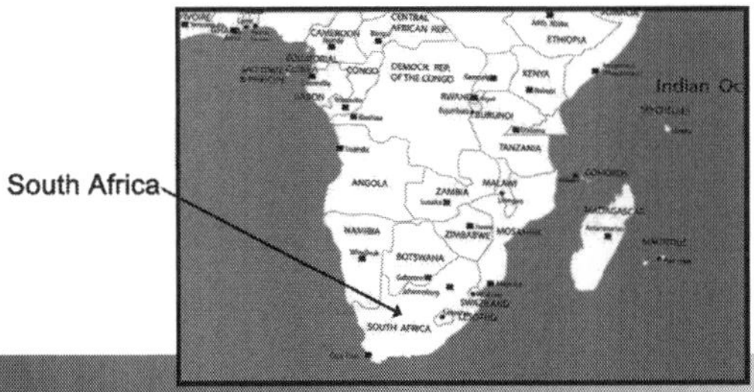

CHAPTER 28

Carving Up Whales & Rental Safaris

Corporate Boy Hits 50 on South African Soil

I was home in Chicago naked and dripping wet when the phone rang as anticipated at 4:40 a.m. Even though I was about to leave for my 50th country, I had once again stayed up all night scrambling to prepare for a trip.

The call was from the taxi driver downstairs who had no way of knowing I wasn't even finished packing, not to mention unclothed. He did know, like I did, that my flight was leaving in an hour and a half whether I was on it or not, and it was a 45-minute drive to the airport. He probably also knew the airlines cut off check in 45 minutes prior to the flight. Fortunately, I had made enough similar trips recently, so the last maneuvers to stuff my suitcase and zip out the door were completely automatic and efficient despite my lack of sleep and blurred-over vision.

With two nights of almost no sleep from pre-trip preparations, I was completely exhausted when I changed planes in Atlanta for my 15+ hour flight to Johannesburg, the first stop on this second of several round-the-world trips for this job. As I staggered onto the plane like a zombie, all I could focus on was the peaceful coma-like sleep I was going to fall into the moment I settled into my seat. I can only imagine the expression of horror that gripped my face when I rounded the corner to find an infant in a huge bassinet in the seat right next to mine. The baby basket was big to the point that for me to pass, the mother had to lift it up and out and back down the aisle.

I knew I was within several weeks of becoming an uncle, so I weakly tried to stay upbeat and tell myself this would be a good character building exercise. That exercise didn't make it to take off. Between the tugging on my arm and the random squeals, I could tell our relationship was not going to work out. The flight attendant was knowingly ready with some alternative seating suggestions. Soon after I moved, the baby kicked into full on Scream Bloody Hell Mode. Ordinarily I would have been peeved, but this time I was blissfully appreciative of the several rows of distance I had gained.

Rent-A-Car Safari

Setting foot on South African soil meant I had reached my 50th country milestone. Vacation Boy made an appearance because I asked for some time off. Having come all the way down to this part of the world, why not take advantage? I had four days to myself before work kicked in.

I ended up renting a car to visit Kruger National Park, South Africa's ultimate game preserve, which is about the size of Delaware. Now I have been to plenty of parks, but this is the first one where they tell you to absolutely never, ever leave your car (even to go to the bathroom) except in approved areas, or risk becoming integrated into the wrong end of the food chain.

This was serious business. Some of the lions in this park apparently even specialize at hunting the illegal immigrants who try to sneak through into South Africa from neighboring countries. Knowing all this, I gulped as I crossed the gate in my little anger-red Nissan. Just past the entrance, there was an ominous Himalayan-sized pile of dung. Jurassic Park images lingered in my mind from that point on as I scoured the brush for menacing eyes. While I saw plenty of wild stuff on day 1, let's skip to…

Animal Overload

Kruger Park is jam packed with very wild animals, but sightings were particularly easy to come by at this time of year—the tail end of a long dry season—since the animals were obligated to stay close to the few remaining water sources. By 8 a.m. I had seen more animals than you could find in the best African section of any zoo. It had been so dry that when it started to rain, I spotted tortoises coming out to lick water

off the road. The weather was nuts. It was well over 100°F on my way in, yet a couple days later I found myself shivering in temperatures under 40°F.

The morning began at sunrise when I accidentally scared off two (what they call) buffalo dozing right on the far side of the electric fence guarding the encampment from where my tent was pitched. They were not as used to people as I had anticipated.

Later, driving around a curve on one remote dirt track, I startled a family of gigantic rhinos right by the road. It sure got my heart going. Theirs, too. These armored-truck-sized beasts scurried off into the brush, occasionally pausing to sheepishly look back over their shoulder. They had it all wrong: I was ready to jump into Reverse Drag Racing Mode if they so much as blinked in my direction. I preferred to not test my insurance deductible policies concerning a rhino horn through the door.

By my observation, the "in" thing to do these days was grazing. Everywhere I went animals of all sorts were chewing on foliage high and low. Among the grazers were plenty of wildebeests, the animals that star as "the victim" in every Africa predator movie. They look like bait. I kept waiting for a Marlin Perkins voiceover and a sinister sound track to fade in each time I saw them. Unfortunately, I did not have the chance to see "a kill".

I witnessed instead a pathetic version of *Trials of Life*. The scene: the banks of a waterhole. The key players: a sad excuse for a buffalo and some lions. The audience: a gaggle of vehicles like my own jostling for good camera position on the nearby road (no one exits their vehicles).

The buffalo for some reason was in bad shape and could hardly walk on its own. The lions—perhaps already full from a recent comestible encounter—were nonplussed by the wallowing buffalo who seemed to cry out "would ya eat me already?" The lions couldn't be bothered and looked like they could easily wait well past dark or maybe the following day before even getting up to give this poor thing a sniff.

I did not learn until later that buffalo tend to gradually go mad from ticks or worms that munch on their brain. I don't know if that was the source of malaise for this particular beast, but it better explained the behavior of another buffalo I saw later circling bizarrely near a pack of elephants, causing them to charge him each time he got too close to their offspring.

As for the above poor lot, I didn't have the patience to wait out the resolution of its demise. Instead, I ended up following an attention-needy lioness on her own personal car parade. She waltzed to the center line and promenaded down the road like she was a movie star before her adoring fans. I stuck with her for over a mile before heading back in the opposite direction. Too high maintenance.

At one point, I passed through a pride of lions lazing about on the side of the road. All traffic stopped. It made me nervous when I saw a couple of them in my rearview mirror come up and sniff my bumper. Their shoulder came up to mine when I was seated in the car and while they were mostly uninterested in the nearby Homo sapiens, occasionally their cold steely eyes flared up at me, giving me the view of the last thing probably many a wildebeest sees alive.

I ended my stay at Kruger with a night drive organized by the park in an open-air jeep. It was amazingly cold, but well worth the suffering. It is astounding how much you can see driving around with a small floodlight. The noise and the light get about anything in the bush to look up at you, and in doing so, their position is exposed by their eyes which eerily reflect the light. A dark tree or bush that would pass by without notice, lights up with moving eyes. You are not alone.

One down side about Kruger is the fact that you cannot get out and do any exercise without the risk of being eaten. You are stuck in a vehicle, which meant that when you add that to the plane flight down, after a few days my legs felt like they might fall off from disuse. I was hungry for exercise.

Kruger National Park, South Africa
Zebra Greetings
For the ladies that want a guy
"hung like an elephant" take note
that this is not his 5th leg.

Post-Cape Town

Once Corporate Boy's work obligations in Cape Town wound down, I had two more days to explore the southern tip of Africa. I elected to head for Table Mountain, Good Hope Peninsula and the wine country. The soundtrack to my outing was provided by Good Hope Radio. In addition to their upbeat mix of African music, I particularly liked their Barry White like tag line: "Good Hope Radio: It's aaaall gooood."

Not far out of Cape Town at an overlook along the winding, beach-peppered coastal road, I came across a curious scene. A crowd was gathered around a large marine something or other on some rocks down by the water. It turned out to be a beached young Right whale. So, what do you do when a whale washes up on your shore? Answer: You cut it up and bury it, which takes hours and hours. They said if they pushed it back out to sea it would wash back up and become a health hazard. This poor baby giant had died overnight and these folks had only recently started the process of standing on top while carving off pieces. I have strong feelings for whales, and I felt honored to be able touch its plasticky wet-suit like skin, its rough barnacles, and its tough baleen krill filters in its partly open mouth.

Cape of Good Hope

There are places in the world that you hear about and dream about, but never think you will ever see in person. For me, the Cape of Good

Hope was one of those places. I remember stories of the world's great explorers sailing in tempestuous waters past this point at the bottom of the Earth. It seemed ironic that I could now pull up to this same spot in a Hertz® Rent-a-Car.

The Cape of Good Hope turned out to be surprisingly beautiful and it had a special calm feeling at the moment I visited as the sun was preparing to set. The peninsula leading down to Africa's southernmost tip is a national park that has its fare share of biodiversity. Here if you got lucky, you could spot land lubber animals like ostriches and zebras with marine species like whales frolicking in the ocean just behind them. It felt like somebody had mixed up the animals and their habitats.

I made a few detours before I got to the apex of the Cape. As I pulled into one parking lot, I noticed something unusual about the car next to me: it had been commandeered by a baboon. The feisty primate was defending his spot in the driver's seat from the two British tourists outside who were more than likely the intended vehicle occupants.

It was all fun and games until the couple tried to reclaim the car and the baboon started to kick the woman's ass. When throwing things didn't scare her off, the baboon got out and chased her, punching her first and then grabbing her shirt from behind as she fled...right into a parked car. Ka-thunk. Ouch.

The situation switched from funny to ugly so amazingly fast there was nothing onlookers like me could do to prevent it, even if there was something for us to do. Then the baboon bolted towards me. Vacation Boy can be pretty fast when he needs to be and this was one of those times. I was back in my car with the door shut before you could say "bananarama". That was one pissed off monkey and one shocked couple. They were OK but rattled. I have a feeling they will follow the baboon warning signs posted all over the place a bit closer next time.

Baboons giving a mating demonstration to the tourists

That night, it felt otherworldly to see a lighthouse blinking on the tip of Africa while standing under the stars and chatting on a pay phone with my soon-to-go-into-labor sister in North Carolina. I camped out on a perfect grassy knoll right by the water's edge. That fairy tale night's sleep led to a dynamic day of whales, swimming with penguins and a speed wine-tasting trip on my way back to the airport.

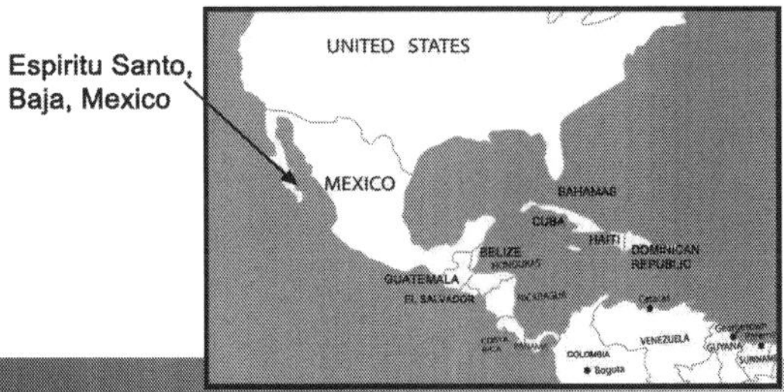

Espiritu Santo, Baja, Mexico

CHAPTER 29

Christening the Crimson Poobah in Baja

I had a distinct sense of déjà-vu. Once again, I found myself soaking wet and naked with someone calling for me to get out the door. But not all was the same.

"Taxi, *señor!*"

Instead of in my apartment in Chicago, this time I was in La Paz, Mexico, a city on the Sea of Cortez near the tip of the Baja peninsula. Instead of rushing for a plane, I was scrambling for a different reason…the wind. It was time for the maritime debut of the Crimson Poobah and a trip that would be one of my best ever.

The name for my new inflatable kayak came during the rush-around lead up to the trip. Only five days prior, I was in Fripp Island near Charleston, South Carolina to celebrate the long-anticipated 60th birthday of my never-aging father. In between golf games, playing with my sister's adorable infant, visiting with relatives and bouts of celebratory indulging, I talked my father into joining me for the first (and what would be the only) test run of the kayak before my approaching trip. Part of the test admittedly was to give my father more confidence in the craft that would be carrying his son for a week on a foreign sea (plus I thought there might still be an off chance I could talk him into joining me). After our paddle against a strong current and a stiff headwind in a nearby inlet, we all felt better about my chances of survival. My sister joined us in a naming brainstorm, but my father gets full credit for the winning name. I discovered later that "Crimsoooon Poooobaah!!" rolls off the tongue just great when shouted as a war cry to the elements.

Some of those elements were front and center in Baja the day I set out. As I mentioned, the wind was a big concern. All the information I read said to expect potentially voracious winds by late morning. With all my last-minute errands, though, my taxi did not drop me off at the departure beach until almost noon. I hopped out of the car and held my breath to see if I could hear taunts from an invisible foe. Nothing. Phew. ...or so I thought.

Between pumping up the boat and doing a final organization of my dry bags, I fumbled around for an hour. When I was finally about ready to load the boat and go, up came the wind. Within 15 minutes the lake-like surface was a field of whitecaps. By the time I was pushing out to sea, waves were crashing over the side of the boat. "Not good," I kept thinking to myself between expletives.

The Crimson Poobah

My backup plan was that if things felt too treacherous out past the breakers, I could turn back and wait until later in the day or even the following morning once things calmed back down. Luckily, once I got past the surf zone, the Crimson Poobah held its own surprisingly well and had no trouble rolling over the wave crests. Once I got past my initial sense of trepidation, the pitching and bucking made for a wild, fun ride.

As the island drew closer, ever so slowly, the "shacks" I had been aiming at ominously came into focus as boats of years' past (or maybe this year) that had been unceremoniously washed up on the rocks.

My destination across this whipped up four-mile stretch of the Sea of Cortez was the desert island of Espiritu Santo. My book said

Espiritu Santo

this was the site for Steinbeck's book *The Pearl* and was frequented by pirates back in the day. I was into it more for the stories of isolated beaches sandwiched between desert vegetation and clear waters. The 40-mile or so round trip circuit would take me a full week to complete.

I had done a number of kayak trips before, but never on open ocean and never in my own inflatable boat. There were several themes that continued throughout my tour of Espiritu Santo. For starters, it was perfect weather every day with clear blue skies, highs around 80 degrees and lows around 60. At night, I shared my chosen cove only with the rising and falling tide and the silent star-painted sky. The water was clear and emerald in color, although cooler than expected. As a result, I ended up doing much of my fish viewing from the comfort of the Poobah.

Sunset on yet another beach all to myself

I was cautious of the sun, particularly since my back was still sensitive from the epic frying it underwent a couple weeks back while on a business trip in Australia. I think my conservative wardrobe would have passed muster in even the strictest of Islamic countries even though I was on a kayak in the middle of nowhere all by myself.

There were crazy jumping manta rays all over the place like floppy fleas on a big watery dog. Sometimes they would simply philander on the surface as if they were doing the backstroke, sticking the tips of their fins up in the air. Others passed their time hurtling themselves out of the water only to have gravity return them to the sea. Each had its own style. One would go for a full triple wing pump. Another for a spiral. A third for a wacky free-for-all. I imagined it was a step in the mating process, specifically the part where they jump up as if to say, "Yippie! She picked me! She picked meee!!"

A school of manta rays passing under me

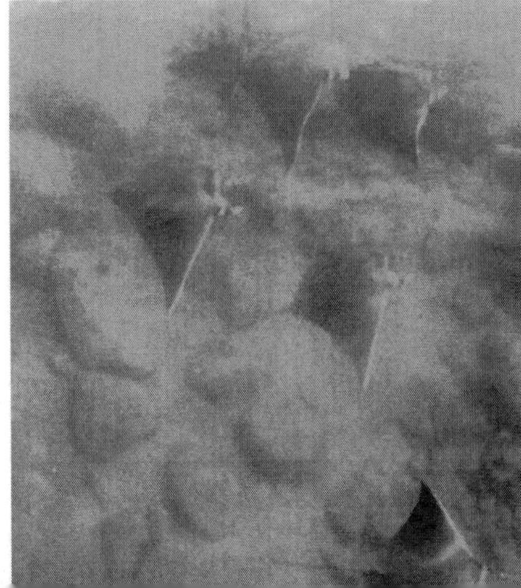

Speaking of jumping, one of the unforgettable highlights of my trip was when I ventured out to the drip-sandcastle like rock outcroppings known as Los Islotes, where a bunch of sea lions and birds make their home. When I approached the islands (along with a litany of tour boats), young sea lion ambassadors came out to greet their new visitors. The urge to jump in and swim with them was irresistible. Right when I plunged in the water, one pup swam right up to me and—I swear—hugged me! He put a flipper around me as if to say, "Thanks for coming to play with us!"

And then the fun began. We (me and up to eight of them) dove and swirled and twisted in every direction. A couple times one charged right at me, and when he got to within a foot of my face, pulled back on a dime into a series of goofy back summersaults.

This spot is the destination for a number of tour boats that come out from the mainland. The tourists that jump into the water for the most part wear life jackets and hover on the surface. The sea lions seemed to appreciate having a playmate that would dive down under water with them. After all that diving and twisting with limited pauses for air, I was a little woozy when I finally pulled myself out of the water and paddled back to the main island. Boy was that fun!

Los Islotes and its adorable ambassadors

This was the longest continuous camping trip I had ever taken. One thing I had not prepared properly for was dealing with my garbage. Granted, it didn't help that the complete lack of refrigeration meant everything I owned spent the day baking in dry bags. On the fifth day, the smell had gotten so bad I caught myself considering sinking my kayak just to make the smell go away. It was kind of pathetic to be sitting there gagging while paddling through pristine waters.

Fortunately, just when I was thinking about taking drastic measures, I came across a grouping of fishermen's shacks. I made a trade of my bag of garbage (which they would take back to the mainland when they took their own) for some of my extra food rations. So great was my clean-air-intoxicated joy to be rid of my rancid trash that—at least at that time—I felt this was the greatest moment of my entire trip.

I once again confirmed my status as one of the worst fishermen on the planet. I knew the gig was up when a parade of over 200 fish of an edible size passed right by my lure like it was yesterday's wallpaper. Poor little squid lure. I felt bad for it. I tried my hand at fishing several times during the trip to no avail. Thank goodness I brought adequate food rations.

It was whale season in Baja. The grey whales are particularly known for migrating here this time a year to give birth to new calves. I did see a few whales, but only one came close to me. On a dead-calm sea I was fish watching from my boat when I heard an explosive 'WHOOSH', unmistakably the sound of a whale emptying and refilling 90% of its gigantic lung capacity in one rushing breath (humans by comparison only with considerable effort can exhale about 25%). I spun around and spotted it for a brief moment before it dove a hundred yards from me. I didn't see it again.

I was wary of getting too close to whales as a friend of mine, during a visit to Baja, witnessed a kayaker who drifted between a mother and her calf. Bad idea. The mother started trying to breach on the guy, who did his best Roadrunner impersonation with his arms, trying to spin himself away from the ire of this big mad mutha.

For my last night on the island, I camped on a scenic stony beach where the water was teeming with fish and had fantastic snorkeling. That evening there was yet another magnificent sunset. Between the persistent bounding manta rays and other jumping fish, it reminded me of the scene in the Little Mermaid for the song "Kiss the Girl," except without the girl.

On my last day, another whale (OK I am assuming it was a different one) waved to me as a sendoff, slamming its tail loudly on the water's surface 30 or more times. The whale seemed only to have wanted to see if he could trick me in to paddling like a banshee all the way out to him (and at this he certainly succeeded) only to then dive and head off to the horizon.

Embarking on my final paddle back to the mainland, with the tailwind and my new paddling endurance, I thought I could shave an hour off my two-and-a-half-hour crossing time coming over. Not so. I ended up barely pulling back ashore in Tecolote as the sun dropped below the horizon amidst a radiant canvas of colors.

After my long endeavor, I was hungry for a celebration. I scrambled to get my tent in place in the encroaching darkness, then went down to the only open beachside café, licking my chops in preparation for a feast. Since the cooks had left for the day, my feast ended up being two beers and some potato chips. Good beer, sad meal.

After saying my goodbyes to Espiritu Santo and the Sea of Cortez, I headed off for Baja's West coast and then down to San Jose del Cabo. It turned out to be right at the time of a major local festival. Take your average State Fair and then plop it into a cute colonial town in Mexico and you have the idea. Instead of elephant ears and snow cones you have churros and flan. Instead of women's mud wrestling, you have cock fights. Instead of ring-the-bell tests of strength, you have mechanical bull contests—all with Mexican music blaring. The seedy game operators, the rides and "See the Two-headed boy!"-type features were, however, remarkably similar.

The final oddity of note was the blanket selling show. There was more than one of them. The main ringleader wore a Madonna-esque microphone, pacing back and forth on a podium. He ordered his two assistants to rush around and throw blankets and pillows up to him. One after the other he unfurled and refolded the blankets until he had a big stack. He jabbered incessantly, "How much would you pay for this? How much would you pay? 800? 800? 800? 750? 750? 700? Right now, not 800! An unbelievable offer: 250! Every word should have exclamation points after it because he was shouting everything. There was quite a crowd of people watching this spectacle and sure enough, time and time again, someone would eventually buy whatever deal he stacked together.

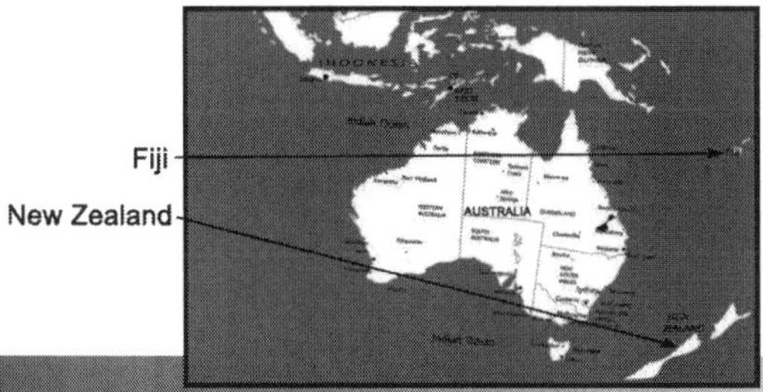

CHAPTER 30

Fun with Unsunken Boats and Dental Hygienists

Fiji and New Zealand

23 Hours in Fiji

I decided to start my third round-the-world trip for work with a stop in Fiji, just because I could. I was heading to Australia and was able to tweak the flight routing so it would offer me a long Fiji layover at no extra cost. Work had gotten crazy recently, so in the end, the only time I could take off there was not even a full day anyway. One day is better than none, right?

On my way to Fiji, I finally executed a plan I had dreamed up at least a year prior. Anyone who has spent time with me in the southwestern U.S. knows how much I love In-N-Out Burger®. From the plane, at one point I spotted an In-N-Out Burger right by the foot of the runway of the Los Angeles (LAX) airport. That's when the idea first came to me, but this was the first time I had a layover long enough to put the plan into play. You see, conveniently located right next to this In-N-Out is a long-term airport parking garage, the one with the yellow and black polka-dotted shuttle busses. Once into the terminal, I rushed down to baggage claim and hopped on one of these busses. That's when I discovered this company operated two different garages. I learned this too late, so I got a lovely tour of the other parking garage. It was fun, though, because I had a nice group sharing moment with the commuters in the shuttle with me. They poked fun at me for getting stuck on the shuttle going to the wrong place, but also shared their own love for In-N-Out burgers and their favorite "secret" off-menu ordering options. I was amongst friends.

Once I got to my intended destination, I was in an urban paradise. The In-N-Out there is right be the end of the runway, so you can sit outside and watch the planes land and take off. All this while the sun stunningly sets as it only can in a place as polluted as Los Angeles. Once I had my fill and the sun was down, I hopped back on the spotted parking shuttle to the terminal—and they even offered a free bottle of water for the ride. It's a plan I'll definitely repeat the next time I have a long layover at LAX.

So then off to Fiji! Since I was only going to be there for 23 hours (arriving and departing around 3 a.m.), I decided there was no point in getting a hotel. I would stay up and explore as much as possible in the time I had. My first step was to gather some information. I had finalized my plan to go to Fiji only a few days prior and had not zero, but negative time to research the place. I started out catching a ride with some Norwegian girls I met in the airport to see the hostel where they were going to be staying. But it was in a quiet area outside of town and I was looking for more activity, so I rode back with the driver to the airport to see what I could find once the sun came up.

Unbeknownst to me, it gets cool in Fiji. The weather during my August stay was already apparently an improvement over the recent rainy, jacket-wearing weather. Sunrise was a write-off with the cloud cover, so I focused on signing up for a boat trip that would get me out to the islands and into the water with the Fijian fishies.

A group of elder Aussies jumped in the shuttle on the way there, saying this would be the eighth time they had taken this same day trip. "Must be good," I thought.

Then they casually mentioned, "A few years back when we came to do the trip, the boat had sunk."

"Say what?"

"Yeah mate, this 60-footer managed to sink right at the dock. One day it was there, the next morning it was underwater."

The Aussies were amazingly nonplussed about hopping back on a boat they had seen being dredged from the bottom.

"No worries, mate she's plenty seaworthy again. We've been out on her a couple times since."

That's the easy-going Aussies for you. Admittedly, the boat seemed fine considering it had spent time under water. The day trip out for a picnic and some snorkeling turned out to be a pleasant outing, although it would be much more enjoyable to try again in warmer weather.

The amazingly unsunken boat

A Hop, Skip and a Jump...to New Zealand

After years of dreaming, I'd made it to New Zealand at last. The scenic superlatives there come so fast and furious you need to pack in glowing adjectives like an overstuffed suitcase to try and describe the beauty.

Milford Sound, New Zealand

Oddly, it wasn't gawking at the magnificent scenery that caused me to have my first ever car wreck in a foreign country. Let me say this, if any of you have been considering running a contest to see which would win in a battle between a mountain and a rental vehicle, let me save you the trouble. I have run the experiment: the mountain wins.

But let me start with the bird. I think I was cursed by a bird…a pretentious parrot I encountered on my way down the road descending into the gloriously beautiful Milford Sound at the southern tip of New Zealand's South Island. When I stopped to take a picture from an overlook, the menacing grey bird with its piercing dark eyes hopped around my car, glaring at me, almost insisting I give it food "or else." I refused to give in and I suspect this accident may well have been the result.

The accident occurred on my return up the same winding road after an amazing kayak trip out in the Sound. Ironically it wasn't from rubbernecking at the amazing views—the culprit was candy. In New Zealand, Cadbury sells a snack called Jaffas, little round, orange-coated chocolate balls. It was their roundness that cost me a thousand plus dollars. Because of the curvy nature of the mountain road, the Jaffas started rolling all over the floor and mixing into my piles of brochures and other road trip muckity muck that was already spread across the passenger floor.

In an effort to save the candies before they all fell out of the box and made a mess of everything, I spent a wee bit too long bent over picking them up. I was jolted back upright to the sights and crunching metal sounds of the car bouncing off the side of the rocky mountainside. The location was suspiciously close to where I had encountered the evil parrot on the way in.

Sigh. The banged up car was quite an embarrassment. At night, my crazy-eye headlight would send up a bat signal on the roadside trees. Blame the Jaffas. Blame the bird (I do!). Either way the car was wrecked. All I could do was drive around sheepishly in my banged-up vehicle. But it did drive, and for that I am thankful.

What had originally brought me to New Zealand was their national dental hygienists convention in Nelson on the northern tip of the South Island. The gala dinner was the most fun part of the meeting. Life-size cardboard cutouts of "Dr. Dan" were spread around the room. It was entertaining watching many of these ladies—well served with the wine provided by corporate sponsors—having their way with this suggestive marketing prop. "Dr. Dan" was a towel-only wearing hunky icon (apparently, also a real dentist) for of one of the toothbrush companies sponsoring the evening. Dr. Dan cutouts made an appearance at many of the dinner tables, danced on the dance floor, and (well beyond my bedtime) apparently toured Nelson's bars and dance clubs later that night.

My Chicago-based dental instrument sales job was going great. I was making decent money, seeing the world and sales were on a steady increase. What would most people do? Leave it all to start a risky cutting-edge orthodontic treatment company in Japan? Yep, that's what I did.

It was an exercise in swinging for the fences, reaching for the brass ring. It could have been huge. How'd that go for me? The expression "That which doesn't kill you makes you stronger" would imply I became Herculean after the mental beating and fiscal dieting that endeavor led to. The moral of that story was, if your entire business is going to rely on the treatment developed by one eccentric Japanese dentist, first make doubly—no triply—sure he is both competent and sane.

After a rough six months in Japan, I retreated home to the U.S. to work on a job search in earnest. I took a couple breaks from my search, using the opportunity to complete journeys I had been dreaming about for years. You know what that means... Vacation Boy was BACK! (at least until I found a new job).

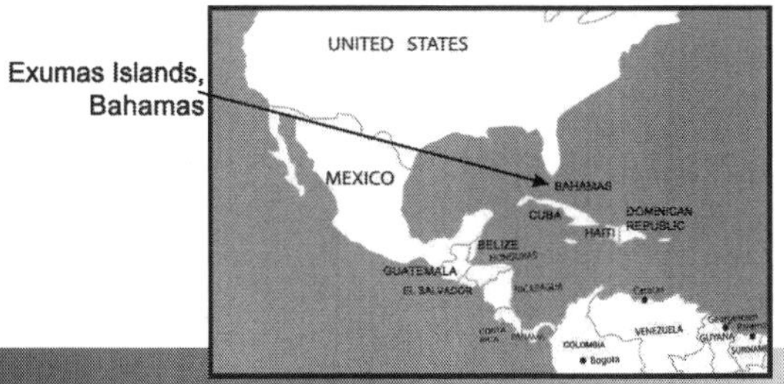

CHAPTER 31

A Kayaking Quest for Conch

Vacation Boy (Finally) Paddles the Exumas

My first flight to the Exumas had forever burned this Bahamian archipelago into my daydreams and left me longing to return. Back then, I was a Caribbean Club Med tour guide, leading groups of Japanese tourists on day excursions out from Nassau.

My jaw dropped on that first flight when the plane began drifting above a chain of scruffy green patches rimmed with stunning white sand beaches and surrounded by the most dazzling array of blues I had ever seen. The crystal clear water made drifting brush strokes with the sand beneath it. The resulting color gradations created a surreal painting that an accomplished artist would be challenged to recreate.

Even before disembarking from that first work-related flight, I began to dream of returning to explore these islands more slowly—and thus the idea of a sea kayaking adventure through this Bahamian paradise was born.

This time, some 13 years later when *Team Exuma* (my friend, Joy Ingham, and I) walked out to the runway in Nassau and laid eyes on pilot Everett Johnson's dilapidated plane, I could feel both of our hearts drop. His duct-taped beater looked better suited to be a comedic punch line than something intended for actual flight. The tattered curtains, and the holes sort of sewn together on the plane's ceiling, did not inspire any additional confidence. Captain Johnson's mention of having made the same flight that morning helped slightly. I kept telling myself, "He's been making runs like this for 16 years; he can make one more."

Joy Ingham was an old friend and over the years has been a recurring character in my travel schemes. I convinced Joy to join me on this adventure simply by baiting her with the trip concept. This enticing voyage was her kind of thing. Raised by missionary parents in Africa and Europe, Joy was no stranger to travel. In fact she was the one crazy enough to lead a group of 14 high school freshmen and sophomores through Europe on a bare bones five-week Eurail and Youth Hostel trip a couple decades earlier. That inspirational voyage she created introduced me to the amazing possibilities of budget travel, a lesson that has stayed with me my entire life.

As we taxied down the runway (with the door next to her open for ventilation) I looked to her for some reassurance like "Sure, I've been on worse planes plenty of times before." Instead she seemed to be quietly tightening her seatbelt and her smile.

Joy had flown in from LA, meeting me at the Nassau general aviation airport for this, her first-ever, multi-day kayak trip—and here I was putting her in peril before we even got into the boats. When we touched down at Staniel Cay 40 minutes later, our shouts of glee had as much to do with still being alive as it was to have arrived at our long-sought destination.

Back during my Club Med days, I headed out on the Exuma day trips with my group of Japanese guests in my flip-flops, bathing suit, t-shirt, a mask & snorkel and a big wad of cash. The cash covered everything from the bus, to the charter flights, to the boat captain who hosted us on the islands once we arrived.

That boat captain had been Patrick Simpson, a muscular local fishing guide, who radiated the relaxed air of the islands. One of the highlights on our outings involved Patrick diving down to grab a couple of conch off the ocean floor on the way to a pristine beach. There, he prepared a fresh conch ceviche which was so delectable I swear I can taste it to this day just by thinking about it. Reliving that conch dream on my own terms became one mission for the trip.

Arriving at Staniel Cay this time, I felt like I had stepped out of a time machine into a future which I did not fully understand. Back when I visited the sleepy, population 60 island, we were always the only plane on the bare landing strip and the pilot would walk in with us to the marina. Now, not only were there a number of planes parked there and others coming and going, but there was even a large shaded gazebo waiting area with a phone and an army of people in golf carts ready to whisk arrivers off to various destinations on now-paved roads. The number of homes on the island had multiplied beyond comprehension. One can only imagine what this island will be like in another 13 years.

The one person in the area I knew from my Club Med days, Patrick, turned out to be one of the people now zipping around on golf carts. He seemed to have transitioned into full-on Entrepreneur Mode in my absence. Once we figured out that we knew each other, Patrick set out to hook me up with his uncle so we could camp out on his island right across from Staniel. He reassured us we would have his full attention once he had completed a few "missions." He zipped back and forth in his golf cart, disappearing for twenty minutes at a time, usually maintaining some form of cocktail in his non-driving hand.

When he eventually took me by the Staniel Cay Yacht Club to load up on water, I was completely blown away. Back during my Club Med days, my manager instructed before my first trip that if there was no one around, I was to go behind the bar and prepare drinks for my guests, and that I could settle the bill later in the day when someone came by. As astounding as that sounds, that is exactly what happened! In contrast, walking in the door on this day there were three busy bartenders, an NFL playoff game on a large-screen TV, sound blaring from the surround-sound speakers, and a bar completely packed with people cheering for their favorite team. Some of them even appeared to be surfing the internet on wireless laptops. I was floored. Here, Patrick was like the mayor seeming to be pals with the boaters and locals alike.

Patrick's uncle, Sid, was quite a character. He picked us up by motor boat to shuttle us off to Lumber Cay, his neighboring private island which he was trying to improve in order to welcome tourists. This arrangement was quite fortunate for us since we discovered Staniel Cay does not allow camping. Upon arriving at his own little Fantasy Island, Sid played the welcoming role of somewhere between Mr. Roarke and Tattoo. I don't think I ever saw him wear shoes. He made great fires for cooking each of the two evenings we stayed there and we invited him to join us for dinner both nights.

Previous attempts to work out the logistics for this dream trip had been vexing, particularly trying to figure out how to get hard shell boats in and out of this remote string of islands. The only publicly accessible transportation was by private plane or by the legendary slow-moving mail boat that passes through once a week when things go well. The advent of high-quality inflatable sea kayaks made things much easier. My craft, the Crimson Poobah, was inaugurated on my trip to Baja a couple years earlier. Joy deeply regretted missing out on the Baja trip and wasn't about to pass up this adventure. On Sid's beach, we christened her proud, new, as yet completely untested craft "The Royal Peapod," a slightly more petite and much greener version of the Poobah.

We used our first full day as a get-to-know-you exercise for the boats and the environment in which we would be paddling, particularly since once we left Staniel, human settlements would be few and far between along the island chain. Most of the islands are deserted. We spent that afternoon paddling to Thunderball Grotto, a beautiful fish-filled network of caves where the namesake Bond movie's underwater scenes were filmed. It is a dramatic snorkeling destination both for the marine life and the topography. You follow crevasses into the rocky mass, weaving into dome-roofed crystal clear water-filled rooms all the while being escorted by multitudes of tropical fish. The ubiquitous colorful coral further decorates the experience.

At the end of the test day, I was uncertain we could make the full 40-mile trip north to Norman's Cay as originally planned. Inflatable boats, while offering superior portability, are slow in the water compared to their hard shell siblings. Combine that with a pile of gear and Joy's "relaxed" paddling pace, I thought we may be restricted to day trips around Staniel. But, to her credit, Joy was resilient and had the resolve to make the full trip. Also—in her defense—through the course of the week her pace increased admirably and there seemed to be fewer times when she was so busy being enamored by the beautiful surroundings that she forgot about the paddling part. Still, we would not know for days if we were truly going to be able to make the full distance.

Joy with the newly christened Royal Peapod

Another major lingering source of stress was the future crossing of the "Wide Opening" (*cue the thunder sound effects and ominous music*). While most of the islands are closely linked one to the other, and it is possible to stay sheltered from the Atlantic, the Wide Opening (*thuuundeerrrr, flash of lightning*) offers a daunting four-mile stretch of exposure to true ocean swells with few options to escape. The stories of kayakers and other "real boats" getting man-handled in this stretch were on the minds of Team Exuma from the start, even on the calmest of days.

Speaking of good conditions, in the "gosh we're lucky" column, I don't think there was a single night or morning during our trip that we were not blessed with beautiful sunrises and sunsets. Each day was as pleasant as anyone could have hoped for—sunny to partly cloudy with highs in the upper 70's and lows in the mid 60's. Most importantly, we were not lambasted by rain nor any of the stiff northerly winds which can rip through this time of year. Every night we camped on a beach (or an entire island) to ourselves. Many nights, I slept out under the magnificent stars. There was no moon, and celestial lighting was out in force.

Back on Staniel that second night, we partook in a conch and fish feast for 17, although there were only three of us there to eat it. Joy and I bought some fresh conch during one of the shopping stops on our paddling outing, and Sid was kind enough to prepare it for us. He also chipped in some delectable leftover fish Patrick had prepared for his guests earlier that day.

Like the previous evening, Sid joined us for dinner and he was in rare form singing Led Zepplin songs a capella and expounding on his theories on fallacies with Darwinism. When he offered to make us a tea that was better than "any tea in the world" using some local plants, we thought for sure he was going to cook up the hallucinogenic potion which seemed to keep him going. It turned out to just be good tea.

Despite whatever misgivings we may have had, the next morning we prepared to head north in the direction of Norman's Cay. Before leaving, however, we had a slightly uncomfortable situation to sort out with Sid and Patrick. While we had anticipated that we would chip in for our stay on Sid's island (despite having fed him both nights), nothing prepared us for the amount that was put forward. "$250??" This was the price Patrick had supposedly suggested to Sid via cell phone the night before. Assuming this was correct, Patrick's intentions were clearly not just to help out an old work buddy. Sid agreed $250 was a bit outlandish. We ended up calling it even at $30—and I had to talk Joy up to that amount. Sam seemed to think that amount was fair, too.

After that brief bit of unpleasantness, our trip was pretty much smooth sailing. Each day we were treated to a new array of beautiful water, beautiful skies and beautiful beaches. We learned early on that currents could play an important factor in our forward progress, or lack thereof. When they were with us, life was beautiful (think "Row,

Row, Row Your Boat…"). When they were against us, it could be an upriver slugfest (more along the lines of "Row faster, Joy, or we'll never make it!")

A couple times when the wind was at our backs, we tried our hand at sailing. We improvised a sail by hoisting up the tent fly attached to the oars and brought the boats together like a catamaran. We made some pretty good time like that, although it was at least as taxing on the arms as paddling.

We also made a scene. One yachtie passing by in his dingy had to double back (giggling) to come get a better look at what we were up to. In this part of the Exumas, particularly this time of year, there are more people living on boats than on the islands themselves. Quite a number of Americans, Canadians, and even a few Europeans come here to winter—some of them every year. The yachties we bumped into all seemed to have interesting life stories, which were usually some variation of falling off the grid. With a VHF radio, you are immediately linked to a community that looks out for one another. Every morning, folksy weather information was preceded by community announcements such as volunteer opportunities at a local school, restaurant lunch specials, as well as mentions about things like dinghies that had gone missing.

At one point, our sailing attempts became fodder for their VHF radio chatter. It is common for Haitian refugees to flee through this part of the world. In fact, the day before we pulled into the Exuma Park headquarters, they had captured a boat of 157 and were in the process of repatriating them. So when a cruiser called in "something like a life raft with a makeshift sail" the park rangers motored out to us post haste, thinking perhaps we were escapees from that Haitian boat. They got quite a chuckle when they figured out what we really were.

We had entered the Exuma Land and Sea Park on our third day out. Since the park rules were strict when it came to fishing or collecting conch, all the conchs which thus far carefully evaded us seemed to have assembled in the park, forming a welcoming committee. The conchs were waving at us, taunting us, knowing full well we couldn't harm them. At one sandbar we walked along to get past an obstinate opposing current, the trickiest part was not stepping on the little guys that seemed to have gathered there like Swedes on a Spanish beach.

The wooden building which houses the Park's main administrative office is perched on a slight hill that offers a 360 degree view of tranquil paradise. Inside was Sandy, our guardian angel of the trip.

I had been in contact with her via phone before coming down, and she had offered lots of helpful suggestions for our trip. She mans the radio for the park so we knew once we were in her radio range that help was near if we needed it. The park was set up to cater primarily to the yachting crowd. Still, I ask you, how many national parks do you know that have NO public toilets?!

Sandy and her husband had been living there five years, the last three of which were also in the company of her aging mother with Alzheimer's. It was touching hearing Sandy describe how perfect this environment was for someone in her mother's condition. There was none of the noise and confusion that are more a part of our daily lives than we realize. No cars, no busses no crowds. Every day was similar to the one before, so there was no need to learn new activities. They had some simple chores they asked her mother to do which kept her occupied, and gave her a sense of value and purpose. Her mother had no idea she had been there for years.

Trader Joe's, while far removed from these islands, was an integral, beloved part of our trip. I never realized how many neat camping-friendly items they have. Imagine looking out at a Caribbean landscape while dining on sag paneer or the likes of dried mangosteens, rambutans, and even dragon fruit. Joy had been in charge of much of the menu planning and she rocked.

Here at the park headquarters we had yet another delectable lunch on the office porch watching the breeze, the beaches and the birds while mentally bracing ourselves for the next critical part of our journey—the crossing of Wide Opening (*Thunnnnderrrrr!, derrrrrr, ominous music*).

On our way out, the park folks were kind enough to allow us to recharge our water supply, knowing it would be the last opportunity to do so before the end of our trip. Sandy insisted we radio once we had made it to the far side of The Opening under threat of her sending people to come looking for us if we didn't. Having someone like this watching over us felt like a warm security blanket where otherwise there would have been nothing but deserted ocean, islands and rocky outcrops to comfort us.

After all the buildup, crossing the Wide Opening turned out to be a cakewalk. The weather and conditions that day could hardly have been more favorable. It was a huge weight off our shoulders—even when setting out—to see the relatively calm sea and light winds. Once we were about 1/3 of the way through, I found myself even cheering "O-VER-RA-TED" in my head. When I hailed Sandy on the radio to let her know we made it across and told her we were disappointed it had been so easy, she responded, "You'd better not be!" Knowing how different the conditions could be out there, she suggested we be real happy with the lot we drew.

Now that we had made it across this portion, we were elated to finally know for certain we would arrive at our plane pickup destination. Joy is one of the people I mention whenever asked about my life's true idols, and getting through this incredibly long day of paddling with a smile on her face put her in even higher standing. More than just this night on this trip, Joy had arrived at our beach for the evening completely exhausted, but then an impressive ten or so hours of sleep later she was up and amazingly raring to go.

Outside of the park staff, the only people we encountered along the entire trip were boaters. They were supportive, often offering to give us water or a ride somewhere if we needed it. Samantha and Paul were a fun couple we particularly enjoyed. We met them on an exquisite beach on the far side of a mangrove estuary on Shroud Cay where there was an opening to the ocean. What quickly put them on the top of our Favorite Boaters list was their offer of delicious chilled rum punch cocktails (with real ice!) that they somehow magically produced from their dinghy.

When I first arrived there, Samantha, an Ironman competitor, was waxing about her philosophical place in the world while Paul relaxed and grinned a lot. While they fit the fallen-off-the-grid pattern, they were particularly fresh in that they had only met a few months prior. At that time she had already quit her successful business career to "find herself," starting by taking some time working as a waitress at a Florida marina following a road trip to Alaska with her aging father.

Paul was a concrete stress tester who had owned his boat for several years but had never taken it anywhere. He had it up for sale when he met Samantha. Somehow Sam's wanderlust rubbed off and they came up with the cockamamie plan to drop everything and sail through the Caribbean together. It seemed to be working fine: they were three weeks in and having a blast. By timing it every night since they left Florida, they had figured out that at sunset, it takes almost exactly three minutes from the moment the sun touches the water to the moment it drops below the horizon. Who knew?

The only chagrin in their lives seemed to be the evil, yarn-ball dog they had picked up on the way out. Not a sea dog by any means, this pet had been a last-minute thought on the way out. Apparently the dog was not thrilled about the ocean adventure either.

As much as we came to like them, before we met Samantha and Paul, Joy and I had plotted against them. Earlier we had seen them pulling away from their boat in their dinghy and we tried to wave them down in hopes of getting a tow up the tidal river coming out of the mangroves. Sadly, they did not spot us and puttered away. When we passed their moored boat, the "Oh-La-La!," and saw the dog aboard, we hatched a fictitious plan to kidnap the dog and ransom it in exchange for a tow. Later when we met them on the opposite side of the island and divulged our plan, Paul said that not only would we have been easy to spot with all the scratch and bite marks on us, but our plan would have backfired completely because they would have been thrilled to have anyone steal their dog.

Speaking of dogs, we had noticed some big ones on some of the boats we passed earlier in our trip. We got to asking ourselves, "How do they deal with the dog using the bathroom?" Almost right after speculating this exact point, we had rounded a corner where there was a couple playing in the water off a beach with their golden retriever Trixie. Talking to them, we learned you are supposed to raise the dog on and around boats right from a pup. Apparently you train them to do their thing on the foredeck, where it is away from the main human hangout areas and is also easy to hose off. Something new to learn every day!

The only time I truly sensed danger on our trip was on the last day before our departure. Once clear of the park boundary, as part of a last ditch effort to live out my thus-far-unfulfilled conch ceviche dream, between two islands I hopped out into a pretty fast moving current to scan for the again-illusive gastropods. In the excitement of spotting a promising shell, I dove down against the flowing current without grabbing the tie-line for the Poobah. When I came up, the current, coupled by a blustery wind, had hurtled my boat away towards a geographical abyss. I had to swim at a full sprint to catch it. I was already pretty tired at this point, being at the end of a full day of paddling. I caught up with my boat within a minute, but it was a cautionary tale of how quickly a situation could become perilous.

To spare you any further suspense, my personal conch dream was never fulfilled, so the conch recipes and preparation methods looked up on the Internet will have to wait until I return again.

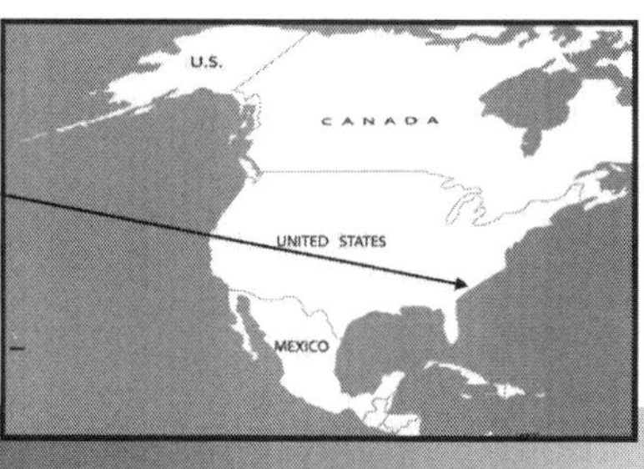

CHAPTER 32

In Search of Gasoline

A Float Down the Savannah River

Trying to contain year-old-feces-water gushing from the hull of a boat was not how I thought I would be spending my birthday. But there I was, the mechanical surgical assistant to my stepfather, Bobby, as he struggled to swap out the pump on the "black water" system on *L'il Lady,* his and my mom's small houseboat. Bobby was crammed down in the hull and taking the brunt of the unpleasantness as I shuttled cup after newly emptied Styrofoam cup to him as he tried to capture the spewing mess as best as possible. Think "Feces Fantasia". Even before this unfortunate phase of the procedure, the smell had already been so awful it made our eyes water. Now we were both howling in disgust.

This horrifying moment marked the beginning of our slapstick family adventure down the Savannah River. *Li'l Lady* had hardly been used during the winter, so in the days leading up to our departure, Bobby, in addition to replacing the pump, had also rewired the boat and completed other miracles of mechanical tinkering to get her seaworthy again.

Then came the packing. You cannot possibly imagine how much stuff my mom can pack for a two-day boat trip. For example, right in the midst of the final scramble to depart on time, Mom decided to break out the 4th of July decorations to better celebrate Memorial Day, and she also insisted on bringing the fresh cut flowers I had given her for my birthday. Bobby and I both rolled our eyes to the point of almost losing them in the top of our heads. But once my mother latches on to an idea there is no letting go. Living with my mother lately has helped me take a fresh look at the traits I see I inherited from her. "Pit bull" was the nickname some folks at my last job gave me for my tenacity when pushing an idea once I latched on to it. Hmm, wonder where I got that from…?

Before I start this story, just know I have already been asked, "How do you run out of gas TWICE in one trip?" It is easier than you'd think.

We launched *Li'L Lady* in the Savannah River below the locks in Augusta, Georgia with little certainty as to how long it would take, or how much gas would be needed, to get to the city of Savannah on the coast. We did know there were no places to buy gas along the way, which made us glad we were starting downriver with a full tank plus full extra canisters of gas. We started out with aspirations of arriving at Savannah, refueling, and then returning to our starting point in Augusta, but even early on we realized this idea was completely delusional.

Due to an afternoon appointment in Columbia, my mother could not catch up with us until late that Saturday afternoon. I took advantage of the time to get an early start down the river in my kayak, the Crimson Poobah, while Bobby meandered about midstream in *L'il Lady* waiting for my mother.

It was almost dark when they eventually caught up with me drifting with the current. I had already seen a deer, a turkey, and an osprey flying with a fish in its claws in the couple hours I had been on the water. It was a great breath of fresh air. Paddling offered a different contrast of sounds. Instead of the din of the motor, the loudest sounds came from the paddle passing in and out of the water and the small whirlpools they would leave behind in the calm river.

L'il Lady's parking spot for the night

We tied up for the night on some posts that extended out into the river. These posts appeared in many places for reasons we never fully understood. All we knew was they were convenient for us. At night we were roughing it, but with all the latest medical advances and a fancy steak dinner. Bobby ran his CPAP ventilator off the generator.

Later the next day, when it became crystal clear we had no chance of making it all the way to Savannah without running out of gas, we set into motion something not much better thought out than the Bush Energy Plan. My mother used her cell phone to call all over the place to try and locate a gas station in the tiny towns we were passing. Bobby tried to get people over the marine radio that could come to us or point us in the right direction of fuel. I prepped my kayak in case I needed to paddle off to find gas or if I needed to try and redirect *L'il Lady* if the motor stopped cold while we were in the middle of the river.

We were sputtering on fumes when we pulled off into a feeder creek, which had a bustling boat ramp with many boaters coming and going. On the dock was a woman relaxing, watching her children swing into the water from an elaborate, multi-story, Disney-like rope swing they had set up on the far side of the creek with complete disregard for the nearby alligators. Winona, as we came to know her, was kind enough to give us a ride––twice––to a nearby gas station to fill both of our five-gallon cans. Considering Savannah was right around the corner, 20 gallons should have been plenty to make it, right?

Fast forward to the next morning on a dock in downtown Savannah with a Hyatt security guard telling us we had to leave their property immediately. He did not seem to fully comprehend our response of "We are out of gas." And we meant it. Not that we could blame him for wanting to kick us off his dock. Compared to the fancy ocean-going vessels in this part of town, ours looked more like the fluvial equivalent to the Beverly Hillbillies' over-loaded camper.

Let me tell you, where the Savannah River runs through town is not a place you want to be drifting out of gas. Gigantic supertankers, big enough to block the sun, ply the waters at amazing speeds considering how narrow and busy that river is.

Somehow the remaining mileage had been more than

we anticipated, particularly since there were surprisingly no marinas in the city of Savannah where you could get fuel. By the time we arrived at the Hyatt's dock, we had figured out there would not be any refueling opportunities until we were all the way through town and out into the marshes, and we were extremely doubtful we would even be able to make it through the rest of town with our empty fuel status. I got some odd and piteous looks as I walked into town with gas canisters in hand to the closest gas station.

Dodging mega tankers through town, dock master Bubba (yes, that was really his name) eventually guided us into his marina in the marshes beyond the city. We had to rent a car to get home. We ended up leaving *L'il Lady* at the marina, giving us a good excuse to come back down to Savannah the next weekend to hang out on the coast a bit more and reminisce about our (everyone decided) never-to-be-repeated trip down the Savannah River.

A Working Stiff Again

After six plus months of searching, I stand before you today to announce that Corporate Boy is back! What on earth is The Boy doing this time? Well, if you guessed managing sales for Europe, Middle East and Africa for a manufacturer of ophthalmic microsurgical instruments, you would have been exactly correct. Having made the transition from dental to retinal surgery, I feel I have definitely moved up in the world (ha ha ha).

This is a real new adventure for me. Based out of Paris, I manage almost three times as many distributors compared to my previous position, plus direct sales in France, Germany and Italy.

It's lucky Corporate Boy is not adverse to travel. My first day on the job had me on a plane to Europe where I spent three weeks in France, Portugal and Holland. The company expects me to be on the road a suitcase-jarring 70% of the time. In September alone I already had trips to Stockholm, Venice, Berlin and the Canary Islands.

A significant component of my position entails me being in the operating room while retinal surgery is being performed. This was VERY new for me. I have to wear the scrubs and everything. I am thrilled I haven't made the rookie mistake of passing out.

Eye surgery the first few times was a bit spooky, but then it seemed to transition quickly to a bit ho-hum. While there are interesting moments, a lot of it is like watching someone crochet a pair of socks. Between the cold air conditioning, the regular beeping of the patient's heart monitor and the dimmed lights—it's my perfect sleeping environment and thus often hard to stay awake.

In one hospital in Utrecht, Holland (a great town!) the view into neighboring surgeries put it into perspective. Retinal surgery requires tiny movements, most of which are viewed through microscopes or on video screens. It seemed dullish in contrast to the neighboring O.R., where orthopedic surgeons were making big excited movements using implements like hammers and chisels, or, looking in another direction, seeing someone's stomach being opened up. It also reminded me of how grateful I am to have not gotten the colorectal (ass) job I had interviewed for earlier with another company.

After Holland, I spent an arduous week in Paris trying to sort out an apartment. The rental market in Paris is tough, especially if you are interested in having more space than a tiny studio, yet are not prepared to forego the price of a new compact car each month in order to pay your rent, or if you are shy about having to walk up six stories of stairs to get to your home. I visited upwards of 20 apartments and easily walked over 60 miles before I finally settled on a place around the corner from the Champs-Elysees.

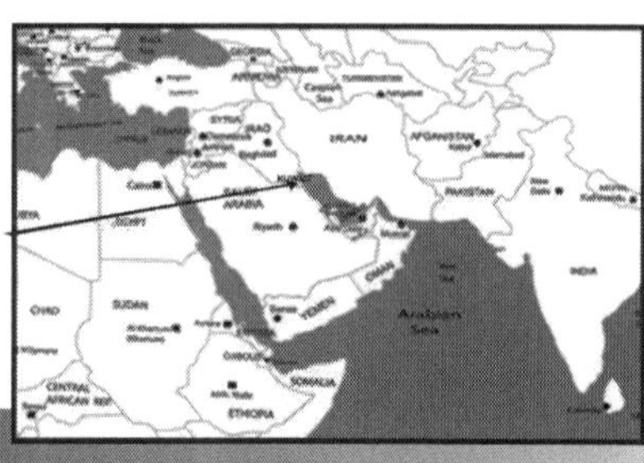

CHAPTER 33

Just Drop Me Off in the Desert

Corporate Boy and the Kuwaiti Hash

"Are you sure this is where you want to get out?"

It was a fair question. The taxi driver had driven me 30 kilometers out into the Kuwaiti desert at night, and here I was taking off at a run into the darkness in shorts and a t-shirt with no one else in sight. And with no flashlight.

I will be the first to admit this was not one of my saner moments. It all had to do with the Hash House Harriers, a group I joined up with in South Carolina and continued to participate in when I moved to Paris. This decentralized organization known as the "Drinking Club with a Running Problem," is found all around the world—there are two in Kuwait alone. Out of my seven hashes to date, the Kuwaiti Hash was by far the most extreme. I had received an e-mail confirmation of the evening's event and location less than an hour earlier, upon returning to my hotel after the day's medical conference. These are excerpts of the exact directions I was given:

> I don't know of anyone coming from that direction. If you take a taxi, come down to the 211 and head west (inland). Go to the end of the road and we'll be there in the desert. Call me on my cell if you're lost…
>
> —Priscilla Queen of the Desert

And she also helpfully added, "You should try and find a red dress if you can – as gross as possible!!!"

Luckily my taxi driver had a cell phone because I was arriving late and without the ability to call "Priscilla", the only group I would have found out there was a group of sheiked-out Kuwaiti men (in traditional dress) gathered near their cars in the dark in the desert for no reason that I could speculate.

Priscilla vaguely guided me to the starting point where their cars were parked under a giant electric power line tower, but she had to break off the call because she, "was going into a ditch and needed both hands". By the time we located the supposed starting point the group was long gone. On the bright side, part of a Hash involves following trail markers left by the "hares".

On the not-so-bright side, it was real dark and as mentioned earlier, I had no flashlight. Rather than trying to focus on trying to locate specific markers, I took off with true reckless abandon as fast as I could go across the uneven soft sand in the direction Pricilla had suggested. When I got around a fence and a patch of trees she had mentioned, it was an extreme relief to make out some flashlights and the familiar Hash sounds of " On-On!" being shouted in the distance. When I came across a ditch, I felt even better that I was getting somewhere, that is until I leapt across and jammed my toe into something hard, so badly I thought I broke it (my toe, not the ditch). Depth perception is tough in the dark.

After all that, it was a tremendous relief to finally catch up with the silhouettes of the men and women in red dresses (+ one child in a stroller + one dog) that were bringing up the rear of the group. It turned out that tonight was the group's Annual Red Dress Run. I was forewarned by Priscilla, but there had not been enough time to go shopping. So here, sweating in the middle of the desert, I was conspicuously underdressed (and had to drink for it later).

The entire run had a post-apocalyptic feel to it. Across mostly sand, the scenic wonders we weaved among (that I could see) included high-tension power lines, trenches, piles of sand, random large holes, a six-lane highway (which we ran under at one point), hubcaps and other random garbage. Many group members commented this place was nice compared to some of their usual places. They also mentioned they had come across a cobra in one of their previous desert outings.

It was a fun group weighted heavily by Aussies, Brits and Bulgarians. I was a significant shade younger than most, which leant towards the (thankfully) slower pace of the group (or I would have never caught up).

Whether for legal reasons or other, the traditional post-run "Circle" took place on the roof of someone's apartment back in town rather than where the run ended. The Circle is a time honored tradition when the run is reviewed and various penalties are paid in the form of guzzled drinks. Alcohol is illegal in Kuwait except in special private clubs. So the "Hash water" which was consumed as part of the post-run festivities was their own home-brewed wine made from grape juice and wine yeast. Like I said, this group is extreme! It was in the circle that I learned this was official Run #787 for them, implying a long-established group.

Once pulled into the middle for one of my many transgressions that night, a British/Aussie-accented dialogue ensued around me:

"Does he hate it here yet?"

"He just got here."

"When?"

"On Thursday" (it was Saturday)

"Well, that's plenty of time!"

"Fair point."

The Circle concluded and then a Chinese delivery meal was served up to the masses. What a great way to spend an evening! It was a bit hard to explain to the doctors I work with why I had to ice down my toe. But now you know the truth.

90-Days' Notice

To recap where we left off, I had been in Paris making a decent living managing sales of ophthalmic surgical instruments across Europe, the Middle East & Africa for an American company. That was all about to come to an end.

My landlord was the first to officially know about my decision to give up this life, because you have to give 90 day's notice before doing anything in France. While many of the plans I was putting together three months prior to now were far from concrete at the time, there was enough evidence that I would be leaving to merit avoiding the possibility of paying for several months rent for an expensive yet empty apartment. If my plans changed, I could always tell the landlord I wanted to stay longer, right? Right??

Before telling you what happened, let me tell you a few things I had been up to in the meanwhile, starting with how I kicked off this year…with a visit from the Parisian paramedics.

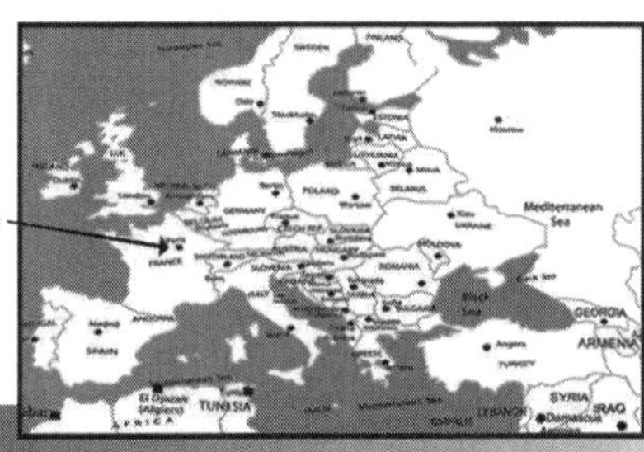

Paris, France

CHAPTER 34

Hosing Down a Naked Frenchman

A Visit from Parisian Paramedics

I, probably like you, did not anticipate starting 2008 by standing in a bathtub hosing down a half-passed-out, naked Frenchman. The fiasco resulted from a house party gone awry.

My New Year's Eve had been off to a great start. My French and Japanese party guests helped pitch in to put together a fantastic meal of tuna and other delicacies… somehow I don't even recall what they were after the events that followed.

This was one in a continuing series of dinner gatherings I had enjoyed with my good buddy Ahmed whom I have known since a college summer when we worked together in a restaurant in the Alps. While I don't think anyone would mistake us as being family, Ahmed is like a brother to me. As we regularly end up in embarrassingly loud laughing fits each time we get together, hanging out with him is one of the main reasons being in Paris was really fun. For this particular party, the folks that joined us were his Japanese girlfriend and three other friends of theirs. With some fun board games to play, plenty of champagne in the fridge and the Champs-Elysees in view from my balcony, the stage was set for a lovely evening.

Skipping straight to the unintended climax…not too long after the New Year rang in, it quickly became apparent that the aforementioned French guy Thierry, had been over served. Mind you none of us ever felt he had drunk all that much, but with his wire-rimmed glasses, meager-framed body and computer techie tan, he was not exactly built to drink anyone under the table.

In retrospect, it should have become clear things were not as they should be when he first tried to explain the unintelligible logic behind his baffling attempt at describing "disco ball" in a failed round of Pictionary charades. From there, his condition quickly declined.

His next act of greatness remains a mystery because to this day no one has figured out how he pulled off the feat that he did. He stumbled into the bathroom and some time thereafter we heard a Bang. Later when he came out, he plopped on the sofa and mumbled something about thinking he had broken my framed picture. Sure enough, upon inspection, he had somehow broken the large picture's glass, which being on a ledge up and behind the toilet, was not in easy reach. Miraculously, he did this without disturbing any of the objects on the shelf in front of it. Whether it had somehow whacked him in the head or if he had swatted it with his hand, we will never know. We were at least grateful the glass did not shatter because that would have made the situation exponentially worse.

Then came his true coup de grace. In a momentary stroke of lucidity in an otherwise increasingly cloudy evening, Ahmed jumped on a grenade. He had noticed in his friend Thierry signs that things were not all as they should be. In an act of unadulterated heroism, Ahmed diverted Thierry from parking himself on my beloved La-Z-Boy couch, thereby saving it from certain ruin.

Ahmed's repayment for this selfless act was to get caught in the crossfire which soon ensued. Approaching the scene, I, too, found myself directly in the sites of a machine gun spray of projectile vomit. It was horrifically impressive how in one sprinkler-system-like stroke, Thierry managed to red-wash (because of the wine) a 140 degree arc of my apartment reaching distances that would have made a medal contender in a long jump contest proud. Faced with this disgusting scene, we all found ourselves stupefied and gagging, but luckily no one doubled down.

The chaos that ensued was coupled with a bird's nest of cultural nuances. While it is hard to explain the subtleties of all this, Thierry's pregnant Japanese girlfriend was instantly buried in several layers of irrecoverable cultural shame because of her partner's indiscretion. This also, in turn, forever lost face for Ahmed's Japanese girlfriend because this girl was a friend of hers, too. It was quite the multicultural drama.

So why did we end up calling the paramedics? Passed out on the floor of the bathroom, it was Thierry's shaking and foaming at the mouth that made us feel we could not wait for him to sleep it off. We had to call.

The firemen were incredible. You could tell it was a big night for them and they were ready. Despite the time and location, they were there within 15 minutes. They did not even wait for the elevator and bolted up the four flights of stairs with their huge packs of gear.

I don't think they were in my apartment more than ten minutes. With one brief look at him, some checks for responses and a few well placed slaps on the cheeks, they assured us he would be fine. You could tell they had seen worse (not that I would like to have seen the other guys). They said they could take him in, but it would mean eight hours in the hospital that didn't necessarily need to be spent there.

Like people unexpectedly left with an adopted newborn, we halfway chased them down the hall asking for how to best take care of our new patient. Their recommendations are what led directly to me and Ahmed washing this guy down in my bathtub while the women tended to Thierry's former stomach contents, which were dripping down the walls and pooling on the floor.

Once we figured out he was going to be OK, I kept finding myself discreetly giggling at the ridiculous situation. The Japanese ladies were decidedly more solemn. You would think nothing could cure a shamed soul like cleaning up prolific piles of vomit, but this was some serious lost face for them. Luckily, I knew culturally I was off the hook on this one.

Thierry was also off the hook until his consciousness (sans memory) returned late the next day (whereupon he was castigated by his Japanese girlfriend perhaps from that point well into his next life). Up to that point, though, he slept like a baby while the rest of us were left to clean up the crime scene.

Once the chaos subsided, the one guest that tried to leave around 4 a.m. couldn't get a taxi, so we ended up somehow bedding down six people in my one-bedroom apartment.

We all gradually returned to life at varying paces. By the time we had a consensus of awake and coherent people, it was night again. As a result, the party ended up running something like 27 hours—a record for me!

CHAPTER 35

The Crimson Poobah Takes on Venice

As the Crimson Poobah glided into the glimmering water bathed in the quiet morning sun, I knew immediately I was plunging into one of the coolest experiences of my life. I was in Venice in a kayak.

I had dreamed about Venice since I was a child. My visions had been a Disney-like version of gondoliers, romantic canals and historic architecture all catering to throngs of tourists—but no actual inhabitants. I was delighted to learn how wrong I was.

I had mailed the Poobah, my inflatable kayak, to my hotel in Venice from Orleans, France. In Orleans several weeks earlier, I had paddled a section of the castle-ridden Loire River Valley with my other French brother-in-spirit Christophe, an actor friend of mine from my high school days in France who later joined me for the Oregon Bike Odyssey.

He and I had quite a challenge sorting out how to pack and ship the Poobah, but the good ol' Post Office turned out to be the best option. Even though it is a common thing to have something you mail arrive at its intended destination, it still seemed miraculous in this instance to have the Poobah there and waiting when I arrived at my hotel. The staff and some guests gave me curious looks as I shuttled the Poobah's various parts across the swank lobby and began assembling the craft on the sidewalk in front of the hotel, which luckily fronted a canal.

On the way back to my hotel that first night, I heard sounds of a rock band setting up emanating from a nearby church. Curious, I ducked my head in to see a poster in the entryway announcing a funk and blues concert that evening. Why not check it out, right?

I returned later to find an energetic chapel full of funk and fun which immediately put a huge smile on my face. With a horn section, tambourines and everything, this group of about ten locals dressed in retro clothes, boas and afro wigs were busting out great renditions of things like "Play that Funky Music White Boy". And they were good! This was a far flung corner of town and the audience was mostly locals, many of whom I sensed were friends or family of those on stage.

When I caught up with members of the band afterward, I learned they were all alumni of the same music school and this concert was a bit of a sendoff party for their guitar player who would be leaving. And in typical Venice form, once the band was done, they loaded up their gear in the band's boat and headed off to drop their instruments in a practice room before heading out for a drink.

These locals, who were about my age, had obviously grown up and prospered, even creatively, in this city. In many ways it was the perfect introduction to Venice because it shattered the preconceptions I came with. And through an interesting coincidence which came later the next day, this connection continued for the rest of my stay.

It was the morning after the concert that I first launched the Poobah into the waters of Venice. As I began exploring some of the tranquil backwaters, I could hear the city slowly coming to life: the sounds of breakfast dishes, showers and morning conversation. I wound around from alley to alley letting curiosity and the magnetism of the beauty around me be my guide.

On this inaugural trip I discovered another aspect of Venice not part of my original sanitized fantasy—the smell of some of the canals. Some of them reeked horrifically of sewage and other fowl substances. I spotted many unknown items drifting in the waters that the Office of Tourism is not likely to mention on a brochure.

People often ask how locals reacted to seeing me in my bright red kayak. It turns out that in a world where everyone is born, lives and dies using boats, one more boat is not a big deal. I caught the eye of more jealous tourists than locals.

Venice, while spectacularly impractical, is stunning to visit. The ancient city seems more designed to be navigated by boat, but you also get a neat perspective exploring by foot the vehicle-free, cobblestone streets, which are stitched together by an endless variety of charming old bridges.

Like my first trip to Australia in the dental business, I knew (correctly) I was at the top of my ophthalmic career on this trip. (Yes, I was actually working there!) The conference was in a stunning sculpture and fresco-drenched venue which was closed off to tourists for the event. Because everything else was full, my company booked me in an obscenely expensive hotel ($800+/night!), a former embassy in the quiet outskirts of town. It turned out to be a perfect location for me because they had a large closet right by the canal where I could store my kayak at night without deflating and folding it up.

I used the Poobah to deliver the booth to the conference location (saving an $80 water taxi ride). When I entered the conference hall to setup the booth, I was pleasantly surprised to bump into to the lead singer from the funk band of the night before. It turned out she was a part of the catering staff for the conference and was going to be working there for the next several days. This human connection to the city of Venice made my week that much richer. It was also humorous knowing the secret that this shy-looking girl wearing a formal catering uniform and serving coffee with the others can, on a different occasion, also get up on stage in a giant afro wig and wail on songs like "Mustang Sally".

It turned out she was also a student of art history. On the last day after the show closed down, she gave me a tour around town, offering a whole new perspective on the history and culture of Venice. A highlight was a stop we made at a chapel whose famous paintings she had studied in school but had never visited in person. She could describe their background in amazing detail.

Trying to describe the magical experience of paddling around Venice goes beyond my abilities as a writer and is something you should experience firsthand if you can. If you ever get a chance to go to Venice, with or without a kayak, GO!

90-Days' Notice: Part Two

It turns out I was a lucky soul that my landlord was unable to sell my apartment as he intended, because I could have been out on the streets of Paris. While three months ago I thought I would be heading to Beijing to work at the Olympics, my next life adventure has superseded that intention. You see, I have decided to become a barbecue salesman.

So why the shift? Soon after entering the eye company and becoming aware of some of the misguided philosophies and managers that lead it, it became clear I would not have a long future there. It wasn't a question of whether I would be leaving, but when and for what.

Even before I started with the eye company, I had begun talks with Ralph, the creator of Auspit®, an Australian outdoor rotisserie grilling system. I came across his unique product during my job search and thought "Wow, that really makes sense to me and I have never seen anything like it in the States or anywhere else for that matter." It wasn't being sold anywhere outside of Australia. And more importantly, it was delightfully more fun than dental or ophthalmic instrumentation. For me, Auspit® was the perfect combination of my love for the outdoors and cooking.

The conversation with Ralph had continued moving forward throughout my new employment. But seeing how the American economy had been tanking and how long it was taking to get the Auspit® business ready, instead of jumping ship I decided only recently to hang onto my day job and my life in Paris for a while longer (and luckily both were still available). Which allowed me to do things like have more parties with Ahmed...

CHAPTER 36

Partying with Parisian Thieves

It was picnic season in Paris. With all the splendid Parisian architecture and the green areas interspersed within, there are many ideal outdoor venues in the City of Lights to gather with friends to share a bottle (or several) of wine and the food which accompanies it. Most nights you can go to almost any particularly beautiful spot and find groups, sometimes many, many groups casually taking part in this rite of summer. If only there was a bathroom, just one, anywhere. But that is another story.

This particular Saturday night started off great. I was invited to a picnic party where there turned out to be a surprising fun mix of several usually non-overlapping groups of friends. The venue was on the Seine River at the point on Ile-St.-Louis facing the sunset. Nice, right?

Ahmed met me there and then called in an extra friend, Marc, for reinforcements right before we joined another already well-lubricated group of friends on the steps of the Sacré Coeur cathedral near the top of Montmartre—another prime picnic location. Marc gets a mention here, because he also played an important role in what came later.

This famished group, enjoying the magnificent night view overlooking Paris, was particularly pleased to see us as we had brought a tasty collection of leftovers from the picnic down by the river. Another bottle of wine or so later, it was getting near time for the metro to close, so all of us (myself included) left except Ahmed and Marc who decided to stay longer, finish off the last bottle of wine, and walk home from there.

Around 3 a.m., not long after I had gotten home, a now completely drunk Ahmed called me from Montmartre to say he and Marc had picked up two girls and they wanted to come over. This is the part where I should have said, "No." Unfortunately, at times my irresistible desire to try things that break me out of my norms (how do you think I ended up in Paris selling ophthalmic equipment?) leads me to trouble, and this was one such occasion. I had no intention of staying awake after they arrived, but it was impossible to explain this to Ahmed on the phone.

I think it was after 3:45 a.m. when they arrived. I helped settle them in and brought out some drinks (Ahmed already had a bottle of vodka in my freezer from a previous night out). Surveying the state of the clientele, I offered light pours on the drinks. Aside from the oddity that these young girls would so easily decide to come to a stranger's house with these guys, everything seemed to going fine. (I had already hidden most of my easily portable valuables before they arrived.) And with that, around 4:30 a.m. I quietly slipped away to my bedroom to try and get some sleep.

From what I could hear through the wall, the four of them proceeded to drink even more, get into various intoxicated arguments, etc. At the point where the conversation crescendoed to an excited peak, I heard what sounded like Marc (who I believe instigated much of this whole event) walking out the door without saying goodbye to anyone. Things calmed down quickly after that.

When I ducked out later to use the bathroom, I saw Ahmed very asleep in the recliner chair, one girl half asleep on the sofa and one surfing the Internet on my computer and no Marc. It was 5 a.m. The girl on the computer was looking up train schedules and said there would be a train at around 5:30 a.m. This is the point where I should have asked them to leave and wait for the train elsewhere, but 5 a.m. is not a safe time of day for two young women to be wandering around my neighborhood.

The awake girl went to lay down with her friend. After straightening up a bit (and taking a few pictures of the future crime scene) I returned to my room to lay down as well. It didn't make much sense that this girl would lay down to nap with the intention of leaving 20 minutes later, so not trusting them, I decided to not go to sleep until they left.

When they did leave, they did it quietly. I almost rushed up to look out the window where they went, but since I had not heard anything unusual, I got up more slowly and surveyed the living room for anything missing or out of place. Nothing registered, so being ready to sleep at this point I went back to bed and did just that.

When Ahmed woke up in the morning, he discovered his cell phone and metro pass had been taken from his pants pocket. Crazy, huh?

It wasn't until much later in the day that I realized these girls had also walked out with a number of the collectables decorating my apartment, mementos I had gathered from around the globe. Coasters from Senegal, a large lacquer box from Myanmar and some other decorative things from Bali that would be hard to put a price on beyond sentimental value.

While I have to say I felt bad for Ahmed, I also chalked up his loss as the price to pay for being such a dumbass. That sense of justice seemed to melt away when I realized I had paid my own price, although I probably deserved it as much as he did for letting all this happen. I am still bitter, because (aside from my displeasure at my loss of sleep and belongings) not only did I host them in my home and make sure they had blankets to stay warm, etc., I was looking out for them by not kicking them out.

Live and learn. I think I am going to have to chalk this one up as having paid a stupidity tax. Can you get a rebate for that?

90-Days' Notice: The Conclusion

Okay, so I mentioned I was working on starting up an Australian BBQ rotisserie distribution company in the US and that I was considering pulling up stakes in Paris and heading for the US by October. Well, that didn't happen—at least for the moment. A combination of the wheels falling off the American economy and the overly slow development of my BBQ business caused me to err on the side of caution and stay put for the time being. That, plus an ever-widening chorus of friends and family took it upon themselves to write me in ALL CAPS—"DON'T QUIT YOUR DAY JOB!"

I hear you! I can say that one advantage of my situation in Europe is that I could work a full day at my day job, then turn around and put in a full shift at my BBQ night job—all without leaving my office/living room— it was a workaholic's dream!

Salt Lake City
Sebastopol
Los Angeles
USA

CHAPTER 37

Introducing...Jonny Rotisserie!

Launching Auspit® North America in Utah

I can't say I have ever had a "vacation" like this one. I blew most of my day job's annual leave in order to go back to the States for an intense two weeks to launch Auspit® at a trade show.

My soon-to-be Australian business partner Ralph flew in for the occasion. Picking him up at the airport in Los Angeles, the Road Trip was officially underway.

On a regular day, Ralph smokes hand-rolled cigarettes almost faster than he can roll them. The guy is a chimney. Our road trip was, thus, a stop/start affair, because on home turf in the U.S. I invoked my No-Smoking policy in the car. We stopped a lot. I mean, a LOT.

With Ralph in tow, we had our share of Crocodile Dundee moments. In Road Trip Mode, during our many stops for whatever, plus an inevitable smoke break, Ralph had a peculiar habit of walking around barefoot whenever he got out of the car. He did this even in the grimiest of gas stations. He also had an uncanny ability to go mix with the locals. In the various campgrounds, hotels, or just about anywhere we passed through along the way, Ralph would come back with at least one or two prospective Auspit® customers, or some other interesting story.

The Outdoor Retailer show in Salt Lake City is preceded by its affiliated "Outdoor Demo" at a lake in the mountains north of the city. This event offers a relaxed atmosphere where buyers have a chance to try paddle equipment on the lake and see other equipment set up in an outdoor environment.

On the way to the Outdoor Demo, in addition to some last-minute shopping in Salt Lake City (for important things like the booth canopy, firewood and food to cook), we had to stop at the Health Department in Ogden so I could take a Food Handler's test to be properly licensed to prepare food and offer samples. I was a bit stressed knowing that if I failed the test, we could not cook. In the end I nailed it, and off we went up in the mountains at warp speed to prep the booth for the show that was scheduled to start in a couple hours.

Once there, in the midst of the scramble to set up the fire pit and the food prep areas, I paused and noticed that despite the car being mostly emptied at this point, there was something important missing: the booth canopy. I grabbed Ralph and we both gazed longingly into the back of it in hopes of seeing something that clearly wasn't there. Oh dang.

We immediately divided and conquered, with Ralph working on fire building and food prep, while I went barreling back down the mountain in search of the closest Wal-Mart, which would hopefully have a canopy like the one we had purchased earlier in Salt Lake (and turns out had left at the cash register ...um...doh).

The show had already officially started when I arrived with our second new canopy. I saw the guys next door glancing at us like we were the idiots that we obviously were. Later, though, once the food was cooking and the smells started drifting around, we made fast friends with these show veterans and we were glad to be each other's neighbors.

Once we were up and running, the reaction from passersby was fun to watch. Most everyone came by for a closer look and the comments we heard were along the lines of "that is cool!" and "awesome!" No one had seen anything like it.

Unfortunately, this was one of the few bright spots for the remainder of the show. Following the Outdoor Demo we rushed back to Salt Lake City to set up for the main show, which started the next morning. Most companies that exhibit at the Outdoor Demo have a separate tradeshow team which sets up the Salt Lake booth simultaneously. But not us (one day...). In many businesses, the mantra is Location! Location! Location! and that could not have been more true in this case. As new exhibitors at the indoor show—we were placed in a distant overflow annex called the ESA Arena (home of the Utah Jazz) which we soon took to calling the East Siberia Area. While the main hall was flooded with attendees, in our area you could have streaked down the aisle naked—or even murdered someone—and there would have been no witnesses. It was eerily quiet.

After the show, on the way to the Pacific coast, we watched the temperature climb to 105 degrees as we descended from Lake Tahoe into the desert valley, and then watched the temperature plunge to the low 40's as we arrived at the fogged-in coastline. California is amazing that way.

Our trip coincided nicely with the timing of the marriage of my friends Evan and Sally. I knew this fun couple from my "orthodontics days" in Ashiya, Japan, and now they were getting married in Northern California, propitiously timed right between the Salt Lake show and Ralph's departure from LA.

They decided to tie the knot surrounded by redwoods close to Evan's hometown Sebastopol. The setting was natural and picturesque. What does not show up in the lovely photos of the peaceful arboreal scene, however, is that there was a military air show being conducted nearby at the time of the ceremony, so you had the sounds of F-16s roaring overhead from time to time loud to the point of drowning out conversations. On top of that, some type of animal had decided to die close to the park and prankishly reveal its odor, but not its location. The wedding coordinators couldn't find it, so from time to time you would get an almost-visible waft of 'dead something' drift through. The minister made some funny comments about both. The wedding still turned out beautiful.

While we had been working on it throughout the trip, Ralph and I were still in the final throes of contract revisions when the wedding day had rolled around. We made the final edits and printed it out at the local library before rushing to the ceremony. We took the time before and after the ceremony to give a final thorough read-through of our agreement. By the time Evan and Sally were fully married and most of the way through the reception picnic, we were ready.

I asked Sally and Evan to join us for a moment to help participate in our own union ceremony. There was a brief awkward moment when Sally—not appraised of the details of my connection to Ralph—thought we were having an impromptu gay wedding. This was California after all. Once we cleared up it was just a business contract and we wanted them be our witnesses, we all had a laugh. With our willing witnesses standing by, it was time.

Ralph and I share a love of Maker's Mark whisky and we even had a clause in the contract that promised him a bottle of it as part of him coming over for this US visit. So with a whirling dervish series of signatures, a toast of Maker's Mark, a flood of French champagne and a rush of merriment, I was officially the exclusive Auspit® distributor for North America.

With the weight of the contract blissfully off our minds, Ralph and I headed out the next morning knowing we had a full day's drive to get him to LA for his departure flight. My No Smoking in the Car rule mostly held up until that last day when I was flooring it to get Ralph to the airport in time for his plane, and stopping to smoke was no longer an option. While I had to stay stone cold sober, I made a successful attempt at getting Ralph hammered before putting him on the plane back to Australia.

At some point in the final stretch, when passing through Malibu, an unusual cigarette smell drifted over despite Ralph's continued attempts to keep the smoke from coming inside. Even though at that point it was going to be touch and go for him making his flight, I almost slammed on the brakes to get Ralph out of the car when I realized he had lit up a celebratory doobie. I guess he had gotten it from one of his campground buddies along the way. So there I was in the dark with barefoot Ralph as he lit up on the side of the Pacific Coast Highway while traffic rushed by and the minutes ticked away. In the end, he made his flight check in time with few minutes to spare. Phew.

Jonny Rotisserie makes his national TV debut!

While bouncing all over Europe for my "day job" as I came to call it, I was burning the midnight oil getting Auspit® off the ground in the U.S. I blew all my vacation days to fly back to the States for the launch in Utah plus trade shows in Orlando and NYC on two other trips. I was working nights. I was working through weekends. It was ridiculous.

Oh…and I moved. Twice. The 90-Day Notice became reality when the landlord sold the apartment and I had to clear out rather abruptly. Instead of relocating to another apartment in Paris for what would inevitably be the first of two moves, with the help of Ahmed, his girlfriend and a borrowed truck I retreated to the beautiful calm of the Alps where I rejoined my old host family and rented the apartment above their chalet in St. Gervais. Being surrounded by the perversely picturesque alpine scenery and snow-capped green mountains was truly a breath of fresh air after Paris.

Knowing my work-focused lifestyle back in the capital city, my actor friend Christophe had aptly described me as "the Hermit of Paris". My move to St. Gervais was a refreshing change of pace—from being my mostly secluded self to one who shared most meals with his former host family. It was great to reconnect both with them and with that gorgeous part of the world.

My second move was a full return to the U.S.. At my day job, sales were good, travel was good and pay was decent. While I would not have minded continuing on with my dual occupation status a bit longer, the people at my American HQ made some unthinkable decisions and I resigned the day I learned of them. Within three weeks I left the French Alps and was back on terra firma Americana, diving into the trade show circuit full time.

The Lounge

But first...let me introduce you to my new home, The Lounge. I had an entire continent to cover to get the word out about Auspit®. Instead of renting out an apartment that would have remained empty much of the year, at the end of September I galvanized my wandering lifestyle by acquiring the penultimate vagabond vehicle: I bought an RV. The Lounge, a 24-footer, became my new official home office. The trailer I pull behind it carries all my show supplies and supplements my main warehouse in Los Angeles. Those who know me well know I am a music junkie, which is why the first thing I did was upgrade to a kicking stereo system, which contributed to The Lounge's eventual name. I love The Lounge. You can't beat the comfort and convenience it provides on the road. My packing and unpacking has decreased significantly, and it has opened up some interesting new ways to explore the country.

As part of getting the word out about Auspit®, the product and I (which are inseparable at times) got in a bunch of magazine and TV shows, the biggest deal of which was getting on national TV. I was on HGTV (unfortunately) right smack in the middle of the Oscars. On the show "RV 2010" I appeared in a segment called "Top 10 Products of 2010". The product I represent, Auspit®...was #4! Boy did that ever help sales! I use "Jonny Rotisserie" as my main meat-handling pen name on the Internet and most anytime when promoting Auspit®. My official title? "Chief Kangaroo".

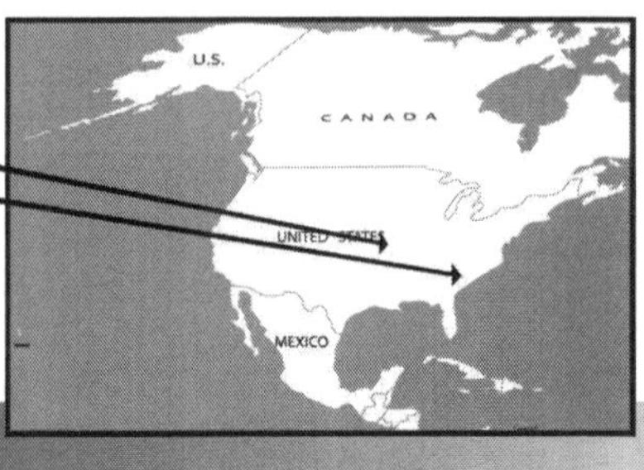

CHAPTER 38

My Butt's on Fire!

Jonny Rotisserie at the American Royal

So there I am, Jonny Rotisserie, wandering around North America in my trusty RV, *The Lounge,* trying to figure out how to sell Australian rotisseries in a myriad of places ranging from NASCAR races to hunting shows to RV conventions.

I also ventured into the world of barbecue competitions.

The American Royal in Kansas City is the world's largest BBQ competition and possibly the largest cooking contest in the world. 500 teams compete for over $50,000 in total prize money. Elite professional BBQ teams come from around the country with elaborate custom-built cooking trailers and sophisticated, even computer-controlled barbecuing contraptions. It's not the kind of venue in which one would usually show up to compete with simple rotisseries over open fire pits (my approach) and anticipate getting anything other than guffaws of laughter from competitors and spectators alike.

"The Royal" as it is referred to, is a big deal and something I had been building up to since June when I decided I should give the world of competitive BBQ a try. I suppose you didn't hear how my first competition went? Let's just say it did not inspire confidence. Let's segue back to that sunny June day in South Carolina…

(cue the time blur sequence)

Jonny Rotisserie's First BBQ Competition

As a general rule of thumb, you know you are not putting your best foot forward at a cooking competition when 1) one of your dishes catches on fire and 2) the category you place dead last in was not the dish that caught on fire.

This, my competitive debut, took place in Saluda, South Carolina which was hosting its first "Saluda Smokin' BBQ Competition." The categories were "ribs" and "pulled pork." As pulled pork is a southern staple and I had never prepared it before, I almost only entered the ribs category. Then I decided since I was going to be there and cooking anyway, I might as well give both a go.

This event was probably the first time an Auspit® (the rotisseries I sell) was used at any BBQ competition worldwide. Most BBQ competitors come to these events as a team, often with an entire trailer/kitchen dedicated to their cooking apparatuses, some of which are so robust they look like they must have military applications.

Contrast that to me cooking with a couple spits over a beat up little open fire pit. I am convinced that one day my setup will strike fear into the hearts of competitors, but this was not that day. In fact, if you asked my neighbors for their reaction to my performance, more likely you would have set them off laughing uncontrollably, snorting beer through their noses.

My day started off early, but not nearly as early as some. Most of the teams start their cooking the night before and have people stay awake all night to monitor and maintain their cooking temperatures. I am not good at all nighters and thus am motivated to find a way to succeed without cooking all night. I know there are people that win without doing it.

So I stumbled out of my RV, *The Lounge* at 5 a.m. (to the heckles of neighbors saying they were wondering when I was going to finally get up and get around to cooking) to get my fire started and put my Boston butts on by about 6 a.m. This is when my troubles began.

The competition was being held on the outfield of a baseball diamond. It had beautiful grass and I knew (from experience) my fire pit would burn a hole in it, so I borrowed cinder blocks from the hospitable organizers to raise my pit off the ground. The problem was that my rotisseries are supported on a post which stakes into the ground. You can raise and lower the spit, but only up to the top of the support post. The cinder blocks were thick, bringing the heat source right up under my rotisserie. There was nowhere higher to go on the support post to raise the spit away from the heat and thus lower the cooking temperature. This was a problem.

My hot hickory wood fire would have been perfect in a larger or lower fire pit, but mine wasn't either of these. I had two Boston butts totaling about 16 pounds, which were to become my pulled pork. These heavier pieces of meat are meant to be lovingly smoked over many hours.

Instead, when I set the meat out over my fire, the intense heat basically scorched it, even blackening some areas. I was horrified! This was not the way to kick off an eight-hour "low and slow" cooking session. While searing had the potential to seal in the juices, it has the disadvantage of blocking out all the delicate smoky flavors you try and infuse into this kind of meat, which is half the point in cooking it slow to begin with.

Not to mention it looked awful. With the continued overly high heat, soon there was a thick burnt crust encasing both of my butts. They looked like two rotating volcanic rocks, with juices percolating to the surface through holes that erupted through the crust.

My fire pit was rickety. In being transported in my show trailer, the screws are perpetually vibrating off and getting lost and I was down to half of the number meant to be holding it together. Onlookers asked politely if it was strategic or accidental that it leaned heavily to one side and if it was meant to be adjustable since it wobbled badly any time I repositioned the wood inside it. Thankfully a nice local couple was kind enough to run home and bring me some smaller bricks to donate to my cause. This brought the fire height down to a much more manageable level.

The scheduled turn-in time for the ribs judging was 12:45 p.m. so I put them on around 9:30 a.m. to allow for ample slow cooking. The way I usually do ribs on a spit is by threading them like a worm on a hook, with skewers on either end to keep them in place. Up to now, I had mostly done beef ribs but they had turned out phenomenally delicious, so I was coming into this category brimming with confidence. I even decided to go a bit extreme with my spices, using only salt, pepper and garlic powder so the flavor of the meat and the smoke I was using would stand out rather than a bunch of slathered on sauce. I would later learn this was pure rookie foolishness all on its own.

I had a few BBQ mentors at this point and I consulted heavily with one of them in Montana about the burnt pork butt crisis, sending him cell phone pictures of the carnage. I am going to go ahead and blame my subsequent rib debacle on him, although in the post-game autopsy he astutely pointed out that while I had latched onto the part about him saying "you can't overheat ribs", in that same breath he did also add, "but you can overcook them".

Truth aside, in the heat of the battle, only that first part was echoing in my head as I approached the final stretch to the turn-in deadline. My ribs were looking good, but I wanted to try and take them to the next level of tenderness, so I dropped them right down near the fire and let them have all the heat that a red hot bed of hickory coals can muster.

When I took them off, the ribs looked great. It was when I went to cut them that I knew I was in trouble. Mind you I have a *very* good knife. My ribs usually have a crispy bite-through skin to them and the meat is usually nice and tender. Here, to my horror, the meat collapsed off the bones into a stiff, sinewy pile. WAY overcooked.

There was no good way to cut them into the eight even pieces the judges were expecting. In fact, the ribs I submitted looked like they had been cut by a blind man with a chainsaw. This was going to be the historic first ever Auspit®-cooked plate submitted for a cooking competition, and it was tough as shoe leather and a plain laughable presentation. A voice was telling me to not even turn it in, but then knowing this competition was meant to be an exercise in learning/humility anyway, I thought, well, might as well see what they say.

I would learn later that the judges agreed with me wholeheartedly. With a rousing 43 points, less than half the score of the guy who won, my first dish placed dead last in a field of about 14 teams. I'd say "ouch", but with the knowingly pathetic entry I submitted it would be like getting upset when your dog wins an Ugliest Dog competition.

So after submitting the atrocious ribs, I was back to my rotating black rocks. With only one hour before turn-in, I realized my efforts to slow down their cooking had been too successful. I had wrapped the butts in foil to lessen the direct heat exposure (and to shield them from the view of visitors).

To get to pulled pork consistency, you want to get the internal temperature to around 200-205F degrees. While at one point sections of my butts had reached around 190 or more, I slowed them down because I still had a long ways to go at that point. Now, however, there were sections that measured as low as 160 degrees, which is below the temperature pork is even considered safe to eat. Fears of the impressions of passersby now cast aside, I removed the foil and cranked up the heat full throttle.

It was in this final stretch to the turn-in deadline that my pork butts burst into flames. The heat was too much too fast. I swung them off the fire, which is usually enough to quiet any flame, but these butts were on fire with the intensity that they seemed ready to be run in their own meat torch relay. I had to pour water on them to put them out.

My neighboring fellow competitors had to love the entertainment value generated from my one-ring circus. It was also a good confidence booster for them knowing they could drop their entry on the ground on the way to the judges table and they would still at least beat me.

Anyway, I shifted my extinguished meat back over the calmed fire, but the meat was still hot to the point that flames quickly erupted once more before finally returning to a benign rotation. This was one of those face-in-the-hands, seated moments where you pause and try and reflect on how to salvage the situation. Despite the pyrotechnics, the internal temperature never got back up to where it needed to be. Still, I felt I could torture my meat no more, so I pulled it off, wrapped it in foil, stuck it in an empty cooler and allowed it to rest for about 20 minutes before I was to attempt the pulled pork preparations.

It was like a nervous Christmas morning as I began taking my competition entry out and unwrapping its thick burnt crust. I was relieved to see the inside looked just fine. It was moist and the pork pulled apart nicely. The flavor was okay, but would definitely need some dressing up, especially since the early searing had blocked much of the smoky flavor it should have had by this point.

As if there wasn't enough drama already, with only minutes remaining to turn in my entry, the skies opened up out of nowhere and began to dump down rain in buckets. I was mostly under a pop-up tent, but everything around me was still getting soaked. My entry box filled up with enough water that I had to dump it out before putting the meat in.

Once all was said and done, the flavor and texture were decent enough that at least I did not cringe when I ran through the downpour to turn it in, although I had serious doubts about how my meat would stack up to the work of Southern pulled pork veterans.

The 15-minute storm-shower-from-nowhere vanished as fast as it appeared. My confidence improved after people started coming by for samples and the sun returned to smile upon us. As part of the event, people bought sampling tickets and came around to try the pulled pork the teams cooked. Maybe they were just being polite, but the tasters consistently said they put mine in the top three out of what they tried, remarking it was the moistest.

There is almost always a gap between what "people" vote for and what "judges" vote for, but I took their comments at least as an indicator of something less than total failure. In saying that, however, the woman who ultimately won the People's Choice award was my neighbor, who—something that would elicit loud unbelieving guffaws from any competitive barbequer—cooked her stuff in an electric Crockpot (connected to a noisy generator) and it was more sauce than meat.

Ultimately I took a somewhat respectable sixth place in this category, and—accounting for the adversity factor—I am going to put a mental trophy on the shelf for this one, my first pulled pork.

(cue the time blur sequence again. Add special effect sound of choice)

OK, so after that confidence builder and a couple more like it, we return to our story about THE ROYAL in Kansas City…

My Kansas City setup was a huge upgrade compared to prior competitions. On the cooking front, I went from one solitary dilapidated fire pit to four custom hand-carved steel fire pits which I had custom made on a farm an hour north of KC. On the personnel side, Ryan—a BBQ wizard and friend in the world of BBQ (and my phone-in coach in the above story)—flew in from Montana to round out the team. Plus we had some Carolinian cameos as well.

While most people show up with a tight plan in place on how they will be cooking for the competition, Ryan and I still had a world of things to sort out in terms of cooking times, temperatures and recipes. Before getting too deep into the whole cooking scene, though, there was a party of epic proportions to take on.

The World Famous American Royal Friday Night Party

Even without the party, our location was not exactly tranquil. We were sandwiched between the main garbage dumpsters—which had an endless array of trucks slamming things into them—and a stretch of five lines of train tracks, the closest of which passing about ten feet from my bed in *The Lounge.* At some points it would have been more peaceful in the front row of a Metallica concert.

The Friday night social scene is notorious for its fervor as the complex fills with tens of thousands of people, all of whom liquidate into one giant well-lubricated party. We were right at the entry point for what many people refer to as "the Dark Side". It is home to the "non-invited" competitors who are renowned for their partying zest. To be honest, it was a little intimidating seeing that some people were ordering six-foot high cattle guard fences to protect their cook areas from the drunken hordes (or to keep them inside their space). That said, seeing things like a disco ball and chandeliers being hung from the highway overpass that cut through the place, I wanted to get out and explore. But once the night got going we were completely slammed with onlookers, and ultimately I was there to sell stuff.

Being one of the highlights on their annual social calendar, my fire pit designers Gary and Kathy come into town from their countryside ranch for this event most every year. For this important social occasion, Gary upgraded his signature overalls with a Hawaiian shirt, sunglasses, a headband and a large flower lapel. With long hair, a long beard, a whisky flask in one pocket and cigarettes tucked into many of the others, he was the charismatic leader of his intoxicated flock. This year they also brought their friend/ work associate "Wally".

(Left to Right) Gary, Ryan and Wally examining the newly arrived fire pits

I had given Wally, a friend of the bottle, a ride home the night I visited the farm where the pits were being made. This was his first visit to the city for this party and he wasn't about to not make the most of it. More than just Wally, stumbling was becoming the primary mode of movement for the masses as the evening progressed.

Even on a normal day, it is not uncommon for people to ask/beg me for samples, because admittedly the food looks and smells mighty tasty when it is out spinning on the spit. That asking can become particularly insistent when the beer kicks in. At more than one event I have had people pull out knives and carve off some meat while my back was turned.

Wally has a big heart and did all he could to try and rustle up business for his friends' fire pits and my rotisseries. When not drifting around to the many parties raging around us, he split his time between trying to generate sales and sipping many beverages.

While possibly not an ideal company representative, Wally seemed to be having fun talking with potential customers, so I went laissez-faire and worried about other things. However, when one gal insistently asked for samples of the food, I felt the thud of my jaw bouncing on the pavement when I heard Wally say he'd give her samples in exchange for something that rhymes with "a grow blob". Aside from being mortified, I thought, "How did he come out with that?"

Ryan died laughing the next day when I mentioned this incident. It seems he had been the instigator behind it. Apparently earlier on Friday, Wally had exchanged one of his beers for $3 and a kiss on the cheek—both of which he got. Ryan suggested he was shooting too low, saying he should ask for more. Wally clearly had taken the message to heart.

Saturday

Saturday, South Carolina high school friends John and Julia were coincidentally in town for a law conference and were crazy enough to let themselves be talked into helping with my fiasco. These guys did an impressive job of rolling up their sleeves and diving into the thick of it. Not bad for folks who usually spend most of their days doing more lawyerly things. I was thankful to have them on the team.

With the intent of showing Auspit®'s versatility, I had signed up for most every cooking category on the docket. On top of still trying to figure out our cooking strategies and recipes for the contest, Ryan and I were being overwhelmed with spectators wanting to talk to us about Auspit® and the fire pits. So I put John and Julia in charge of two of the main dishes up until the point they had to run catch their flight back to Atlanta. I am not sure how we would have gotten through it without them jumping into the fray. I only wished they could have stayed the whole time because in some ways, we didn't get through it all as evidenced by...

The Dessert Debacle and Walk of Shame

Ryan and I conceived a brilliant dessert to submit. Brilliant—at least in theory: we had never tried preparing it. It was Bananas Foster on a caramel-chocolate cookie and topped with whipped cream and a flourish of garnishes and sauces. That all sounded beautiful, delicious and well-conceived in our minds—before we were sleep deprived and under the gun in terms of time.

I had signed up to be part of the American Royal official tour, where they bring groups of people by to observe and get presentations from the cooks in action. Earlier in the day when they came by, we already knew we were at risk of missing deadlines for the three dishes we were turning in that day. So I asked the tour group to come back later, anytime after the last turn-in: dessert.

Fast forward to the dessert turn-in. You have a ten minute window to turn-in your entry or you are disqualified. At the moment the dessert turn-in window began, our dish was still in complete disarray. Ryan and I were inside *The Lounge* fighting about raspberry and whipped cream placement and what to do with the Nutella-bourbon chocolate sauce which was supposed to be drizzled on but instead was almost solid in its consistency.

It was over a three-minute walk to the turn-in location, and at two and a half minutes before the final deadline we were still struggling to decide what to do with the mint leaves and powdered sugar. It was also at this point that I noticed the tour group had returned and was peering around our setup. Not something I had time to think about.

At The Royal, dessert is the one category you are not required to turn in enclosed in an anonymous Styrofoam box, but you do have to turn in your numbered box with it for tracking purposes. Our colorful ceramic serving plate would not fit into the box so I had to carry the two items separately.

With less than two minutes left, I turned to the door knowing I was going to have to sprint to make it in time. The next 120 seconds switched to extreme slow motion in my mind. As I reached for the door, I hear Ryan calling out, "waaaatch oooout for the wiiiiind!" Before arriving at the "d", I was already part way out the door and being buffeted by an intense blustering wind. I don't think I made it two paces before all the mint and powdered sugar were whipped off the plate. I glanced up to the wide-eyed tour group while spinning around to yell at Ryan, "briiing mooore miiint!"

Not breaking my stride, I sprinted past the group and turned into the headwind towards the turn-in area. I was going Heisman Trophy style with the Styrofoam box tucked under one arm and the plate outstretched in the other hand. The wind was so strong, though, it literally ripped the box out of my hand and flew away behind me and past the aghast tour group. One of them was heroic enough to chase down my escaping turn-in box and stomp on it before it could go another 20 yards in the wrong direction. Once they baton-passed it to me, I ran as fast as my legs could carry me, trying to hold onto the box—which was still shredding in the wind—while also trying to activate ancient waitering days' muscle memory to keep our entry intact as Ryan chased me down the street with replacement mint.

The next thing I remember was arriving panicked at the turn-in area, heading upstream in a river of people that had already turned in their dishes. In a blurred mix of me frantically trying to re-plate the dish while simultaneously figure out where we were supposed to turn it in, one of the judges walked towards me with a stern face holding up an outstretched clock, saying that the time had expired and they would not accept any more entries. We were disqualified. We had missed it by seven seconds.

Exasperated, I thought about leaving the dish anyway and walking away, but then I thought, "Why should I let THEM eat it?" Thus began our walk of shame back to our cook site. Seeing us carrying our dish back in hand (as a sad hymn played in the background of my head) people shook their heads and gave us their condolences. They all knew we had been DQed.

Upon returning to our spot, the tour group was still there, I think still talking about what had just unfolded in front of them. They ended up being the direct beneficiaries of our disqualification as we gave them most of the Bananas Foster. They loved it. It was cathartic sharing it with them and then getting back on the horse to tell them about our cooking setup.

Ryan sadly examining the dilapidated remains of our disqualified dessert

Luckily the Saturday events are a wash as they do not affect the scores for the main competition on Sunday.

Ryan and I spent much of Friday and Saturday debating how we were going to cook the chicken. Considering many options, we settled on cooking whole chickens and then cutting off the best parts—most likely the thighs—to turn in. Saturday night, however, we got caught up in a potluck party and by the time we realized it, the place to buy the chickens was closed. Oops. At that point we were committed to using what I already had in the fridge, cooking pre-cut thighs, something I had never attempted on the rotisserie. Gulp.

Sunday - Game Day

The day of the main competition was blessedly calm. There was a lot less foot traffic, there was a lot less wind, and the sun was out. It was a great day to BBQ. Our cook session had its stressful moments, but overall all four of the main meat categories—beef brisket, pork, chicken and ribs—went pretty smoothly.

Once we handed in our final turn-in at 1:30 p.m., I felt a huge weight lifted off my shoulders. Between working out the logistics, and figuring out what and how to cook, arriving to this point had been stressful. Now that we were done, looking around our cook site, it looked like a bomb had gone off in a restaurant kitchen, blowing off the walls. Instead of touching any of it, Ryan and I sat down, had a drink (possibly several) and a good laugh about the whole experience. It was the first time I felt relaxed all weekend. I think we meant to get everything cleaned up and packed away before the awards ceremony a couple hours later, but somehow little of that was accomplished. (I know this only by having seen some embarrassing video footage from later in the day.)

Our chicken entry

The Awards Ceremony

BBQ Awards ceremonies were already a practiced exercise in humility for me. I would applaud the winners and wait for my scores, which they pass out at the end, to see if I took last place or not. Here was no different.

In terms of chances of winning, The Royal offers the worst odds in BBQ. There were 499 teams. About 130 of those are invited because they had been Grand Champion at another competition(s) during the year—the best of the best competing with the most advanced barbecuing equipment around. My goal for the competition was to not place in the bottom 50 in any one category, and to not finish in the bottom 100 overall. These goals would appear extremely ambitious had you seen any of my earlier results.

Once the awards ceremony was over, it was time for Judgment Day. When I got a copy of the score sheet—knowing my usual place—I started looking through the sheets starting from the back. Up to now, it had been a quick study as I had never been further than sixth from the bottom. Here, I flipped through page after page without seeing my name. A voice of reason in my head politely suggested I go back to the end and start over since surely I had missed it.

And then I saw it: Jonny Rotisserie and the Auspiteers: #224. I had to pause and reread this several times. And then I erupted. And I mean erupted. Amidst my shouting and hugging the people around me, I overheard voices saying, "You'd think he won the whole thing." And I hadn't even reread my score carefully because someone nearby soon pointed out it wasn't 224, it was actually 223. 223!! Posts on a popular competition BBQ forum later mentioned people's appreciation at seeing "that kind of unbridled joy".

The Drunken Victory Lap

"Sober" is not a word I would have used to describe myself, even at the beginning of the awards ceremony. After finishing in the top half of the pile at the world's biggest BBQ contest, this descriptor was not going to be returning any time that night. In cooking our non-traditional way, we were trying to show what could be accomplished with my simple outdoor rotisseries. Placing in the very respectable top half was a statement indeed, meriting some serious celebrating.

And I hadn't even gotten the best news yet.

When trying to figure out where my teammate was, I got the text, "Meet at *The Lounge*... SHOTTZ!!!"

When I returned to the site with arms raised in triumph, Ryan called out, "Hey did you see our score in chicken?"

"Nope"

Without saying a word, he handed me the sheets where I discovered our team name was on the very front page. We were 31st place. 31st. Out of 500 teams. 31st!

I "lost it."

If memory serves me correctly, Ryan and friends picked me up off the ground where I was rolling around shouting "I can't believe it!" I'm pretty sure I continued shouting that same refrain (plus "223!!") for the next several hours as Ryan and I made our victory lap, which took the rest of the evening as we visited friends, colleagues and strangers around the sprawling venue, celebrating as one should on such a magnificent occasion.

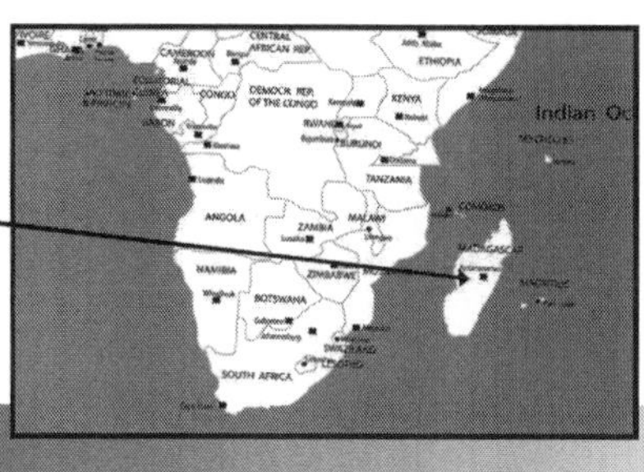

CHAPTER 39

It's a Mad, Mad, Mad, Madagascar World!

Not on my list of New Year's resolutions this year was to have copious amounts of blood gushing from my head. Yet by the second day of the New Year, there in a Madagascar rainforest, that is exactly what was happening. But I am skipping ahead…

With its exotic, eye-popping flora and fauna, the island nation of Madagascar had always been a dream destination for me. It was upgraded to my "must visit" list ever since my friend Dave Ingham moved there with his family to be missionaries 15 years earlier. Previous attempts to get there failed due to a lack of money and/or time, but at last the stars aligned for me. My time had come.

Despite having a fairly robust travel resume at this point, every trip I take presents some kind of new wrinkle. My trip to Madagascar offered a few firsts, even before leaving the United States. It started with something as seemingly simple as parking. While it seems like a benign challenge, it was the first time I'd left a vehicle at an airport for more than a couple days. The ordinary challenges of airport parking are compounded when trying to find a spot for something like *The Lounge* my 25-feet long,10-feet tall RV. For starters, it doesn't fit into any of the covered garages. Additionally, I was attempting this at the Los Angeles airport during the peak Christmas vacation period. Knowing this could be a tall order—in a rare move for me—I called over a week ahead to reserve a spot.

With the stress of an impending international departure already on my shoulders, imagine my angst upon arriving at my selected parking lot only to have this one critical piece of the departure puzzle yanked away from me. The people there told me they couldn't find my reservation and they were full (despite the fact I had a confirmation number)...but they could still somehow find a way for me to stay there if I paid double the amount I had reserved it for.

Travelling to Africa, one expects a healthy dose of nefarious dealings, but you don't expect them to begin before you leave American shores. Considering that most of my life's belongings were represented in *The Lounge*, this violation of trust was a deal breaker. So, I had to frantically find a place from scratch with only a couple hours before my flight was scheduled to leave. Time was ticking fast.

I tried calling maybe eight different places before finally reaching someone who would take me in. The place *The Lounge* ended up was not ideal, but it had to do or I was certain to miss my flight. In an alley between two covered parking garages, I left *The Lounge* in a spot clearly marked by a "No Parking. All Vehicles Will Be Towed" sign. Would you sleep easy even though the Afghani lot owner swore up and down it would be fine? Never mind that this was right in the midst of the U.S. invasion of Afghanistan. It was a risk I decided to take.

Once I got in the actual airport, everything went much smoother. I was using my mileage points to travel and the only seats available were in business class, so that is what I took. For a journey like this one, where I had four flights totaling over 24 hours of flying time, plus a seven-hour layover in London, the upgrade from my usual back-of-the-bus surroundings felt well worth it. Also, just a couple days prior to my flight, that terrorist idiot had tried to blow up a plane with a bomb stuffed in his underwear, so security was on high alert. Being able to check in via business class probably made the difference between making my flight and not.

I encountered another traveling first after arriving flustered at the check in counter, then stopping to giggle when I realized I did not know how to say the name of my destination. "Antananarivo" doesn't exactly roll off the tongue like "Paris". Sheepishly, I had to show the agent the printed reservation to communicate it correctly. Wow, this guy is prepared!

I was met at the "Tana" airport—as locals thankfully call the unpronounceable Madagascar capital—by Samid, a charming young man my hosts, the Inghams, had sent to meet me because they were out of town the afternoon I arrived. Samid made the innocent mistake of negotiating with the taxi driver *after* he came out with me the *vazaha* ("foreigner") and he was flabbergasted by the price the driver insisted on, especially since we were only going to a place a couple kilometers away. Welcome to Africa for outsiders!

We bumped down the red dirt road to the house where my friends live. Their neighborhood seemed laid back, unquestionably poor and unquestionably happy—themes that were later reinforced throughout the country. At the house, I was greeted by their dogs and the friendly housekeeper & cook, Luluna, wearing an IHOP apron. She offered me some just-out-of-the-oven delicious banana bread made with bananas from their garden. Yummy!

After that delightful refreshment, Samid then took me on a walk so I could stretch my legs and check out the neighborhood, a quiet hilltop missionary compound surrounded by bucolic rice fields. Wikipedia claims Madagascar has the highest per capita rice consumption in the world. In some parts of Madagascar I saw rice cultivation which unexpectedly appeared as refined as anything I saw in China—and I saw a lot of rice in China.

During this particular stroll, I took the opportunity to learn some key phrases in the local language, Malagasy, such as "Don't worry I speak Malagasy" (azamatar miteni malagasia ahoo) and "What's news?" (Manaona inan vo vo) and "Don't worry, I don't bite" (azamatar qi manaikitra ahoo)—all of which came in handy later. French is the other official language and it got me through many situations, but Malagasy is arguably much more dominant.

Throughout the country, the Malagasy people were much friendlier and more laid back than anywhere I have been in Africa. In many aspects, including the music, Madagascar feels much more like the Caribbean than Africa. My theory is that being an isolated island nation with abundant natural resources, they did not have to deal with the much more competitive—at times antagonistic—realities of mainland Africa. The faces of the people show amazing diversity, showcasing the clear mix of Africa, the Middle East, and Indonesia, which have all played integral roles in the country's history.

Malagasy New Year's Eve

I had known Dave Ingham growing up as the brother of Joy (from the Exumas story) who would drop in from time to time on breaks from running the Ingham Bros.Trucking business in central Africa. He always had jaw-dropping stories involving tough roads, reptiles and uprisings. Now with a family of his own, he and his wife had been missionaries in Madagascar for 15 years.

My arrival in Madagascar was just prior to New Year's Eve, so I had the treat of experiencing this annual tradition in a way truly different from any year prior. I walked with Dave and his family to a neighboring school/chapel where sounds of music, dancing and happiness radiated into the darkness. Here I had my first tastes of the delightful camaraderie of the locals and their Malagasy music—which had a delightfully upbeat Caribbean feel. When the popular dance tunes came on, everyone formed a long circle and marched/danced around in a rotating processional, which conveniently ran alongside a big table of snacks. People reached out and grabbed refreshments as they pranced around. A group of young girls sometimes grouped independently of the main circle, gyrating their booties to the music like there was no tomorrow.

The dancing was broken up by storytelling. One of the favorite storytellers, a group leader, asked around the room for names of hated insects and animals and then reinserted them into his story like the old Mad Libs books, which got the room howling with laughter.

I followed Dave and his family outside prior to midnight to see what the capital had for pyrotechnics. Not much. It was a pretty quiet celebration with the sound of barking dogs overpowering the various bottle rocket-type fireworks some people shot off in the distance. It was just as well that things weren't too crazy as Dave and I had a big road trip waiting for us in the morning.

In his 15 years in Madagascar, Dave has done some incredible work building tree nurseries focusing on cash crops such as trees which produce food, as well as local decorative plants. His work also alleviates the problem of people planting foreign exotics. During my visit, I got to see several places around the country where his work is being carried out by locals who are often equally passionate about the work. On our road trip kicking off New Year's Day morning, we stopped at one such place several hours outside of the capital. It felt apropos to start a new year planting trees. It was also neat seeing Dave interacting with his staff and seeing his work in progress.

A spectacled, curly-haired *vazaha*, Dave is fluent in Malagasy to the point it catches people who don't already know him off guard. One of my favorite moments was when we pulled off in the middle of nowhere at a roadside stand which sold nothing but bananas.

Wide-eyed just at seeing foreigners stop, Dave got them all laughing when he asked, "Do you know where I can find some bananas?"

Beyond trees, Dave is equally fervent about Malagasy politics and he would talk about it constantly. Madagascar, particularly Tana, was in the midst of a simmering political upheaval. He knew many locals, expats and players in the diplomatic community who were involved with what was going on. Clouds of further turmoil were lingering low and heavy.

Hiking in Mantadia and Andasibe National Parks

After planting trees at the nursery, we continued down the road to stay at another nursery Dave had established outside of the Andasibe and Mantadia National Parks. He had previously explored Andasibe plenty, but took the day off to join me for his first ever visit to the neighboring Mantadia rainforest. As Dave has discovered and named several new tree and plant species in Madagascar, and is probably one of the top naturalists in the country, it was like having Dali join you for a museum tour.

We also hired a local guide to accompany us for our seven-hour hike. You are required to have a local guide with you in all of Madagascar's National Parks, which works out for preserving the parks, the visitors, and supporting the local economy. And the guides were amazing. Their eyes could spot things lay folks like you and I wouldn't have a chance at seeing on our own. Not only that, but some of them could do impressively effective bird and animal calls. I'm not talking about whistling a simple bobwhite song. I am talking about intricate whistling growls and barks which must have taken years to perfect and were good enough to get the lemurs to respond, or at least lean in for a closer look.

During the Mantadia hike, we were treated to a mix of many things this place is known for: lemurs, chameleons, frogs, snakes, crazy bugs, etc. Madagascar's insects push the envelope of believability. Some focus on design innovations and others focus on size. In the Best in Size category were snails the size of your fist, rollie pollies the size of golf balls, and spiders purpose-built for menace. For Best in Design …innumerable colorful creatures that surpass my ability as a writer to describe them.

Golf-ball-sized rollie poley

So that bloody head thing I mentioned at the beginning? I got leeched. Right at the beginning of our otherwise magnificent hike, the first sign of something being amiss came with a casual touch to the back of my head, returning a red hand. I had never seen so much of my own blood.

This was my first time to be leeched, which is almost surprising considering the life I have led. Mind you, we never saw him/her, but the leech calling card seemed to have been left behind. I think this guy (or should I presume *female*??) must have still been reeling from New Year's parties because s/he got carried away with the anti-coagulant dose.

Leeched Vacation Boy (after I had already cleaned it up some)

The blood formed what felt like big clotted blood dunes on the nape of my neck, and there were no signs that the bloodletting would cease. The wound continued bleeding until later that night. Had it been on my ankle I think I would have been a bit less concerned, but it was right on the back of my scalp and I had an inner fear that maybe it wasn't a leech at all, but instead some sort of skull-boring worm that was busy gorging itself on a brain buffet at my expense. Meanwhile Dave, a longtime Africa veteran, was completely nonplussed by the event, commenting I must have lived a pretty cushy life if that is all the blood I had spilled up to now. Dave can be pretty hard core.

The next day while Dave was tied up with his work and attending the local church, I visited Andasibe National Park alone with a local guide. With some rain having fallen in the morning, the leech red carpet was rolled out in full. Still sensitive to the horror scene of the prior day, my concentration switched from looking for all shapes and sizes of cool critters in all levels of the forest canopy to looking for leeches on me and my guide. Another one of these pesky inchworm-like beasts almost got me. I spotted it licking its little lips about to smear his anesthesia and anticoagulant cocktail on my arm when I swatted it away.

Andasibe is known for its lemur populations, especially the unique and rare indris. With less than several thousand remaining, indris are the largest living lemurs. No one has been able to keep them alive in captivity. While they share the fuzzy teddy bear ears and big eyes of their lemur brethren, the indri have a stubby little tail instead of a regular long prehensile tail. Their call can take on many expressions, but the most common one we heard sounded like a loud, sometimes piercing whale song. Like all lemurs, they are ridiculously cute.

I love chameleons. They were one of the things I was looking forward to seeing most in Madagascar and I was richly rewarded. During my stay I saw close to 20 of the 75 or so species endemic to the country. They look like they each had their own eccentric personal costume designer and they have the ability to change colors like Cher changing outfits. In addition, they have the characteristic eyes that can move independently of each other, cool little lobster-claw-like feet, a prehensile tail, and a bug-grabbing tongue that can shoot out double their body length. They also never seemed to be in a hurry. Even when they decided to escape, it was always a slow-motion getaway.

People kept saying chameleons were easier to spot at night. Blending perfectly into their surroundings, I could rarely spot them during the day (sometimes even with the guide pointing right at them), so I couldn't imagine how the veil of darkness would make it any easier.

I felt like I was going through some silly new-visitor hazing ritual when, flashlights in hand, Dave and I went out one night for a walk by the park entrance in search of them. It felt like ghost hunting. I wasn't far off. It was an "aha!" moment when we spotted the first little guy sleeping away: it was all white. At night in their natural environment their camouflage was no longer needed, so they let their skin switch to a ghostly white as they slept.

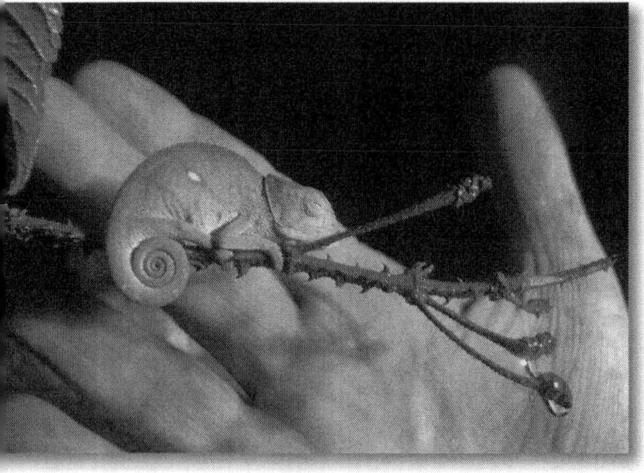

Sleeping chameleon

Flashlights were a great way to spot lemurs and other critters at night, too, because they would look towards the light out of curiosity and their eyes would light up red.

Sometimes all you could see were an eerie collection of red glowing eyes which appeared to be floating in the tree canopy.

In addition to numerous chameleons, we had the fortune of spotting an amazingly well-camouflaged leaf gecko, whose skin perfectly mimics the bark of trees it frequents. I felt bad for illuminating the little guy's wide night-vision eyes with a camera flash. At least we didn't accidentally catapult him off his tree like we did one poor sleeping chameleon whose branch we had pulled down for a closer look. Felt bad about that one, too.

Leaf gecko

A variation on this nighttime activity was one of Dave's favorite driving games, cruising slowly down the road at night and seeing who could spot the most chameleons. When he spotted one, he often pulled over and proudly shined the headlights at them.

The Remote Nursery Search

Dave had heard there was a plant nursery up a nearby road on the way back to Tana, so how could he not check it out for himself? This road was not a good one. It was muddy, heavily rutted, flooded in areas and was stitched together with dilapidated bridges that were scary to even walk over. Dave brought a couple employees from his Andasibe Nursery along for the adventure.

It was not at all reassuring when Dave took this opportunity to tell me the story of when he had a trucking company in central Africa and was held hostage by the village elders after his truck slid down a muddy embankment in a heavy rainstorm, crashing into their main bridge, wiping it out.

After a jarring couple of hours, we did make it to an end of the road. A barrier gate kept us from advancing further, but after talking with the locals Dave determined the nursery we were seeking was about four kilometers off the road from this spot anyway, so he sent someone with a note to try and fetch them.

We waited for an hour or two as the local community gave us curious looks and some amazing bugs wandered about. Because of possible rain and the time required to get back to Tana, we eventually had to give up and head back.

For whatever reason, Dave was less cavalier about the bridges on the way back. At some that we had breezed over the first time, we now stopped and worked to assemble enough beams to make it feel like there was enough real estate to handle a vehicle's weight and tire width. It was a wonder how we had gotten over them the first time.

Reassembling bridges on the return trip

It was great to do this first excursion with Dave, because it gave me a nice introduction to the country before striking out on my own for the remainder of my travels.

Evatra and onto Lokaro

One singular sentence in my Madagascar guidebook changed my entire travel trajectory. The author wrote that a certain trail in the Andringitra National Park was "one of the top 10" best hikes she had ever done. I could not let that go. After researching the public transportation options, it became clear that in the timeframe I had, the only way I would be able to reach Andringitra plus some other areas in the south that were also calling out to me, was to fly to the south, then take a 24-hour-or-so bus ride to this park on the way back to the capital.

After flying down to the coastal town of Fort Dauphin (a.k.a. Taolagnaro), I hired a guide to take me on a cool two-day excursion to the little paradise of Lokaro. The trip involved a seven kilometer dugout-canoe paddle, then a hike to Lokaro's jewel of a beach area where we camped before returning to the city via a lengthy hike, mostly along a beach.

My guide, Olivier, hired an assistant to help with the paddling section. We paddled in a canoe carved from the trunk of a tree. The bottom had a worrisome persistent leak, so instead of paddling, I spent much of the trip bailing out the water collecting on the floor of the canoe.

Olivier said crocodiles could be spotted in these waters up to two or three years prior, but they had since been hunted to extinction. Prior to their disappearance, he said one time when they were paddling this same trajectory, a big croc had followed behind them for a half hour, looking for an opportunity to turn a mistake into a lunch.

After several hours, we arrived at our intermediary destination: **Evatra.** Evatra had everything going for it and nothing going for it at the same time. It's situated in a stunning location where a river lagoon meets up with a fantastic surfing beach, but something about the village was just not right. It reeked of an unpleasant poverty I had not encountered elsewhere in the country, but not because of the banana thatch huts and the sandy paths which served as roads. One red flag was instead of hearing the common greeting "Bonjour vazaha!" the ubiquitous little children here called out from every corner, "Bon bon vazaha!" holding out a hand.

This was clearly a habit taught to them by French tourists who basically trained them to beg for candy. It was off-putting and sad and seemed to be a symptom of a larger civic illness.

Olivier talked about how he had tried to coordinate donations from foreigners to improve nutrition and infrastructure in the town, only to have the mayor pocket most everything for himself. It's sad, especially because Evatra looks to have so much potential to be a better place.

From Evatra, we climbed over the hill behind it and down onto the crescent-shaped beach paradise of Lokaro. My guide had an arrangement with a local family in which they made us dinner before we camped amongst the palm trees lining the beach. We were the only ones there. This was true of most everywhere I visited in the country. The ongoing political turmoil had thrown a wet towel on the fragile tourism market.

A frog we passed on the way to Lokaro

The next morning before heading back, I waded out to explore and snorkel off the island which dotted the middle of the crescent. The most curious creatures I saw were some ugly little fish that seemed to be right in the throes of an evolutionary step forward. They hung out on the rocks while the waves occasionally crashed up and over them. They were extremely agile out of water, hopping from rock to rock despite an obvious lack of arms and legs.

We took the long way back around to Evatra, exploring a rocky coastline punctuated with palms and blue-water beaches. After passing through Evatra again, the walk back to Fort Dauphin was along a continuous ten kilometer stretch of beautiful beach. The beach was littered with shipwrecks—both intentional and accidental.

I counted close to seven large ships. Some of them were apparently wrecked there intentionally for insurance claims. Others were being salvaged for parts and scrap metal. Barefoot laborers worked like bacteria breaking down rusting vessels with bare hands, basic tools and cutting torches.

One ship that was mostly still intact had a guardian living on it and was apparently there in anticipation of going back out to sea once the next tidal storm came through. I thought it odd that some locals walking down the beach asked this guardian guy to give them water to drink. I thought it even odder that he actually gave it to them, especially since most likely he had to bring his own drinking water there himself.

I witnessed something along this beach I had never seen in any tropical community anywhere: people running. And they weren't jogging for a recreational activity. Most often, they were carrying heavy loads of things in baskets either balanced on a shoulder pole or on their heads. Their loads looked destined for the markets of Fort Dauphin. Some talked animatedly or were singing as they trotted past. It seemed cheerfully industrious.

The Overnight Bus Ride from Hell

Trying to reach that Siren-like hike calling to me in Andringitra National Park, my commitment was tested by a serious bus ride. One thing I didn't count on when I signed up for 24 hours on a bus with no toilet, was having a severe case of the trots. At least my body gave me a bit of advanced warning, so I was able to taper off all food consumption to zero ahead of time. I decided to load up on Imodium and fast for about eight hours before eventually consuming one Pringles chip per hour later during the bus ride. The plan held up pretty good for awhile.

I was nervous about more than my bowels. My health was already far from top form, and we would be traveling overnight through a remote part of the country where the quality/navigability of the roads was never a given. Oh yeah, and there were reports of fairly recent violent bus robberies. Busses tended to travel in convoys overnight in this region to reduce the risk of being robbed by highway bandits. So once our bus was fully loaded with people and luggage/stuff piled on top—almost doubling the height of the bus—it joined with another bus before heading down the road.

After pulling out of the bus stop, much of my pent up angst melted away when the driver turned on the stereo. He had a surprisingly great sound system and the joyous Malagasy music resonated to my soul, warming it like sun rays shining through a winter bay window. As we rumbled into a landscape of rice fields and jagged green mountains, the happy music became the soundtrack for what was once again a welcomed adventure.

I thought it a bad sign when we broke down only 30 minutes outside of town, but in the end the bus required significant work only twice during the whole trip.

I was pleasantly surprised I got the window seat I had reserved the day before. Getting the window, however, turned out to be a mixed blessing. On one hand, I got the great views and fresh air I hoped for. But with that came the dust from the road and the exhaust from the belching muffler below me, particularly when we slowed down (constantly) to navigate around—lets go with an all-encompassing generic term—hazards. These hazards ranged from lakes and streams posing as the road; to impressively eroded and rutted areas; to herds of goats and zebu, the (delicious!) humped-back cattle common throughout Madagascar.

We were packed in like sardines. In one row I counted six adults and four kids. I found with some climbing and gymnastics, I could use my window as a door and did so on many occasions, as it would have been an even more death defying feat to try and climb out over all the bodies between me and the real front door. My immediate neighbors were Delice, a cute, awe-inspiringly well-behaved five-year-old and his aunt, Perle, a college student returning to the capital. Bus rides such as this are brutal for adults, but can feel like a lifetime low for some kids. The crying and throwing up I had anticipated from Delice (from experience) were blessedly replaced by his adorable smiles, occasional spontaneous singing, and an inordinate amount of sleeping—sometimes resting his little head on my shoulder and eventually sprawling completely across my lap during the night.

Perle giggling at her droopy-eyed nephew Delice just after or before one of his many naps

Space was tight to the point I felt like one of the ducks whose body had been tightly bound in a burlap sack with just his head sticking out, which I had seen being loaded on the roof at the beginning of the trip. There was no way to access anything down by your almost unmovable feet or even in your pants pockets. In one sense, my body was happy about this sensation of being in traction. As I mentioned before, the last ten kilometers of my hike the day before was along the Lokaro beach while carrying a full backpack. At stops during the night, when I would meander about in the dark, I felt like I had a pit bull clamped onto each of my calves from the sore muscles.

I found it impossible to sleep. The seatback was too low to lean straight back, even using a travel pillow. The road was so bumpy that when I let myself relax towards the window, my head would slam violently into it. Letting my head drift downward or to the right, I felt I would surely get whiplash from the jerking motions.

We stopped at a number of villages and spots in the middle of nowhere so people could go to the bathroom, stretch their legs, shop or get a bite to eat. At one stop around 2 a.m. at a small village where trucks and busses stop to eat, a vendor had built a fire on the ground just off the side of the road. It was interesting to see they made their cooking fire much how I like making mine for rotisserie cooking. They had their main fire for warmth and then fed the coals off to one side which they used to cook their skewers, which they rotated manually. The crowd around it reaffirmed that fires and food bring people together the world over.

Part of me was pleased to be fasting so I didn't have to seriously contemplate the only food options that were available at these kinds of roadside stops, where hygiene and quality of ingredients were definitely on the "iffy" side. As an aside, I heard a statistic that 90% of cooking in Madagascar is still done over charcoal, which is part of why they have suffered so much deforestation.

At one stop—thankfully before sunrise—it became clear it was payback time for the ten potato chips I had indulged in over the course of the last ten or so hours. In a mostly asleep Nowheresville town, still under the cover of darkness, I wandered with intent down a dark alley, passing the silhouette of a woman clearly (by sound) with the same agenda. There, I committed one of my greatest acts of civil desecration to date. Granted, the amount I had eaten didn't add up to much more than a chicken squirt, but oh the guilt of doing that outside someone's fence. I did cover my tracks and can rationalize that I did some free composting for them. One irony that made me giggle (I love irony!) was that in climbing out of my bus window to go on my alleyway errand, I had to first pause the audio book I was listening to: *Think and Grow Rich.*

I realize I sound like quite a whiner, but this is not to say I regret the bus voyage by any means. The scenery you could see in the daylight hours—from the spiny desert forest in the south to the mountain highlands further north—was spectacular, and the people I encountered both on the bus and in the various villages along the way made it all worthwhile.

One such encounter was with a scrappy young boy in a pit stop town who approached my window. At first I ignored him, lumping him in with the mix of persistent sellers and beggars who regularly do the same at these types of places. But there was something about his smile and demeanor that made me decide to open the window and say hello. It turned out all he wanted to do was an Obama-style fist bump with me, the foreigner. When I did that, he sauntered off with a smile. How cool.

For the record, my bus was WAY better than the alternatives. As an "express" to the capital, it made significantly fewer stops to pick up people and stuff, and it had much bigger tires (a big plus on an unforgiving road) than the smaller regional busses, which would have taken three to five days to make the same journey in less comfort throughout.

Andringitra at Last (Barely)

Even once I arrived near Andringitra, my trip to the park was in danger of not happening because I had run out of cash. There were no ATMs or places to exchange money in Ambalavao, the bustling picturesque highland city closest to the park. There was also virtually no regular public transportation up to the park entrances. Knowing I couldn't afford to hire a driver just for myself, I checked around town for options such as renting a bicycle or finding tourists heading there in a hired car. I was fortunate to visit the park's city satellite office at the right time. A crew of workers was about to head back to Andringitra after having had some respite in town. They let me ride up with them, packing me in with their replenishment supplies for the roughly 35 kilometer scenic ride to their main park office.

Ambalavao school bus in action

It wasn't until I began my return trip a couple days later that I realized the road ended there and there wasn't a single other car (or bicycle) in the village or anywhere else for miles. With the savings on transportation, I had just enough cash for the park entrance & guide fees, plus return bus fare. Thus, the next morning I headed out with my guide, Edu, on truly a hike of a lifetime.

One of my favorite parts was just leaving town. Their office was nestled in a picturesque valley scalloped with fantastically refined rice fields surrounded by rocky-topped green mountains. The trail in places required you to balance on narrow rice terrace walls with water flowing on both sides. It was a closely knit community, and my guide could not simply walk through without stopping to make extended sing-song greetings with everyone we passed. I felt an extraordinary warmth from the people. Smiling children not only came out to wave hello, but some of them even spontaneously sang a song to me. It was such a refreshing change from the bon bon beggars of Evatra.

Some women we came across working a rice field were excited that I wanted to take their picture. But they wanted to make sure I didn't take a picture of them on break, so a couple of them got up and started working just for the picture. They were all laughing and carrying on. It was great.

The rice fields became smaller below us as we made our way out of town and up the slope of the mountain, which was the last remaining obstacle between us and the border of Andringitra National Park. I was elated when we crossed the summit and officially entered into the park, as there were so many moments during this trip where I was almost certain I wasn't going to be able to set foot here.

For dinner that night we had a mix of Edu's rice, which he had grown himself, some meager food items I had purchased, and a couple of freeze-dried meals I had brought from America. Edu had never heard of Mexican cuisine, or Mexico for that matter, but that night I gave him most of the Chicken Enchilada meal. He enjoyed the Turkey Tetrazzini one, but he REALLY liked the Mexican one. I enjoyed the treat of being able to eat the rice he had grown himself.

Edu boiled the water over a fire inside our shelter for the night, a thatch-roofed cabin which wasn't fully walled in. He kept the fire going during the night for warmth. He did an impressive job of sleeping on a mostly rock bench. I was in my hammock which I had strung inside the hut in a way that I could see out over the wall. Before calling it a night, Edu thought me a bit weird that I wanted to go walk around with a flashlight in search of critters. I think he was surprised at how much we spotted for the little effort we put into it. We encountered a couple sleepy chameleons, a praying mantis, a hissing cockroach and a few other little guys.

Try crushing one of these guys and you may lose a limb

Madagascar hissing cockroaches are hilarious in their malice. First, they are huge, getting up to the size of a cell phone. Apparently they bite. And their name isn't for naught. I didn't even realize until half way through our hike the next day that it was them making the prevalent noise which sounded somewhere between a hissing cat and air squeezing out of a wet hole in a shoe sole. Even when they were completely out of site hidden away under bushes and rock ledges well off the path, they challenged angrily from all sides.

Another of my favorite creatures from Andringitra was one chameleon in particular. He was perched way up on a vertical dead-end branch. I was having some trouble getting a decent profile picture of him. It was only when taking some video that I realized that as I shifted around the branch to get a better vantage point, he was slowly, almost imperceptibly rotating around the twig so that he kept the branch between him and me. It was a crafty but laughable defensive technique since he was about five times wider than the branch he was hiding behind.

The scenery was magnificent. At first I had been disappointed with the clouds that had rolled in, but the way they rose and fell and wisped about gave a much more interesting perspective to the texture of the rocky landscapes and the dynamic flora within.

After a full day of exploring the park and a long hike back, our arrival at the park office was marked by a giant, arching, complete rainbow stretching across the valley, magically galvanizing my feelings of this village being a perfect little paradise.

Knowing I was flat broke, the park administrators were kind enough to let me stay in a dorm room in the building free of charge. Seeing firsthand the meager resources these guys had at their disposable at one of the top national parks, it was no surprise that the country is losing the battle against poachers and other ne'er-do-wells who have been destroying the forests at record pace.

With my wonderful hike in Andringitra complete, it was time to head back to civilization. The first step was to get to the town near the main road where I could catch a taxi-bus. Locals talked about this bus stop like it was around the corner, but it was actually a ten kilometer hike away. The interesting sights and sounds along the way, though, made the time pass quickly. Rocky cliffs lined the picturesque valley which was filled with rice and other cultivation. As a reminder of the beach runners near Fort Dauphin, here I was passed by school children literally running to school (also barefoot) as a group.

When I first started out, a couple men coming the other way stopped to say hello and warmly shake my hand. One of them even seemed to thank me for visiting. Did I mention the people here were friendly? The people's effervescent warmth did taper off to more normal levels as I proceeded towards more populated areas closer to the main road.

The one time during my entire trip to Madagascar that I felt a real sense of danger came during the last leg of this hike. An adolescent boy and what looked to be his young brother were walking in the same direction as me, but much faster as I was weighed down by my backpack. They slowed considerably when they got close to me. When they caught up to me, the older boy took what I felt was an unhealthy interest in my backpack and asked for me to give him some kind of handout. I declined. Food would have been the only thing I might have considered sharing in this situation, but the little food I had left had to last me for many hours. All the cash I had left was barely enough to get me to the major city I was heading to. The older boy was carrying a bag hanging over a stick, which could have easily doubled as a bat-like implement.

We began a bit of a casual cat and mouse game over the next 30 minutes or so, where I tried to not show any concern while attempting to put distance between them and me. I started by slowing down more and more. Eventually the twosome did continue on, but once past me they did not pick up their pace. They could walk much faster than I and they should easily have left me in the dust. Instead they lingered in much the same way I had done and after awhile stopped off the side the road for what looked to be a non-errand. It gave me a bad vibe, reminding me of times when I had been robbed in the past.

I passed them quickly and tried to put distance behind me. Once they started back down the road, though, their pace was back to its original fast speed and I realized there was no way for me to outpace them. As they approached, I ducked off to the side and acted like I was fiddling with something so that they would have to either pass me or stop walking. They did pass me, but slowly. I was relieved when we finally got into more populated areas and the chance of something happening dissipated. It may have been nothing, but the encounter definitely gave me the creeps.

Once I got a taxi-bus, I was whisked along a well-trafficked route through the middle of the country. I rejoiced upon finding an ATM in Fianarantsoa (try saying that three times—take your time) the regional capital with about $2 to spare in Ariary, the local currency. Phew.

Post-ATM visit, I felt like a king. Flush with cash, I hit an Internet café to see what was up elsewhere in the world. It was a relief to learn *The Lounge* was indeed in good hands. A week after I headed to Madagascar, my mother and her husband Bobby flew into Los Angeles, picked up *The Lounge* where I left it, then proceeded to take a multi-week trip up the West Coast. It sounded like everything was going well and they were having a blast. Phew for that, too.

Ranomafana

After Fianarantsoa, I made one detour before heading back to the capital. Ranomafana, aside from being fun to say, is one of the most popular rainforest destinations in Madagascar. It is also another place where Dave had established an arboretum outside of the national park there.

Botanical gardens guardians

There were three things of particular interest in Dave's park. 1) a single palm tree of a variety that has never been seen anywhere else in the world. 2) a cool boa constrictor 3) the cicada hunters. These kids would place the sticky innards of a durian fruit on the end of a long stick and then use their implement to pluck cicadas off of trees. Speaking to a local about this later, he told me these giant ugly screaming bugs make a great snack once they are fried, but I insisted I witnessed those boys not waiting to get all of their prey back to a frying pan before consuming them.

The following morning I visited Ranomafana National Park. Here the guide had an assistant who went out in search of lemurs. During our visit to this famous park, shockingly, we didn't see a single chameleon or lemur, although I did see some cool bugs and another round of leeches.

One insect that I was quite proud to have spotted was a huge, ridiculously well-camouflaged walking stick. The only way I saw it was because my guide had gone off in search of an audible troupe of lemurs, leaving me in a small clearing. While nothing jumped out at me, I had the distinct feeling that if I stood still and looked carefully, there were things around me. My gut feeling was rewarded when I focused on some moss on a tree. Something about the pattern of the moss seemed off. As I approached, I saw one of the most magnificent living creations I have ever encountered. Evolution has gone to awe-inspiring, painstaking detail to help this walking stick replicate is surroundings.

Another particularly interesting creature was a bright orange, wasp-like bug that had black stripes along its wings and unusually long antenna. It used these feelers like two independently-moving blind man's canes, probing the holes and surfaces of a log as a way to forage for food.

After exiting the park, the "lemur spotter" assistant passed me where I was having lunch on the way back into town. She directed my attention to a bright green chameleon stumbling across the road beside me (they aren't built to walk on asphalt). We both laughed that this chameleon was here in plain view when we couldn't find a single one in the national park.

Once back in Tana with Dave and his family, it was fun recounting my stories and sharing the pictures of the different things I had encountered in the place they call home. He was particularly excited to see the pictures I had gotten of his various projects.

After a bit of shopping in town for local music, a cool musical instrument, flip flops and Malagasy booze, it was time for the return home. Once back to LA, I was tremendously relieved to be reunited with *The Lounge* parked right in the tow away zone where I had left it. My folks had returned it there the day before I got back, and had already flown safely back to South Carolina.

For what it's worth, since I used frequent flyer mileage and traveled on the cheap, my entire one-month trip cost only about $700 for everything. It would probably have been more expensive for me to have stayed in the US. And I can't wait to go back!

CHAPTER 40

Racing in Istanbul Traffic to Kayak the Lycian Coast

A Birthday Trip through Turkey

Had I been born 48 hours later, the start of my birthday trip could have been explosive. The shopping mall in the upscale area of Istanbul, where I met my friend Gül, was bombed two days after I arrived. Sometimes, it's just good to be lucky. As it was, I simply had to undergo the embarrassment of receiving a big silly Happy Birthday balloon at the mall's Starbucks, blissfully naive of the carnage that would take place there in a couple days. I benignly drank my blissfully bitter Turkish coffee—the first of many I would have during the trip—and then headed off to get ready for a fun dinner out.

Gül is a friend from my days in the ophthalmic industry. A rising international star in the world of retina surgery by day, a petite tango-loving, percussion-playing adventurista by night and on holidays, Gül and I had already had shared other trips such as kayaking off Vancouver Island and exploring the southeastern U.S. This would be the first time that I got to spend time with her on her home turf when neither of us was working.

I was elated that she decided to surprise me with a birthday dinner at the chic open-air restaurant, Sortie, right on the Bosphorus Strait, the ancient water passage which connects the Mediterranean and the Black seas. The water splits Istanbul into East and West, thereby also separating Europe from Asia.

I had seen this restaurant from the water on a sunset cruise of a previous business trip, and I remembered hearing how Sortie was one of the top hot spots in Istanbul. Jet setters sometimes flew in just to party for the night. It is a spectacular venue. There are multiple restaurants under one (non-) roof. We went with the Lebanese one. The tasty dishes seemed to never stop coming as well as glasses of raki, the Turkish version of ouzo. We saw everything from barges to cruise ships to tiny little fishing vessels passing by as we ate. Giant bright red Turkish flags fluttered proudly on the bridges, boats and colorful hilltops as the sun slowly set on the magical scene.

The restaurant converts into a dance club as the night progresses. I wanted to stay out and party like a rock star, but this jet setter's jet lag was getting the best of him and my pillow was a Siren I could not refuse. Is that a sign of getting OLD?

I usually don't make a big deal about my birthdays, but 40 was one I wanted to go all out for. This special evening out was already the second of what would be many celebratory birthday meals which spilled across multiple countries, and even non-countries. The first such meal was on the plane ride over, somewhere over the Atlantic. I washed down my food with champagne right at the moment I first turned 40 (as best as I could calculate).

This birthday originally—since I first conceived the plan at age 23—was meant to mark the day I retired, but *that* didn't work out. Not yet, anyway. More recently, I had also decided I wanted to be in the best shape of my life. After months and months of an intense workout and diet regime, I can say with confidence that I did accomplish my goal. It felt great, too. I was excited to get out and put my reinvigorated body to the test, using muscle strength I never had before and a well of energy eager to be tapped. A kayak trip on the Mediterranean and a bike trip through the Alps would be the perfect release.

So back to Turkey… where we had a plane to catch.

Our post-arrival morning was complicated, both by me oversleeping (until 11:30 a.m.) and by Gül being caught up on the computer, sending big video files to the American Ophthalmic Academy. She'd been asked to submit case presentations as part of being an invited speaker for their next conference (a big deal, especially since she would be the first Turkish retina specialist to receive this honor) and she needed to get the files off to them before we went off grid.

Oh, and Gül was completely delusional about how long it would take to get to the airport. She talked as if it was a five-minute stroll around the corner. In reality, we had to get all the way across the entire busy, ancient Istanbul metropolis. It was frightfully less than two hours before our flight was to DEPART when we tried to launch at breakneck speeds into the city's taffy-thick traffic quagmire. It was an impossible attempt.

Undeterred, Gül drove in a way that—if I had ever experienced something like it before—I must have blocked it out to better preserve my mental stability later in life. Overlaid by cell phone calls and streams of cursing and waving in Turkish, Gül's darting and weaving through every lane—including the emergency lane—would have white-knuckled even veteran NASCAR racers if they were sitting where I was. She even went for the classic pull-behind-the-ambulance maneuver, following so close no one could possibly cut in. I could have easily reached out and polished the ambulance's (and many other cars' along the way) bumper.

With all the guardian angels of Istanbul working overtime (one or more of them just to keep my heart pumping properly), miraculously we tore into the airport with 30 minutes to go before our flight. Gül tossed her keys to a startled valet as we sprinted for the entrance... which was blocked by a line of people waiting at a security X-ray screening just to get into the lobby. I had gotten there first with the bags, but Gül ran past me, almost scrambling over the top of people in line to race to the check in counter, getting there at the exact minute they were cutting off check in. We made it. Unbelievable.

And where were we flying to after all that? Antalya, on the southern Mediterranean coast. We did not stay there, but rather rented a car and right away headed east down the mountainous coast. Life there in the south was moving at a palpably more relaxed pace.

You could feel the summer season slowly awakening. At the seaside cafe where we stopped for (of course) Turkish coffee, the employees were going through their annual ritual of taking out the lounge chairs, getting the parasols in place, and laying down a walking deck to get closer to the water when the sand was hotter. There would be hoards of beachgoers here in the months to come, but for now those working at the counter seemed to still be in full hibernation mode as it took the better part of an hour to get our coffee despite being some of the only customers there. It was a good way to get us to adjust our clocks to "island time" despite not being on an island.

I quickly instituted a rule to reflect this new reality: NO ISTANBUL-STYLE DRIVING. One can only ask so much of the guardian angels. It was time for them to go on vacation, too. It took some reminding, but at some point, Gül found a way to relax at the wheel.

One of our main goals in coming to southern Turkey was to go sea kayaking, which ended up being folded into a road trip. Like any good road trip, the experiences along the way weave themselves into a unique fabric incorporating the journey's many individual threads. Roadside attractions are quintessential road trip fabric memory fodder, and in Turkey those detours can lead to things like...flames coming out of the earth? Really? Surely they jest.

Sure enough, a 15-minute climb up a mountainside brought us face to face with Chimera, a place where flames have apparently been coming out of the ground for hundreds of years. Our curiosity was brimming when we arrived at Chimera's rocky clearing in the pine trees overlooking the Mediterranean in the distance. The intriguing flaming phenomenon occurred in several spots and amazingly wasn't marked off at all. Being daylight, you had to be careful to not burn your leg on little ones that weren't easily visible. They were not violent eruptions but rather more like a pleasant gas fireplace—but coming out of a bed of rock.

From there we wandered back down and across this same seaside town Cirili, to see the ruins at Mt. Olympus, which brings up the question of Greek vs. Turkish heritage overlap/confusion. It reminds me of the varied religious narratives coming out of a singular Jerusalem, except here there are similar histories that stem from separate locations. Doesn't it seem like it would be a lot easier to light an Olympic torch off of a flame that is always going (near a Mt. Olympus) rather than having to rely on solar power and mirrors like they do for the Olympics nowadays?

Another clear source of confusion came later in the trip with my moussaka debacle. At some point, I developed a craving for moussaka, an eggplant dish I have always considered a Greek food staple and a good litmus test to differentiate the decent Greek restaurants from the great ones. Here locals were claiming it was a Turkish specialty, not Greek. I could see wars starting like that.

After seeing it appear on enough menus along the way, though, I entered a town for lunch with a mission to try out the moussaka and see for myself. With visions of layers of eggplant, spicy ground beef coated with a béchamel sauce spinning in my mind, with Gül's help I interviewed one restaurateur after another about their moussaka formulation. Averaging about $20 a plate, the prices weren't cheap and I wanted to be sure to get it right. (Turkish food by and large is absolutely delicious, but not inexpensive). The preparations varied, but were consistently distant from what I would consider moussaka. We ended up at a quaint outdoor restaurant overlooking a sweeping bay, dining on some sort of tasty eggplant dish, but I did not end up with anything close to what I would consider moussaka. Want good moussaka? Go Greek.

But back to Mt. Olympus...with intricate stone carvings and aqueducts, Turkey's Mt. Olympus ruins reflected a high level of architecture and the transitory nature of humanity as the forests slowly reclaim it.

The ruins were in a gorgeous seaside location nestled next to a tranquil stream full of ribbitting frogs. The only things disturbing the idyllic setting were the vacationing Russians. When we Americans imagined the Red Invasion, I know that most of us were not envisioning it in the form of red Speedo bathing suits slightly eclipsed by hairy belly rolls folding over the top of them. Inconsiderate, loud and tacky to the point of humor, these groups of tourists with their poorly behaved kids put the Ugly American stereotype to shame.

Tuning them out to reflect back to the past, though, I was perplexed about how such a great spot could have been abandoned. I was also wondering how the current government could leave these precious ruins unguarded. Later I came to realize there were ancient ruins EVERYWHERE and it would be a Herculean task to guard them all.

So then it was time for our long-anticipated kayak adventure. We rented a hardshell double in Kas, a quaint little port town at the base of a mountain amphitheater. The biggest challenge from the get-go, aside from trying to figure out how to cram all our stuff in this one vessel, was getting past some menacing geese blocking the water. Luckily, our guard was up because we had already heard from an American couple about a duck that attacked one of them at a nearby beach to the point of drawing blood. We played it cautious until the web-footed contingency decided they had made their point and arrogantly swam off.

We jumped in our kayak, glided out onto the water and soon pulled out past the protected harbor and into open (albeit calm) seas where I experienced something new for me on a kayak: hearing a Muslim call to prayer. Like a road trip, each kayak trip has its own unique pallet of sensations and the crackly speaker reverberating its solemn song from the town's mosque across the calm water seemed to christen our voyage. Another sensation that struck me then and throughout the trip was the intoxicating, piercing deep blue color of the water in this part of the Mediterranean, occasionally shifting to a rich emerald green. I had been itching to get out on a kayak and this magical combination of sensations was instantly exactly what the doctor ordered.

Here at the beginning we also had a look at Greece. By some fluke of history Megisti, a beautiful island within a healthy but doable swimming distance of mainland Turkey, remains firmly in Greek hands. The place sounds like an odd Greek outpost that is worth a look around, but with surprisingly irregular ferry service we weren't able to make it over there after our kayak trip.

We spent much of the first day investigating the rocky shoreline and occasional caves we could paddle into. We stopped at a scenic beach cove for lunch where Gül went for a swim and I went for a nap. Napping seemed to be the theme of the day, as later in the afternoon between the gentle rolling of the waves, the sunshine, and the sounds of the ocean, Gül was pulled into a brief deep sleep in mid paddle. Yes, it was that pleasant.

A few hiker groups passed by our lunch spot. Considering how remote it already felt, I was wondering why there were so many folks in the area. It turned out we had stopped at a wayward point on the Lycian Way, a path which coincidentally would be a constant ribbon ultimately connecting most everywhere we visited along the Turkish coast.

Threading from Antalya (where our southern trip began) to Fethiye (where our trip ended), the Lycian Way is a 509 kilometer footpath along the coast of Lycia in southern Turkey. It is said to be one of the "Top 10 Long Walks in the World". The trail is marked by a red-and-white-striped mark painted on rocks and trees all along it, a telltale sign that became like bumping into a familiar friend as we spotted it over and over again even in pretty remote places.

That evening, we camped on what we called the "Isle of Gül". It turned out to be the only place we overnighted in the south that was not directly on the Lycian Way. Gül spotted this beautiful little rocky island on our way in to camp at a beach on the mainland. Not only did we have it to ourselves, it looked like we were the only ones to have had this idea as we could only find one spot suitable for a tent on the entire island and that site took some excavation to make it tent-ready. Upon disembarking, we were nervous about the ubiquitous unfamiliar yellow lightning-bug-like insects buzzing about until we figured out they had no malevolent intentions other than using us as occasional landing pads.

We celebrated the end of sunset with a bottle of wine on the 360^0-view rocky summit. I enjoyed watching a fisherman puttering about the silent bay setting his nets while his wife, in a traditional headdress, drove the boat as goats wandered around on the headlands behind them. He'd grumble at her for not driving where/how he wanted her to, but you could tell they enjoyed each others' company. It was touching to see their interaction as it is rare to see a couple working together at sea.

We set up our candlelit al fresco dinner on what we jokingly referred to as the "Level Two Restaurant" as there were several waterfront rock shelf options to choose from. Some fishermen passing nearby must have been curious to see lights here as we heard them putter over in the dark for a peek before their sounds circled back away.

In the morning we departed the Isle of Gül at a relaxed pace, ready to bathe in the glory of another beautiful day. Gül and I tried our hand at sailing the kayak on the way into our evening's destination. The kayak company we were using, Dragoman, had developed an interesting sail rig with PVC pipes forming a V which was attached to a hole in the center of the cockpit and held up windsurf-sail-like material to catch the breeze. While not too big, a nice benefit of their design is you can paddle while the sail is doing its thing. It took the edge off a full day's paddling arms.

That evening we made it to Opalais where there are some interesting ruins dropping down the hill side all the way into the water of the cove. You can even swim over part of them. I was aghast to see these magnificent historic structures completely unguarded and without any signage or anything. In the US, this place would be nothing short of a national monument.

While Gül was off in search of a hot shower, I had these ruins to myself. Climbing around the half-toppled walls and buildings as dusk quietly approached, it was fun to imagine the sounds and what life was like there when it was fully intact and inhabited. I was particularly intrigued by the above-ground tombs, some of which had ancient writing carved onto their walls. A couple of these, oddly, were sitting right at the water's edge.

We were treated to glistening smooth water for much of our third day out. Our first stop was to explore the olive-tree-and-goat-inhabited island soon named "Isle of Jon" to warm up after snorkeling in the nearby "aquarium" area. The ruins at the top of the hill-shaped island offered stunning views of the inlet, home to the ruins of Kekova and Simena, the still vibrant medieval city across from it.

We arrived at our next stop—a U-shaped cove fronted by a beautiful beach—just as it began to rain for the first and only time it would rain on our entire journey. Fortuitously, an ancient arched room beckoned to us from above the beach, so we retreated into it to have lunch and watch the serene rain. Coincidentally, as we were finishing up, Jeff and Kelly, the duck-attacked Americans from Montana we had met at the Dragoman office, arrived and joined us to swap stories. We worked out a plan to meet up the next day so we could share a ride back to Kas.

From there Gül and I paddled around the corner to the top draw of the region: Kekova, the famed sunken city. Like in Opalais, there were structures on land which spilled down to and beyond the water's edge. The day's glassy smooth waters made it an ideal day to visit as we could easily see deep down to the bottom from the comfort of the kayak. This was particularly important because Kekova is the only place on our trip where snorkeling is prohibited due to the highly valued ruins and the heavy tourist traffic. Through the piercing blue, I could see possibly 1000+year-old urns sitting mostly intact on the bottom 20 feet under water. It was hard to believe that relics in such good condition, and that accessible, would still be there. Who knows how old they really were.

As we wound down our Kekova visit, across the inlet from the castle-topped town of Simena, the sounds of crowing roosters and a call to prayer drifted lazily across the water. Along the green rugged mountain ridges, multiple above-ground sarcophagi formed the vertebrae of a spine that led to the castle wall from one side of town. We

Simena

pulled into the docks like ancient mariners to have dinner at a waterside café. From there we headed up through town to the walled castle at the top. While the castle itself did not offer much to see, it did offer a spectacular view of the town, the port and the deep blue inlet beyond it.

On the way down, we came upon a ridiculous brand new turnstile gateway and kiosk that looked to be the most recent structure in the entire city by at least 40 years. With its air conditioned office, digital light boards and laser bar code ticket scanners, this modern affront to the senses screamed (excessive) "foreign donation". Mind you, the turnstile entry didn't even block the whole path, so you could walk right by it if you so chose. We only encountered it on our way down, since the path we originally wandered up had no such faux barricade.

That night we were lucky enough to find a campsite just before dark where we could walk (along the Lycian Way) to the Smuggler's Cove bar. We figured it would be better to be where we could stumble home rather than paddle in the dark, particularly after the number of drinks we thought we might be consuming.

Smuggler's Cove reminded me of the bars we pulled into all over the Virgin Islands when sailing there, oh gosh, almost 20 years earlier with my party hardy Club Med buddies. I'd guess the ubiquitous and relatively affordable Blue Cruises that ply these waters fill this place on a regular basis during the summer. Tonight, however, perhaps too early in the season, it was quiet and the staff invited us to join them for a family style dinner (for no charge). We resisted, but ultimately took them up on some soup which turned out to be some of the best chicken soup I have ever had.

A somewhat lurid sign posted in the bar suggested that when the place was in full swing things could get much crazier, and go much later in the night. As it was, Gül and I seemed to be the only customers that night and closed the place down by ten. So much for our big night out.

The next day our trip wound down in a marshy river where we met the guys from Dragoman, and the Americans, for a ride back to Kas. Great trip! After welcomed long, hot showers, Gül and I celebrated our kayaking success at sunset with a takeout dinner and cold beer. Our hotel balcony overlooked the harbor as the lights of the town glimmered steadily brighter in contrast to the falling darkness.

We were back on the road in our rental car early the next morning, winding along the radiant blue waters down the coast to Fethiye. One highlight en route, in addition to the before mentioned moussaka fiasco, was visiting Patara's impressive ancient amphitheater ruins and its perfect running beach. Patara's wide magical beach has ten kilometers of the most blissfully springy/soft sand one could wish for. It begged to be run upon. I left Gül to her sunbathing and swimming, and I ran for a glorious hour, passing along the undulating dunes in one direction and the water in the other. It was a truly magnificent experience.

Seeing the vast sprawling dunes which backed the beach, a 1970's porn-like soundtrack arose in my head... bow chika WOW wow... I speculated the way they were laid out sprawling for miles with no buildings anywhere near them these were surely heavy duty nookie dunes. I imagined that over the centuries, the population equivalent of entire cities had been conceived in them. They were that inviting.

That night we stayed at a bizarre camping resort on a lagoon in Oludeniz. The camping was cheap but the food in the empty restaurant (which we passed on) was inexplicably obscenely expensive. It was much cheaper for us to take a taxi to and from town and eat at a decent restaurant there. The next morning I had a laugh seeing Gül getting startled awake by chickens pecking her through the side of the tent.

We decided to kick our heels up and be pure tourists, taking an island day cruise from Fethiye to see the 12 Islands of Golcek. For some reason, the British tourists piling onto the bus that morning were having trouble with the critical life skill of *walking*. Two different people ate it getting on and walking in the bus aisle, and on the walk from the bus to the boat one very obese woman fell on a completely flat sidewalk in such a dramatic fashion as to possibly have broken her nose. It was quite disconcerting.

The best thing all morning were the panini sandwiches and fresh pressed pomegranate juice Gül and I ducked away to grab for breakfast before boarding the boat. Delicious.

Once the boat got under way, it turned out to be a pleasant day. The tour boats plying these waters have a unique feature I have not seen anywhere else in the world. Upon talking to the captain, I found out why. They are equipped with a water slide which starts at the top of the stern of the three-story-high boat and tunnels through most of the ship, kicking thrill seekers out to the side of the boat near the front. It was well designed, giving a fun ride. A cute life-jacket-wearing Korean newlywed couple must have gone down it 20 times or more.

The captain said it was a local design that originated from one of the captains of these boats being in prison at the same time as a ship builder. They put together the concept while doing hard time and now several boats of varying sizes from this town have the same feature. He said that in summer, groups of 15 or more people would go down it together as a chain, which sounded dangerous but fun.

The following days we did some further explorations of the spectacular remote coastline south of Oludeniz (bumping into the Lycian Way once again), but soon it was time for us to catch our plane from Dalaman back up to Istanbul.

My stay in Turkey ended on a high note with Gül and her brother (despite my protests) treating me to dinner at another spectacular Bosphorus-front restaurant which had its own boat to get you over to its location on the eastern side of the strait. The non-foodie in me will simply say, "Wow, it was yummy," which also summarized my entire trip to Turkey.

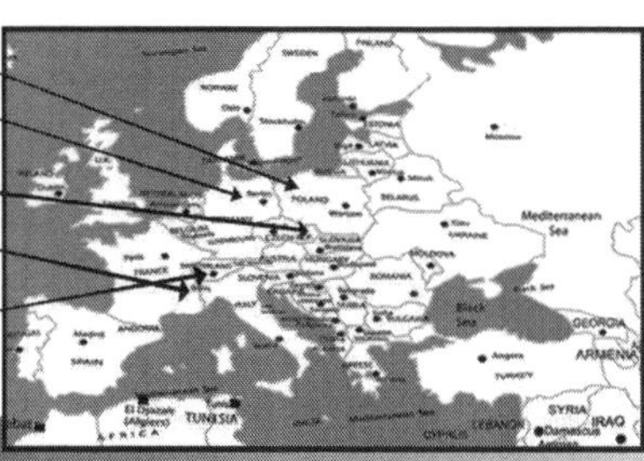

CHAPTER 41

Strawberry Underwear and Rainbow Wigs

A Birthday Reunion in France

When word got out I was having a 40th birthday party in St. Gervais, a magnetic tractor beam kicked in, attracting friends and family from near and far to come join in the fun. It doesn't take much to get my father to want to jump on a plane to Europe, especially to St. Gervais, as he had visited there many times and was familiar with the wonderful people and magnificent setting. I knew he would be excited to introduce his new life partner, Valerie, to this part of the world. More challenging was getting my sister to join in as she had not been out of the country in 20 years. Her task was complicated by having two young children. She worked out a family compromise in which she brought my adorable niece, Tabatha, for her first-ever international voyage while hubby and son remained (gladly) at home.

Other people who joined the festivities included the infamous Ahmed, Christophe (from "The Krishna Bike, the Frenchman and the Comfort Biker" story), now three generations of my French host family, and a collection of their local friends I have gotten to know over the years.

The culmination of special people, good weather, and a beautiful location made for an event that—even in the midst of it—felt like a lifetime highlight. Rather than imposing the festivities directly on my French host family, we splurged on renting a beautifully renovated wooden farmhouse in St. Gervais' valley floor (thanks Dad and Sis!). The home served as a base camp for adventures into town and the surrounding countryside, as well as a dormitory for all who decided to stay the night. One night I think we had 14 people slumbering about.

I couldn't help reminiscing and wishing my friend Joy Ingham could be here to celebrate with us. Joy had been instrumental in introducing me to the love of budget adventures. She was also top of mind because just before everyone arrived for the party, I had completed a five-day bike trip which started in St. Gervais and wound through the storybook French and Swiss Alps up to Leysin, Switzerland, the village where Joy used to teach. Friends Evan and Sally (from the "Introducing Jonny Rotisserie!" story) coincidentally were currently teaching there, too, and were arriving for the party with their newborn, Colleen.

I recalled another great journey Joy and I had shared many years earlier which also started in Leysin. Back then I was looking for work in France during my summer break from college. Joy had just finished teaching her classes at the Leysin American School and was planning to head to the States for the summer. When we realized she had both a car and a four-day window before taking off, we came to an inescapable decision...ROAD TRIP!

The only question was where to go. It had rained for almost the entire month I had been in St. Gervais. Our inclination was to look at a weather map and go anywhere at all that was sunny, which meant the Spanish or Italian coast. Nice options. But it was 1990 and six months earlier the Berlin Wall had come down, ending a decades-long Cold War. It would be a noble pursuit to see this history unfolding, despite the depressing weather that was sure to accompany us throughout the trip. Once the options were laid out on the table, there wasn't even a decision to make. Berlin it was.

I hitchhiked over to Aigle, the town in the valley at the base of Leysin's mountain. Joy met me with her alpine-green Subaru bubble-top minivan, and off we went. In this pre-Google Maps era, we had heard it would take up to 24 hours of driving to get to Berlin, so with her four-day window we were not even sure we would make it the entire way before having to turn around and head back. Our vehicle was far from the fastest on the road. It was especially frightening on the West German *autobahns* where, at our top speed, cars passed us like rockets.

We had to cross through East Germany to get to West Berlin. Upon crossing, the East German skies and everything underneath seemed to have the color sucked out of them, leaving only depressing shades of grey. The East German highways were atrocious and increasingly dangerous to drive on as night set upon us. The loud jarring from the constant potholes and bric-a-brac paving was nerve racking enough, but the rain caused additional problems. Water pooled on the road enough for ducks to swim around, causing Joy to continually swerve and slam on the brakes. At some point we just gave up and pulled over at a rest stop to sleep in the back of the van, a pattern we kept throughout the trip.

To our surprise, by 11 a.m. the next morning we were in Berlin watching people chip off parts of the remaining Berlin Wall for souvenirs. We did the same. And because this was as far as our plan went, and we still had almost three days left, we had to decide what to do next. Joy suggested, despite not having any visas (which were required), perhaps we should try and venture into East Berlin and even see if we could get into Poland. Why not?

We got lost in West Berlin for several hours trying to figure out where to go before we found a small side street passing through a hole in the Wall, which had clearly been only recently punched through. A makeshift guard station stood on the opposite side of the road—but not on ours. We went with the classic ploy of not stopping, but smiling and waving at the machine-gun toting guard as he started tentatively approaching us from his building. After hesitating, he chose a course of action, namely stopping and waving back at us. We were in!

More specifically, we were in a time warp. Entering East Berlin felt like going back decades. The buildings and the people's clothing harked of a time gone by. We were driving without maps at this point, just trying to figure out how to get to Poland. In doing so we passed near one of the official East-West Berlin border checkpoints (as opposed to our hole in the wall route), with traffic backed up for blocks on either side. Had we gone that way, we would have never gotten in.

But we did, and the next thing we knew we were at the East German–Polish border. THIS was a tough border. No one there spoke any English, so Joy navigated diplomatic waters using her broken German. It took us an hour and a half in a place that was otherwise not busy, but we did somehow get through and when we did, we were like giddy school-children getting let out for recess.

Poland was extremely poor but seemed exponentially livelier and happier than East Germany. My first impression was seeing people at the side of the road waving up and down with arms stretched out straight from their side, trying to get us to stop and buy things like blueberries. When we entered cities, they were alive with people out and about walking everywhere.

The myth of Polish women being homely hairy beasts (per American jokes) evaporated before my eyes as I saw one drop dead gorgeous woman after the other. I surmised that the stereotype images I had been carrying in my head had been planted there by smart Polish men who wanted to keep prying American eyes away from their women.

Apparently, Japanese bubble-top minivans were none too common in Poland at the time because it felt like everyone stopped to watch us drive by, pointing us out to their friends or family like we were a UFO. Something else not common there was unleaded gas, which proved to be problematic down the road.

We stopped for a delicious three-course silver service meal served by waiters in tuxedos in the quiet, colorful main square of Wroclaw. It was the only restaurant open. Including wine, I still remember it cost only $8 for both of us. I hear things are different there now.

When we first entered Poland, Joy mentioned she had heard of a jewel of a city on the far eastern side of the country called Krakow. At the time, we were just exuberant to have gotten into Poland at all, and still assumed we would have to turn south before getting too far in the country. Going all the way to Krakow was pure fantasy. And then amazingly enough, there we were.

Krakow, Poland

With its beautiful and varied architecture, and its main cathedral housing hundreds of years of kings, Krakow is stunning. The ancient city is situated on a river and was the capital of Poland up until about 400 years ago. The entire Old Town section was on UNESCO's original list of World Heritage Sites when it first came out.

After a walk about Krakow and purchasing some cool handcrafts, it was time to head south to Czechoslovakia (yes it was still one country at the time). The border crossing here was mild in comparison to our previous one. Entering Czechoslovakia, I was particularly excited to see the impressive mountains I had heard about in the northern part of the country. They never materialized, despite being obviously in our path according to our map. I learned later that maps in Czechoslovakia were often purposely misleading so they could not be used by invading armies. Great.

One army that would not have been terribly successful invading the country—good maps or not—was us. Our vehicle only ran on unleaded gasoline, which was hard to find in this part of the world. At one point (perhaps over an hour before it would happen) we figured out there was no possible way we were going to make it to the next place where we anticipated finding unleaded. Sure enough, eventually the motor started coughing and sputtering unhappily and we coasted off to the side of the road, out of gas.

I don't think we were hitchhiking more than ten minutes when an amazingly nice gentleman pulled up in a Mercedes and offered us a ride 45 minutes each way to the closest unleaded gas station. Luckily he spoke some English. He was a product of the times: a government official who had just been tossed out of his post along with the rest of the communist old guard. He was upbeat for being recently unemployed. Not only did he drive us in both directions, but he also followed us for more than 30 minutes once we were refueled to make sure we found the right road to get us towards our next destination: Brno.

We decided to drive via this impossible-to-pronounce city only because Joy knew a woman there from her days of volunteering in some bizarre volunteer work camp which involved shoveling a lot of sand. We amazed even ourselves when we found the woman's apartment with only a shaky address to go on. But our quest ended in disappointment when her neighbor from across-the-hall told us she was out of town for the weekend. We'd tried.

It was time to get back to Geneva so Joy could make her flight back to the States. It was clear the only way she would make her flight would be by driving all night. Joy did the heavy lifting as the overnight driver. I remember trying to sleep in the back and getting rolled around on the windy mountain roads. The first great disappointment during the trip occurred in Poland when we realized belatedly that we could have routed our trip differently to have paid a visit to Auschwitz. Here occurred my second great disappointment of the trip: missing Lichtenstein. I was hoping to get a stamp in my passport from this tiny country, but Joy made one wrong turn in the middle of the night and we missed it completely. Dang.

As the sun came up, we were still unsure if Joy would make her flight. But she gunned it as much as her poor little Subaru could go. As the stress mounted, we came screaming into the Geneva Airport with just an hour before her flight. She made it!

Back in St. Gervais, two decades later, I was making more great memories—and dinner. With friends and family here to celebrate my milestone birthday, I wanted to treat them and myself to a regional specialty. The main course for dinner was my request, a local dish called *farcement*. An amalgamation of shredded potatoes, bacon and prunes, this hearty (not to be confused with "good for your heart") dish is only found within about 20 miles of St. Gervais. I have fond memories of my petite wrinkly yet adorable host grandmother, Clémence, preparing *farcement* for special occasions. She took me under her wing to teach me some French recipes, but this is one I had never gotten to try.

Clémence

Apparently back in the day they used only year-old potatoes to achieve the correct texture and they would put it on to cook in the morning when people headed out to work the fields. They would have a nice high-energy meal waiting for them when they returned home. Due to some technology advances, shortcuts can be made, but the preparation is still not a simple process. Despite not being originally from the region, my French host sister Delphine's husband Luc has become the family specialist at preparing *farcement*.

I made a morning appointment at their house the day prior to the party to learn how he does it. On the way, I picked up a groggy Ahmed from the station, who had come in on an all-night train ride from Paris. Apparently his neighbors on the train decided to party like rock stars all night, which didn't help his state of consciousness. But he was still game to jump into the *farcement* preps.

This was one of many times when I wish the people who rant and rave about Muslims being the scourge of the earth could meet Ahmed. Being a faithful practitioner of his religion, he avoids pork at all costs. It makes his stomach turn even talking about it. But once we entered the Beaufils home—now converted to a den of bacon for the *farcement* preparations—he came to life trying to capture every aspect of the recipe on film and video. He was careful to not touch anything, but shared our joy in trying to recreate this ancient recipe. How cool is that?

Later that day, a group of us hiked up for a Sound-of-Music-esque picnic in the flower-infused grass of the pastoral glacier-capped Miage Valley. Cow bells clanged lazily around the valley as our bovine counterparts in the surrounding fields grazed away the day.

It was touching seeing people from all different parts of my life coming together and genuinely enjoying each other's company. Every time I turned, I saw different pairings of friends and family chatting away while soaking up the scenery.

Delphine's husband, Luc, drove up in his 4x4, which came in handy for shuttling those who were too tired or feeble to hike the full distance. That transportation was even more welcome for the descent after the wine consumed during the picnic and the homemade blueberry tarts we stopped for at the ancient little stone and wood farm house café catering to hikers.

Vacation Boy with French host parents Jean-Claude and Brigitte

My actual birthday party the next night was a blast. As I knew many people were coming a long way to attend this event, I asked that instead of giving me any presents, they simply wear a ribbon of any design at the party, since they were all the present I needed.

The party evolved as the sobriety levels lowered. First some party-themed t-shirts my Dad and Valerie had brought from the States made their appearance, then a bunch of crazy rainbow afro wigs materialized courtesy of the French. I wore anything anyone handed me, shirts, wigs, banners, underwear with strawberries on it…

I will pause here to say that this would be the final birthday party I was to share with my fun-loving host father Jean-Claude as he passed away the following summer while I was putting this book together. A professional ski instructor by trade, he was a charming man unlike anyone I have ever met. He treated me like his own son ever since the time I lived with him and his wife Brigitte for a year as a high school exchange student. He adored food, wine, these mountains in which he was born & raised, and everyone around him. When Jean-Claude passed away, many people at the funeral in St. Gervais told me about how much fun they remembered him having at this party weekend and we loved giggling at the pictures of this usually hairless man wearing a huge rainbow afro wig. Jean-Claude, may you rest in peace…when you are not merrymaking with the angels or teaching them how to ski.

Back in the moment, after we devoured the *farcement* and other delectables, it was inevitably time for dessert. My Dad, a notorious sweet tooth, specifically requested the cake for the party: a tower of cream puffs connected together by crispy caramel. He must have been lusting for this style cake for the entire 14 years since he had it at Delphine and Luc's wedding. I wasn't about to object to that monument of deliciousness, yet my Dad's insistence on it months before the event made me snicker.

Jean-Claude with his granddaughter Eline

The champagne and food eventually became more than Ahmed could keep up with and he somehow managed to fall asleep on his back on a narrow wooden bench in the midst of all the revelry. This, of course, turned into a group photo bonanza as we gathered around him snoring away contentedly, posing empty champagne bottles and other props around him.

In the end, this gathering of friends and family in one of my favorite places in the world seemed to be an excellent bookend to my first forty years on the planet. Part of the reason I made my fortieth birthday party a special event is because I see this milestone as life's halfway point. Life has been a blast so far and it is amazing to think I may have a shot at another 40 years of this. I can't wait!

THE END (for now)

Epilogue

To bring this book to a close, I thought a quote from my early journals would be appropriate:

> *September 14, 1993*
>
> *"As I head out on this new adventure, also known as a job…I am sitting in the Charlotte airport feeling pretty groggy as I await my flight to Nassau where I will begin working at Club Med. It feels good to have a journal and pen in hand. My life has gone off in too many directions to tell everyone I know about everything. Some of the time I wish there was somebody I could talk to all the time to share some of the neat experiences I have been having. I guess for the meantime this $1.99 journal can fill that void."*

I hope in reading this book you have enjoyed being my ear for some of these cool experiences life has presented me.

A Parting Thought...

> Stop putting off your life and/or personal happiness! So many of us put off personal happiness waiting for some external result like "I'll be happy when I lose weight, when I pay off my debts, when I get a better job." The truth is, you deserve to enjoy your fabulously imperfect life right this very minute! When you stop putting off happiness, you start attracting happy people, healthy relationships,

exciting and new opportunities. Instead of postponing joy until something external happens, today's the day to start celebrating the joy in your everyday life.

— Lisa Steadman
Bestselling Author, TV
& Radio Personality

Amen to that!

About the Author

Growing up in South Carolina, **Jon L. Sattler** was always curious about what lay beyond the horizon. Spending a year as a high school exchange student to the French Alps only fueled that fire. During college he was also an exchange student in Japan for a year, living with a Japanese family while attending school in Nagoya, Japan.

After graduating from the University of Southern California, he started out as a tour guide at Club Med in the Bahamas followed by the Dominican Republic. From there, newly anointed "Vacation Boy" worked a series of seasonal jobs in Colorado, Alaska and Hawaii before changing gears to work for a Japanese newspaper at the Atlanta Summer Olympics. This opportunity flowed into a position with Coca-Cola in Japan relating to the Nagano Winter Olympics, which led to a job in France relating to the World Cup Soccer tournament.

Then came Corporate Boy. Jon received an International MBA at the University of South Carolina, which included studying and working in China for a year and a half. From there, as "Corporate Boy" Jon delved into the world of international dental sales, covering Asia, South Africa and India. Later, he transitioned to a position in Paris, selling ophthalmic microsurgical instruments around Europe, the Middle East and Africa.

Finally the suit and tie had to go. Jon became BBQ Boy a.k.a. "Jonny Rotisserie", returning to the US to start his own company selling outdoor cooking equipment, travelling around the US full time in his RV "the Lounge" promoting a line of outdoor cooking equipment while occasionally participating in BBQ competitions.

Throughout this "career", Vacation Boy would reemerge, casting off to explore the world at ground level, which led to this collection of stories.

Currently in winter, Jon teaches skiers with disabilities in Park City, Utah as part of the professional staff at the National Ability Center while maintaining his role year round as "Chief Kangaroo" at Auspit North America (www.AuspitBBQ.com).

Jon's articles and photos have been published in USA Today, Sports Nippon Newspapers, the Park Record, Xiamen (China) Evening News, Snow Country Magazine as well as several university alumni publications. Jon speaks fluent Mandarin Chinese, Japanese, French, Spanish and "Southern," plus he can do a horrible Aussie accent.

Full size color photos from the book can be seen at www.vacationboystories.com/bookphotos (this special page is not linked from the main page). While there, if you sign up for the mailing list, you'll receive a free bonus section straight from Vacation Boy's handwritten journal about hitchhiking to participate in a crazy Japanese Naked Festival.